About the

Ray Knowles is a retired pharmaceutical advertising executive. He lives in Henley-in-Arden with his wife Tracy, has three grown-up children, loves writing, fishing, playing the guitar, and is a co-presenter of the podcast "The insane ramblings of crazy old men."

FOREWORD

I've been asked many times to write up Jack Kiely's story. As his grandson, I knew him well and I suppose I have a unique inside track. To date, I've shied away from it. It would be far too easy to define him by the events of 2nd February 1934.

They were certainly a sensation, reported in almost every newspaper across Ireland. The huge public interest generated, however, was the culmination of a much more intriguing tale. The struggle for Irish independence and the role his family played in achieving it.

For at least two hundred years, the Kielys ran a small mill just a couple of miles from Borris in County Carlow. The income kept the wolf from the door, but a few crumbs of economic success were no substitute for freedom.

By the time Jack was born, the Irish had been relegated to third class citizens ruled over by a dictatorship with no plans to change the status quo. It seemed their sole purpose was to rent-roll a largely foreign gentry, who cared little for them.

His father and grandfather had told him their secret history of cruelty and oppression. In the early half of the 20th century, he experienced it for himself.

Not surprisingly, he was determined to secure full Irish independence. A Republic that encompassed the whole island, and kowtowed to no one. He was prepared to risk everything to achieve it, and in the end that's what he did.

To paraphrase Cromwell, this is the story of Jack and his family, "Warts and all."

ACKNOWLEDGEMENTS

I'm greatly indebted to the following people and resources:

John Nolan — historian extraordinaire. Mick Kinsella, whose generous sharing of local knowledge helped put flesh to the bone of 1920s Borris. Jim Cody for his invaluable insight and encouragement.

Kilcumney '98: Its Origins, Aftermath, and Legacy (Kinsella, Moran, and Murphy), which provided much background for the early chapters. The anonymously written book *I Did Penal Servitude* for descriptions of Mountjoy and Portlaoise prisons in the 1930s. The online British Newspaper Archives and published military records.

Also, my son Rupert, my wife Tracy, Trevor Powell, my mother, Birdie, my father, Peter, the Archive staff in Wexford, Sherry Mooney, and of course, Josie and Jack.

CHAPTER ONE
The Accused

On Friday, 9th June 1934, three men sat side by side in the dock at Wexford County Court. Nineteen-year-old Jim Treacy — tall, blond, with gangly good looks — and the more worldly-wise Kiely brothers.

At thirty-seven, Jas Kiely had what some reports described as "the air of a gentleman." He was slim, almost delicate, with aquiline features and a dark, receding hairline. The shortest man by far was his younger brother, Jack. At 5' 4", he was three years younger than his brother, heavily built and pugnacious with an unruly mop of thick black hair.

Unlike the fresh-faced Treacy, the Kiely brothers had been hardened in the flames of the 1919-21 fight for Irish independence and the savage civil war that followed. Both had previous form.

The courthouse was relatively new. Twelve years earlier, the original building at Commercial Quay had been burnt to the ground by what became known as the anti-treaty IRA. Commanding officer Francis Carthy and nine members of his 4th Wexford Battalion had managed to break in through a window, sprinkle petrol through the rooms, and set them alight. Even if Jack and Jas hadn't been involved, there was little doubt that as anti-treaty men themselves, they would have been close to the project.

The courthouse had been built inside the grounds of the old Wexford gaol. With its high, grey, featureless walls and small, barred, rectangular windows, it looked as most early nineteenth-century gaols had been designed to look: formidable, impenetrable, and intimidating. At the start of the trial, when Jas and Jack had been driven into the courtyard under heavily armed guard, it must have crossed their minds that only ten years previously, three of their comrades had been executed there by a firing squad — men they knew well.

June 1934 was one of the hottest months on record. The higher windows in the courtoom had been thrown open and two large electric ceiling fans turned on to stir up the air. Most men in attendance looked distinctly uncomfortable, stretching their collars and mopping their foreheads. Many had taken off their jackets or loosened their ties. Almost all the women had removed their hats and many more were fanning themselves with newspapers, handkerchiefs, and anything else that they could lay their hands on.

The oven-like heat was matched by the smell: a fetid, earthy stench of sweat and livestock, the inevitable consequence of a court packed mainly with farmers and agricultural workers who'd queued for hours to get a seat in the public gallery.

Because Jim had turned King's evidence on his co-conspirators, he was obliged to appoint his own solicitor. John Foley of Bagnalstown, an old friend of the family, was the obvious choice. In his mid-forties, balding with a friendly face, he was both experienced and tenacious. Since he'd established his practice in 1916, he'd built a reputation for generosity and integrity. On his advice, Jim entered a plea of "guilty."

The Kielys' representative was their usual go-to man when they were in trouble, the street-wise, middle-aged, red-faced "Rumpole-like" R. J. Brennan. On behalf of his clients, he submitted a plea of "not guilty."

Presiding over proceedings was Circuit Judge Michael Davitt. When Brennan was asked to write the judge's obituary two years later, he said that Davitt had been a great Irishman, an engaging conversationist, and an extremely fair and sympathetic judge. The Kiely brothers must have hoped that the obsequious praise their lawyer heaped upon him throughout the trial would hold them in good stead.

The state prosecutor was the highly experienced King's Counsel, Joseph McCarthy — not to be confused with his namesake, who decades later would conduct the notorious witch-hunt trials in America. He sat, as was traditional, across the court and to the right of the defence.

McCarthy had worked throughout the twenties for the Irish Attorney General, mainly on conspiracy charges and civil actions. A year earlier he'd prosecuted the case of the young, unmarried Bridget McCormack, who had strangled and buried her newborn baby in fear of what her father might do if he found out. He'd laboured remorselessly to secure a guilty verdict and it paid off when young Bridget received the maximum sentence of three years hard labour without remand. It seemed likely that he was hoping to exact an equally punitive sentence for the men in the dock.

Throughout the three-day trial, the public gallery had been packed. The sensational evidence reported over the previous few months had caught the public imagination. Already hundreds, if not thousands, of people had flocked to Kilcloney to see the mill and the hole in the wall where the much talked about climax to the manhunt had taken place.

Behind the lawyers sat many of the police officers and witnesses who'd played such an important role in securing the capture and prosecution of the three men. George Love and his wife Elsie; Edward Conry; Garda Wall, the chief photographer; Sergeant McNamara, the fingerprint expert from Dublin; Sergeant Angus, who found the tyre tracks; Sergeant Pat Summeries, who took the plaster cast of the boot; Sergeant Rabbit; Sergeant Kinsella; and Superintendent O'Brien, who made the final and unexpected arrest.

Behind them in the gallery sat the families of the accused, among them Jack's wife, Josie. Well-dressed, with a full figure, fair hair, and blue eyes, she was a woman who could turn most heads. Right now, however, she wasn't concerned about how she looked. Should Jack be sent down, she'd be left with no money, no way of earning a living, and two young children to raise on her own: six-year-old Birdie and her sister Maureen, still in nappies. Josie wasn't the sort of woman to wear her heart on her sleeve. She wasn't going to let anyone see her cry. She'd save that until later, when she returned to her parents' house in Clomoney to pick up the girls. For the moment she was determined to show a brave face and keep her emotions to herself while internally raging at the pig-headed man who couldn't keep out of trouble, the man who'd made it impossible to walk down the main street of Borris without people whispering behind her back — the man who, despite all his faults, she loved dearly.

As a relative of one of the accused, she'd been spared the long queue to get in. She'd taken the opportunity to secure a seat with a good view of the dock — but not the best. She'd left that for Anastacia Treacy. It seemed only fair. After all, it was Jack who'd got her son into trouble and she fully understood why the other woman was so hurt and angry. Their families had known each other for years and as she peered through the sea of well-wishers, ill-wishers, and those just there for sheer titillation, she was pleased that Anastacia had found the seat she'd left. Sitting beside her was her husband, James. He had a comforting arm around her shoulder as she leaned forward, face flushed, trying to catch the eye of her son in the dock.

Directly ahead, and positioned just in front of Davitt's bench, was the reporter's desk. Behind it was the man from the *New Ross Standard*. He was young—in his mid-twenties—and as he wrote his tongue flicked between his lips. He'd been frantically scribbling away on his notepad throughout the morning, and she wondered how he'd report what he'd heard. Would he be sympathetic? Would he be venomous? Perhaps he'd already written alternate "guilty" and "innocent" verdicts to speed up the process of getting to print.

To his left was the jury box. Currently, it was empty. An hour or so earlier, the twelve good men and true had been instructed to leave for an anteroom and deliver a verdict. Davitt was also absent, presumably waiting in his chambers for notice they were ready.

As her mind drifted, she wondered how he might be filling his time. Rehearsing his summing up speech perhaps or weighing up a possible sentence if the men were found guilty. Maybe he was smoking a cigar or drinking a glass of porter brought in from Mulligan's across the road. Perhaps he had his feet up on his desk, catching up on the latest news from America about the ambush and shooting of Clyde Barrow and Bonnie Parker.

While Davitt might have been able to stand by an open window and get some fresh air, there was little relief for the defendants in the dock. Jim in particular seemed to be suffering from the heat. As she watched him wipe beads of sweat from his forehead, she noticed he was wearing his father's best Sunday suit. It was loose and baggy around the chest, the elbows were frayed, and the sleeves were too long. His tie didn't quite reach the neck, but at least his mother had made sure his shirt was ironed and his hair neatly cut. He reminded her of a schoolboy waiting for one of the Christian Brothers to return and give him a good thrashing. In contrast, Jack and Jas seemed perfectly relaxed. Jas had seen the inside of a court many times before and she knew it would take more than the antiquated robes, wigs, and other paraphernalia of justice to bother him. Jack didn't seem too concerned either. In fact, he seemed the more bullish, grinning from time to time and occasionally whispering something in his brother's ear to make him crack a smile.

She realised it wasn't a good look. The perception most people had formed of Jack during the trial was that of the archetypal tough guy — the sort of "Tom Powers" gangster James Cagney had recently portrayed in the controversial movie *The Public Enemy*.

The irony of it was that he wasn't really like that. That tough guy exterior was just a front. He might have been reckless — he might have been bull-headed, but he wasn't a monster. Under that façade of devil-may-care bravado, he was as frightened and anxious as anyone. She'd known him since they were at school, and she'd been married to him for six years. If anyone in the world knew the real Jack Kiely, she did. He was intelligent, well-read, idealistic, and passionate. Passionate about her, passionate about their children, and passionate about Ireland — which is what had landed him in this mess in the first place. What's more, he was kind and often overly generous. After his arrest, didn't he beg Superintendent O'Brien to make sure she got the few pennies he had in his pocket? Didn't he offer Elsie Love 10 shillings for the children?

James Cagney in Public Enemy

This passion for Ireland ran through the Kiely family like a seam of emerald in a mine. His father and grandfather had been the same — and certainly his sister, Nell. She and Nell were both a year younger than Jack, but that's where the similarity ended. Nell rarely wore make-up and had little interest in fashion. She was sitting next to her right now, taking on the stare of anyone who had the temerity to stare back. Heavily pregnant and with a face like thunder, she was wearing bottle-bottom, horn-rimmed specs and, despite the heat, a shabby grey cloche hat and thick woollen coat.

Nell was as tough and protective towards her brothers as a lioness to her cubs. A few days earlier, McCarthy had issued a formal complaint about her to Davitt. According to the prosecutor, she'd approached his key witness outside the court — a man called Coburn — and allegedly screamed,

"You aren't much of a man are you...to let Jack down after he was on the run with you."

During the trial, the court heard that he and Jack had fought in the same IRA flying column back in the twenties. Jas had allegedly asked him if he'd give Jack an alibi. For one reason or another Coburn refused and gave evidence that Jas had tried to bribe him. This hadn't gone down well with Nell, who allegedly went on to shout, "Jack can do you if he wants. You carry on but trust me — you'll get bumped off after."

It was a serious threat and Davitt called her before the bench for an explanation. Under oath, she maintained that she'd been misunderstood. "That's not what I said," she backtracked. Coburn must have misheard. She hadn't threatened him with being bumped off — merely that Jack would do him a bad turn. "...and he would," she added, to the amusement of the gallery.

On Nell's left sat Biddy, the Kiely matriarch. Crippled from years of back-breaking work, she was in tears. It wasn't the first time she'd seen her sons in trouble. Encouraged by their father, they'd been fighting against what they saw as British oppression since 1916. Her husband had died ten years earlier and if Jas were to go to prison, she had no idea how she would manage the farm. To her right, and tightly grasping her hand, was her eldest daughter, Mary — the sensible one. Mary's husband had died three years earlier and since then she'd been a godsend. While Nell had been going through marital problems in New Ross, Mary had been virtually living at Kilcloney, helping wherever and whenever she could.

That morning, Josie had made her way through the Rosary at least five times. Feeling for the beads in her pocket, she was about to embark on another round of "Hail Marys" when she heard the call of "All rise."

As Davitt returned to the bench, everyone rose to their feet. For a few seconds, he busied himself shuffling a sheaf of papers. Then the door to the anteroom opened and the jury began to file back. As soon as they'd returned to their seats, he lay the papers down, wiped a film of sweat from his forehead, and peered over his glasses. "Have you reached a verdict?" he enquired.

The Foreman stood, "We have, my lord."

Davitt nodded slowly and turned to the dock.

The three men got to their feet, Jim was visibly trembling, Jas seemed more concerned with straightening his tie. Jack caught her eye, smiled, and shrugged his trademark "Inshallah" shrug.

She wanted to run down and throw her arms around him — reassure him everything would be alright. She also wanted to wring his neck. He was right about one thing, though — whatever happened now was in the lap of the gods.

CHAPTER TWO

The secret

From very early on, I knew my Irish grandparents had a secret. My mother warned me not to be curious and not to ask too many questions. I suppose there are secrets in every family, unspoken rules of engagement. Things that shouldn't be said or shouldn't be asked. Yet, despite the seemingly impenetrable wall around them, I sometimes caught a tantalising glimpse of their past — a past that seemed dark, mysterious, and exciting.

To the outside world, Jack and Josie appeared an unremarkable, respectable, elderly Irish couple. I'd been told they'd moved the family to England in 1945, telling my mother and her sister as they boarded the cattle boat in Dublin, that they were just off on holiday for a few days. As it happened, they were embarking on a new life in a new country with little prospect of seeing their old friends and relatives anytime soon.

My father, who was English and a bit of a history buff, told me that the war years had been difficult for most of Europe. Ireland as a neutral country should have come out of it better than most, but as it turned out, the reverse was true. It came as a surprise to me to discover that back in 1940, Churchill asked De Valera if Britain could re-occupy its old naval bases on the South and West coasts. The idea was to use them to defend against U-boat attacks; in return he offered De Valera Northern Ireland.

I would have thought it was a great deal for the old Republican but, convinced Germany would win, he refused.

When Britain, short of supplies itself, then began to cut down on exports, Ireland was the first to suffer. It soon experienced severe shortages of coal, manufactured goods, and fuel. With soaring inflation and increasing poverty, diseases like typhus reappeared and within a year, De Valera had to start planning for a famine. As John Betjeman, the British press attaché in Dublin, quipped, "No coal. No petrol. No gas. No electric. No paraffin. Guinness good."

From the little I knew about Irish history, De Valera's reluctance to help Churchill was understandable. On the other hand, it did little to improve Anglo-Irish relations. There was much public anger at the loss of so much shipping and many people in Britain saw it as a direct consequence of the Long Fella's intransigence and insistence on neutrality. To make matters worse, the newspapers were full of stories about IRA collaboration with the Nazis.

Subsequently, I discovered they were true. In 1938, an explosives expert called Jimmy O'Donovan was tasked by the IRA leader Sean Russell to draw up a plan of sabotage — what he called the S-Plan. It was aimed at terrorising mainland Britain and the idea, as usual, was to attack their old adversary when it was at its weakest.

Just days before the Second World War kicked off, Russell's IRA detonated a bomb in Coventry, killing five people and injuring seventy. The chief suspect was Dominic Adams — a man I'd never heard of — but whose nephew, Gerry, became infamous in the 70's as leader of Northern Ireland's Sinn Fein. Because of food shortages and the fear of inviting in a fifth column, Irish immigration to Britain was temporarily halted. It wasn't until Hitler invaded the Soviet Union and Britain needed more labour in its armaments factories that it was reluctantly resumed.

Russell's S-Plan resulted in three hundred explosions, ten deaths, and injuries to almost a hundred people. By the time Jack and Josie stepped off the boat in Liverpool, the Irish were considered personae non gratae. To make matters worse, De Valera had just sent German High Command his condolences on the death of Hitler. The zeitgeist in Britain at the time was neatly summed up by the infamous caveat of its landlords, "No blacks, no dogs, and no Irish."

Fortunately for my grandparents, there were parts of Britain with strong ex-pat communities. One was Birmingham, where Josie's brothers were already working. With severe labour shortages, jobs for Irish immigrants were relatively plentiful. Within a week or so, Jack had found his family a flat in Stratford Place and a job at the United Wireworks factory near the city centre.

I would have loved to have been a fly on the wall when he discovered my mother had fallen for an Englishman. At first, she said, he hit the roof. Then he threatened to throw her out. When that didn't work, he resorted to bribery — offering her money to ditch him and find a nice Irish lad. Thankfully, for me, she stuck to her guns and in 1951 she and my father tied the knot.

Jack was in his mid-fifties when I came along. By then, he and Josie had saved enough to buy a terraced house in Sparkhill. He seemed to take to grandparenthood well and, according to my mother, he liked nothing better than to push my pram up and down the streets of Sparkbrook to get me off to sleep.

When I was seven, my mother returned to work. Although it was a part-time job, she was required to work Saturdays.

With my father working weekends too, it was left to Jack and Josie to take care of me.

That's when I really got to know them. Josie taught me how to make soda bread, made me go shopping — invariably to Marks & Spencer in the city centre — cooked mouth-watering stews, and conjured up the most magical sherry trifles. Through my child's eyes, she looked old, but even so I could appreciate that in her youth she must have been quite pretty. Certainly, she took great care of her appearance, always well dressed and usually wearing a large, stylish hat when we went out anywhere special.

I was never shown any old photographs of my grandparents. The earliest ones I saw were when they were in their fifties, usually ones of them holding me as a baby. Even when I was in primary school, I thought that unusual. Perhaps, I concluded, cameras hadn't been invented when they were young. When I got a bit older, I discovered they had. My other grandparents had photographs of their wedding — they even had photographs of their parents and grandparents. In fact, when I looked it up, I found out that cameras had been around since the 1830's.

Years later, when Josie died, my mother discovered an old sepia photograph of her. She was standing with two other girls in front of a building called The Salutation Hotel. She looked extremely elegant, with a long white coat, white gloves, and a strange white hat, and she was by far the prettiest. In the foreground was what looked like a marina, and I decided to try and find out where the hotel could have been. It took me a while, but Google eventually revealed a photograph taken a hundred years later. The building and the name were the same — the typography on the sign had changed, but everything else matched up. When I started my search, I was convinced that the hotel would be in

Ireland, but to my astonishment it was in Scotland. A small coastal resort in Fife about fourteen miles south-southeast of St Andrews called Anstruther. As to what she had been doing there, I had no idea.

Josie (far right)

Josie and Jack looked after me well on Saturdays. At first I missed my mum and dad, but then I came to look forward to my weekly visits to their house in Ivor Road. There was always a hearty lunch of mince and potatoes and I always had fun playing with the two boys who lived next door.

Josie wasn't one for telling stories, but Jack was.

Noticeably short at about 5' 4", he was bald and thick-set. Despite his height, laid-back style, and easy smile, he didn't look the sort of man you'd want to tangle with. He was also a million miles from the typical Irish stereotype of the time. He never drank, he never swore, he didn't gamble or smoke. He was extremely well-read and quoted lines of poetry at the drop of a hat. When Josie forced us both out shopping, he would always carry her bags, doffing his trilby and opening doors whenever there was a lady around. To all intents and purposes, he was the perfect gentleman.

Jack, aged seventy, in Sparkhill.

He retired when he was sixty -five. After that, he kept himself busy around the house — digging out foundations for a new extension, fitting a new bay window to the kitchen, and generally beavering away on various odd projects.

One such project was the excavation of a hole under his garden shed. Once it was dug, he covered it with a neatly fitting wooden hatch. Over the top, he placed a sheet of lino. He showed it to me when it was finished and of course I asked him what it was for. To his great delight, he removed the hatch and revealed what I recognised from school as a Liebig condenser. It was for making poteen he told me — but it had to be our secret.

I discovered later that poteen — or "Poitín" in Irish — is an extremely intoxicating type of whisky with somewhere up to a 90% alcohol content. My favourite drink as an adult is

Chardonnay, which comes in at a mere 12%. No wonder then that the Irish word for hangover is póit.

As to where he got the condenser, I don't know, but every Christmas he would boil up a pot of mashed potatoes and distil it into a crystal-clear, odourless fluid. Even Josie's alcohol-hardened brothers would baulk and splutter as they downed a glass and, not surprisingly, apart from a little sup, I wasn't allowed anywhere near it.

The more I got to know him, the more fascinating he became. Even watching him shave was an education. He would strip down to his vest and braces and sharpen a razor on a thick piece of leather. Then he'd lather up some soap, contort his face this way and that and scrape away until he was done. I never saw anyone shave like that before — not even my father — and apart from in films, I haven't seen anyone do it since.

In the afternoon, we'd settle down to watch wrestling on TV. While Josie made bread and scones in the kitchen, he'd make himself a cup of tea — usually with at least five spoonfuls of sugar. We'd watch Mick McManus and Jackie Pallo throw themselves acrobatically around the ring well before WWE fighters like "The Rock." Sometimes, when I was bored, he would take me off to his workshop so we could make something together. Thanks to Jack, I discovered how to use a lathe, turn wood, and wire a plug. Once, he showed me how to connect a battery between the face and hands of a clock to make a bulb light up at a chosen time. It wasn't until years later that I realised that this was how you made a timed detonator.

When he got flu — which was usually every year — his jaw would swell up. Sometimes it happened when he got stressed, although I only had that on hearsay as I rarely saw him get stressed about anything. He had a firm view of how the world should and would be. He assured me that, by the time I was his age, there would be a cure for cancer, the common cold, and baldness. Men would have landed on Mars, there'd be a base on the moon, and everyone would have a flying car. He was fascinated by the newspaper reports of Walt Disney being cryogenically preserved and he was sure that I might be one of the lucky ones for whom death would be a thing of the past. He had his pet theories as to why Kennedy was shot, he wasn't too keen on Harold Wilson, and he had a reluctant admiration for the monarchy.

Like men of all generations, we would talk rubbish for hours, but the chats I preferred most were the intimate ones — the ones where he'd tell me about his childhood in what seemed to be an idyllic, almost mythical place called Kilcloney.

Kilcloney, he explained, was a small townland in Ireland — what the English might call a hamlet — and his father had owned a mill there. It stood on a crossroads where a fresh-water spring flowed from a spout across the lane. Because of that, his family became known as "Kielys of the spout."

The Mill had been owned by his family for as long as he could remember. It ground corn and made a variety of woollen goods — and it had been a highly successful business. When he was a boy, he used to travel with his father on the train to collect rent for a row of houses they owned in Dublin. He remembered how generous his father had been with his tenants — granting them extra time to pay or sometimes waiving a month or so's rent. Jack also told me how much he loved working at the Mill, learning how the machinery worked and how to keep the pulleys and wheel in tip-top condition.

It seemed he was quite mischievous as a child, always in some scrape or other. And he was stubborn. He told me that one day he arrived at school with a new coat his mother had made. It was wool, of course, spun in his father's mill, and it had new shiny buttons she'd sewn on for him. When his teacher told him to take it off, he refused point blank — earning him a rap across the palm with a willow cane.

Jack had many stories to tell and sometimes, when Josie was out of earshot, he'd tell me ones she would have preferred me not to hear. Like how he tried to make nitroglycerine in a secret room under the mill. I didn't ask him why or how, but even as a child I suspected it wasn't a good idea. When I asked if he'd been worried about blowing up his parents, he just grinned and gave me that characteristic shrug of his.

As I grew up, he began to reveal more. He had two sisters. He'd been a good cross-country runner. He won a silver GAA watch chain in 1916 — which he eventually gave to me — and he'd been in the IRA. Apparently as a quartermaster, the man who stores and dishes out weapons. He told me how he'd spent a lot of time on the run, sleeping in ditches and marching through heavy rain across mountains and muddy fields. I had no idea what he might have been doing, but I'd heard of the IRA. My father told me it was a terrorist organisation out to cause trouble — he'd also told me about those bombings during the war. It was inconceivable to me that Jack could have been involved with anything like that. It seemed totally out of character, and I decided that I should take most of what he said about his IRA days with a large pinch of salt.

My favourite program at the time was Dr. Who. It came on after the wrestling and as soon as it started, Jack would leave his chair by the fire and head off to join Josie in the kitchen. When it finished, they'd both rush back to the living room to watch the news. It was something they never missed and as soon as it started, they were glued to presenter Richard Baker's every word — especially when he was reporting on Northern Ireland.

Before 1968, news items about the province were few and far between. Occasionally, however, there were one or two. After one broadcast, I remember Jack trying to explain to me why a Stormont MP called Austin Currie was squatting in a house in Co. Tyrone. He said he was protesting against discrimination, but it seemed the BBC's view on it was that breaking into a house — whatever the reason — was wrong.

Back then, I didn't know what *discrimination* meant and it was only years later that I understood what he'd been trying to tell me.

The house Austin Currie had been squatting in wasn't just anybody's house. The local council had allocated it to a single nineteen-year-old Protestant girl who happened to be the secretary of a local Unionist politician. Nothing wrong with that except she'd been moved to the front of the queue ahead of two large Catholic families with children. This wasn't a one-off. Currie's gripe was that Unionist-controlled councils were regularly discriminating against Catholics — and it went further than that. It was only possible to vote in a local council election if you owned or rented a property. As most Catholics couldn't rent and — like blacks in the southern states of America — were too poor to buy, they were effectively disenfranchised. To make matters worse, landlords with multiple properties got multiple votes — and most of them were Unionists.

Over the years I spent with Jack, I got to know him well. My mother even complained that I knew more about him than she did. It was true he'd shared a lot with me, but with a child's intuition I suspected there was more he hadn't. What it was, I didn't know, but I had the feeling that if I discovered more about the old mill at Kilcloney I'd be a step nearer to finding out.

CHAPTER THREE

The massacre

Almost a hundred and fifty years before Jack was led into the Wexford county court, his great grandfather, Johannes, was woken early. It was 1794 and his father James told him to get dressed. As his father disappeared back down the steep wooden stairs, Johannes yawned, slipped out from under his thin blanket, and walked barefoot to the little window. He was only five, but his mother told him he was strong and tall for his age. Already he was doing little jobs around the family mill, and he knew it wouldn't be too long before he could help out with some of the bigger tasks.

As he looked down into the yard, he could see his father loading up the wagon. His mother was helping, as were his uncles, aunts, and grandfather. In the distance, Mount Brandon loomed grey and cold on the horizon. Dark clouds hung above it and a few fields on, near the river, he could hear occasional shouts and the clanging of picks from the men digging.

His father said they were building a canal — whatever that was — and they seemed to have been doing it forever.

He rolled up his blanket, pulled on his clothes, and ran down the stairs. His mother had left him a bowl of porridge on the kitchen table. He was her only child, at least for the moment. She had another one on the way and every day her belly grew bigger, he looked forward to its arrival — a new brother or a sister to play with.

He quickly gulped down his breakfast and ran out into the yard. The last of their furniture was already on board the wagon. His father had taken the tools to their new home a few days earlier. Now there was just the dresser, a table, a few chairs, and the beds. His mother smiled when she saw him and headed up to his room to bring down his blanket.

While his father fetched the donkey, his uncle lifted him onto the cart. He placed him carefully onto an old chair next to his grandfather. The donkey brayed as his father hitched it up to the wagon and Johannes prayed it wouldn't rain and ruin their furniture.

When everything was roped in place, his father climbed on board. As his mother pulled herself up beside him, he could see that her eyes were red. No one had told him exactly where they were going — only that once they got there everything would be alright. With a crack of the whip, the wagon began rumbling forward with his aunts and uncles walking on behind. He'd never left Templanaboe before, but he knew where they were heading. Out on the narrow dirt track that led out towards the small settlement at Borris.

It wasn't until he was in his mid-sixties and had time on his hands that Johannes thought back to that day. His birthplace, Templanaboe, is a small townland in St. Mullins, a village only two miles square. It sits on the river Barrow — the second longest river in Ireland. He'd been taught by his father and grandfather that it had an interesting history — or more accurately — mythology.

Before it was called St. Mullins, Viking pillaging trips regularly stopped there because of the weir. As they sailed up to Dublin from Hookhead in Wexford, they'd have to get out of their boats and drag them a few yards across land to resume their trip. Boatmen for time immemorial had done the same and it wasn't surprising that over the years it had become a sacred place.

Johannes was told that one such boatman was the famous navigator St. Brendan, the man who allegedly discovered America before the Vikings. According to *The Book of Tighe Mulling*, he sailed to St. Mullins with the idea of setting up a monastery. When he arrived, he was told by an angel that there was no need, as a man called Moling would make a much better job of it. Brendan took the angel's advice, lent his name to nearby Brandon instead, and sailed off.

St. Moling himself was supposedly a Kerry man. He worked hard at his devotions and after becoming a monk, the King of Munster offered him a site for an abbey. However, that night an angel —possibly the same one who visited Brendan — told him not to do it. There was, it said, already a place earmarked — on the stream pools of the Barrow, and in the same spot that a fire lit by St. Brendan thirty years earlier was still burning.

St. Moling took the advice. When he finished building his abbey, he turned his attention to feeding his followers. The best way to do that, he decided, was to build a mill and grind corn.

Legend has it that he was a strong man. So strong that he single-handedly dug a mile-long water channel to power his mill. Apparently, it took him seven years and he refused to wash or drink until he'd finished.

Johannes wasn't convinced that was the whole truth and nothing but. Certainly, someone had built an abbey there — maybe a St. Mullins — although in later years he came around to thinking that Mullins might not have been his real name. *Muileann* in Irish and *Molino* in Spanish translate to *mill* — surely too close to be a coincidence.

As to why they'd moved away from St. Mullins, he'd never had the opportunity to ask his father. Perhaps there'd been a problem with the landlord. Perhaps the family had fallen out with a neighbour. More likely, it had something to do with the new canal — all that banging and shouting he'd heard when he was a lad. Certainly, it would have caused huge disruption to the water supply.

Either way, when his father found a plot of land ten miles down the road at a place called Kilcloney, he announced that this would be their new home.

As to whether a mill was there already or his father built it from scratch, Johannes was too young to remember. Certainly, in terms of location, location, location, it was the perfect place — sitting astride the Black River, a tributary of the Barrow, and next to a stone bridge that forded the main road from Wexford in the east to Kilkenny in the west. A few yards on, a narrow dirt track cut across it heading north towards Dublin and south to the settlement at Borris.

His father took him around to explain the grand plan. The house with its three stories and two bedrooms had been built into a slope running up from the river. Where the Wexford road dipped down towards the bridge, traffic could be driven into the lower yard. This is where he put the entrance to the kitchen and dairy. If the house was approached from the higher Borris track, the way in was through a grand front door on the second floor.

This slope construction allowed James to have both a posh and not so posh entrance to his house. It also had a more practical application. A cart of grain could be driven off the higher Borris track to a shed housing a kiln. Once dried, the grain could then be fed into a hopper and dropped onto mill stones six feet below. The flour produced could then be bagged up at yard level without the need for expensive hoisting equipment.

He'd built the stables in the lower yard and made sure the water wheel was sited behind the mill house so it couldn't be seen and barely heard from the family home. He had also commissioned a canopy to keep it dry. Even though it was made from water-resistant wood, it could still warp or be badly damaged on a frosty night.

When the work was complete, James invited their neighbours over to celebrate. There was plenty of food and even more poteen. A few weeks later, the sluice gates were opened, and the new mill began grinding corn.

1798 was exceptionally hot and should have been a good year — but that was the time of the massacre.

Johannes' grandfather blamed Dermot MacMurrough Kavanagh. In fact, he blamed him for most of Ireland's woes.

In Irish, *MacMurrough* means monarch and back in the twelfth century, Dermot had been locked in a power struggle with a rival Irish king, Tiernan O'Rourke. To break the impasse, he invited the Anglo-Normans over to help. When O'Rourke was defeated, they decided Ireland was a great place to live and started to annexe huge tracts of the country.

Over the next two centuries, the power of the Kavanaghs declined. Then Richard II decided to beef up security for his main highway through the country — the River Barrow. To make sure it didn't fall into the wrong hands, he appointed

Dermot's descendant, Arthur, Keeper of the Roads: the man responsible for river security between Carlow and Kilkenny.

With Richard's backing, the Kavanagh star rose again. Arthur became King of Leinster and things seemed to be going well until a spat over property led him into direct confrontation with the English monarch. Richard met him on the battlefield with one of the largest English armies ever assembled and within days Arthur surrendered, falling to his knees and begging for forgiveness.

Johannes felt he should have shown more backbone. To add insult to injury, when Richard rewarded Arthur with a knighthood for his change of heart, he obsequiously grasped it with both hands.

According to Johannes' grandfather, he wasn't the only Kavanagh who had no shame. A hundred and fifty years later, when Henry VIII demanded the Irish kings renew their pledges of loyalty, Arthur's descendant, Charles, was one of the first to volunteer In a face-to-face meeting with Henry, he famously renounced "the title and dignity of the MacMurrough." To ingratiate himself further, he converted to Protestantism and packed his children off to London to be educated.

It wasn't the way Johannes thought Irish kings should behave, but it was a wise move for the Kavanaghs.

Over the ensuing years, the Tudors gave away over 70% of Ireland to friends and family. When the Irish decided enough was enough, they rose up in revolt. In the ensuing rebellion, the Kavanaghs were spared because of their ancient Irish heritage. When Cromwell turned up to put the rebellion down, they were spared again, this time because they were Protestant converts and quick to pledge loyalty to the new commonwealth.

While Cromwell punished the big Catholic families who'd fought against him, "men for all season" dynasties reaped the rewards. In return for sitting on the fence, Cromwell granted the Kavanaghs' thousands of acres of prime arable land — including a small hamlet of mud cabins beside the Barrow. The area had previously been owned by the Catholic O'Drones and called *Buirgheas Ó nDróna*, the borough of the O'Drones. After the Kavanaghs took over, the name was anglicised to "Borris."

Oliver Cromwell, warts and all

Cromwell's invasion changed the face of Ireland. By the time the uprising was quashed, over six hundred thousand people had died from fighting or disease. 41% of a population of 1.5 million.

New penal laws meant Catholics could no longer worship, vote, teach, marry Protestants, own land, or do much else.

More insidiously, they were required to bequeath property to their children equally, rather than to just the eldest. This dilution meant that within a few years, practically the entire population had been reduced to a nation of subjugated tenants.

After the English Civil War, Cromwell was considered by many of his countrymen as a hero. Portrayed in the newspapers of the day as a sympathetic and reluctant leader who had wrestled with his religious conscience, uncertain how to deal with the intransigent Charles I.

Johannes' grandfather and most of the Irish population's impression of the man were a lot different and neatly summed up in the lyrics of a folk song of the day called, "Young Ned of the Hill."

> *"A curse on you Oliver Cromwell*
> *You've raped our motherland*
> *I hope you're rotting down in Hell*
> *For the horrors that you sent*
> *To our misfortune forefathers*
> *Whom you robbed of their birthright*
> *"To Hell our Connacht," may you burn in Hell tonight."*

Cromwell's atrocities seemed an age ago, but Johannes was about to experience a whole new set for himself. As he celebrated his thirteenth birthday, a mainly Presbyterian group called the United Irishmen decided the country needed to rise, rid itself of the penal laws, and throw out the big Protestant landowners. Inspired by the recent revolution in France and the American War of Independence, their idea was to strike when Britain had a bigger fish to fry — in this case Napoleon.

Unfortunately for them, the British military was as geared up for war as it would ever be. In stark contrast, they were not. Not only were they inexperienced and badly organised, but after the French failed to land weapons for them at Bantry Bay, they were also poorly armed.

They planned to start by taking Dublin, but the British soon discovered what they were up to. An hour before the rebels were due to mobilise, the Redcoats moved in. Most of the rebel leaders were arrested but insurgents in other areas of the country, unsure as to what was happening, rose as planned.

Itinerant workers who travelled down the course of the Barrow and occasionally provided additional labour at the mill kept the Kealys up to speed with the latest news. Fighting was quickly spreading through Leinster. The rebels had gained control of much of Kildare. In nearby Carlow, the hill of Tara and Country Meath, they were on the back foot. In Wicklow, things had gotten particularly nasty, with Loyalists massacring any Catholic they could lay their hands on.

Sixty years earlier, Charles Kavanagh's descendant Morgan built a big fort cum mansion in Borris. Unimaginatively, he called it Borris House and left it to his son Thomas. By virtue of the Kavanaghs' support for the Loyalists, the House became fair game for attack. The first assault came on 24th May and was driven off by Thomas' personal "Orange" yeomanry. A second attack, led by the rebel leader General Thomas Cloney, also failed but resulted in parts of the house being destroyed.

As Thomas and his son Walter bemoaned the damage, another rebel leader, Father John Murphy, found himself in trouble. A few days earlier, his men had taken Wexford, but on 21st June an overwhelming British unit moved in and routed his forces at Vinegar Hill.

His escape plan was to lead his men through a passage in the Blackstairs Mountains called Scullough Gap. From there they would march to the Midlands and join up with other rebel units. On his retreat from Wexford, he'd managed to take the garrison at Killedmond. Heartened by this success, he decided to make a detour to Gorsebridge and attack the heavily defended bridge. To get there, he needed to cross the river at Kilcloney.

Johannes' first inkling that something unusual was going on was when he saw a dust cloud on the horizon. Then a sound like thunder in the distance. As Murphy's army drew closer, the dogs in the yard began to bark furiously. Then they came into view. Around five thousand men, women and children, some on horseback. All looked tired, wretched, and dishevelled. It was a blazing hot summer day and when they reached the bridge, Murphy and some of the other leaders dismounted and led their horses to the river.

As the men bathed in the water, Johannes noticed how emaciated they looked. Their clothes were virtually rags and their weapons just old swords or pikes. The women and children with them were presumably their families who had followed on from Wexford when their homes had been burnt out.

It took the line all day to pass. The next day, on the 23rd, Murphy took Gorsebridge as planned, and continued on to Castlecomer. At first, things went well; then, beleaguered with desertions, exhaustion, and lack of ammunition, he decided the best thing to do was to head back to Wexford.

On the night of the 25th, Murphy ordered his men to make camp at a field in Kilcumney, just a mile up the road from Kilcloney. The area seemed relatively secluded, and Murphy assumed they'd be safe, at least for a while.

He was wrong.

The next morning, they woke to a thick fog. Then the blast of cannons. Thirty-six-year-old Charles Asgill, one of the British commanders who'd been tracking them, now began to attack.

Kilcumney monument

Asgill was a battle-hardened survivor of the American War of Independence. Back in 1782, he'd been captured by George Washington's patriots. Just a few weeks earlier, an American soldier had been murdered by the British and Asgill's name had been drawn out of a hat as the Brit to be hung in reprisal.

His mother, who was a French Huguenot, asked Marie Antoinette to intercede. She in turn pleaded with George Washington to spare Asgill's life. Because he was keen to keep the French on side, Washington agreed.

Asgill had been treated mercifully — which was a far cry from how he intended to deal with Murphy's men.

Outnumbered five to one, but with fresh, well-armed troops, he began adding artillery fire to the canon barrage. Murphy somehow managed to escape, but in the confusion, his men started running back towards Scullough Gap.

What happened next would stay with Johannes for the rest of his life. Tales that for years afterwards he would tell his children and grandchildren in hushed tones around the fireside.

Drunk, angry, and out of control, Asgill's troops began to systematically massacre the locals. They rampaged through the district, roaming from house to house out to cause trouble. The Kealys managed to escape to the relative safety of St. Mullins. Many of their neighbours weren't so lucky.

A group of drunken yeomen broke into the Neil's house next door. After ransacking it, they forced the family into the yard. Then they used their bayonets to gut five brothers and two of their little sisters. To complete the job, they assaulted and murdered their mother and grandmother.

Another neighbour, Peter Kinsella, was severely beaten up and then shot in front of his wife and seven young children. On their way out, Asgill's men set fire to his house.

In sixty-year-old Tommy Myron's case, they shot two of his sons as he was forced to watch. Then they tied his hands behind his back and lifted him onto a mule. For the next hour or so, they jabbed it with bayonets to make it buck. Every time he fell off, they lifted him back until eventually his spine was broken. Then they dragged him outside and bludgeoned him to death.

A hundred and forty of Johanne's neighbours were murdered that day, three-quarters of the local population.

On top of that, nearly five hundred children were left without parents or a home to go to.

For the next few days, the road from Kilcumney to Wexford was strewn with corpses. Johannes sat on the bridge watching carts coming in from New Ross and Wexford, mostly driven by single young women desperate to recover the bodies of their men. Opposite the mill, in a field called the Sandpits, human remains were being thrown into trenches and covered with lime.

One of the women got into trouble when she tried to wash her husband's body in the river. James managed to pull her out and in return, she gave him a cavalry sword, complete with scabbard. It had probably been stolen from a British dragoon and eventually it wound up in pride of place above the stove in the kitchen.

The uprising ended in disaster. Two years after it was crushed, the British parliament and the quasi-independent Irish Parliament — ultimately controlled by the British — passed the Act of Union. The idea was to keep a tighter control of the country by seamlessly merging it with Britain. The new entity was called the United Kingdom of Great Britain and Ireland, and to hammer home the takeover, Ireland's St. Patrick's cross was merged with the Scottish and English flags to create the Union Jack.

The new Parliament attempted to sweeten the deal by repealing some penal laws. Catholics were again allowed to sit in Parliament and, if they so wished, marry Protestants.

The Kealys and their neighbours weren't impressed. Having the option of marrying a Protestant in exchange for losing their last vestige of independence was a raw deal. However, from Johannes' point of view, there was an upside. As the eldest son, he was now able to inherit the mill in totality without his father having to distribute the proceeds equally between him and his brothers.

As for Walter Kavanagh, he decided to make the most of a bad job. Employing some of the best architects in the country, he set about restoring his beloved Borris house. It wasn't cheap to construct an ornate Stapleton ceiling, build a new chapel, and procure some of the most expensive antique furniture in Europe. Fortunately, he had his tenants to foot the bill and to keep the rents pouring in he used middlemen to collect it.

In an official report submitted to a Royal Commission, Middlemen were described as "land sharks," "bloodsuckers," and "the most oppressive species of tyrant that ever lent assistance to the destruction of a country."

Their modus operandi was to lease large tracts of land from landlords like the Kavanaghs and sublet them. To maximise their return, they divided them into parcels just big enough for a family to feed itself and sell whatever crop was left to pay the rent.

For landlords, it was an easy and reliable way of getting paid. For absentee landlords, it meant fewer visits to a country they considered dirty, unpleasant, and hostile.

For tenants, it meant a hand-to-mouth existence. The only saving grace was the potato. It had been introduced to Ireland in the sixteenth century, but its true value wasn't appreciated until the famines of the 1700s. Originating in central Peru, it was ideally suited to the climate, it could be grown in poor soils, and, at a push, a single acre could support a family of six.

Even so, the life of a tenant farmer was miserable. The same commission observed, "It would be impossible adequately to describe the privations which the Irish labourer and his family habitually and silently endure ... in many districts, their only food is the potato, their only beverage water ... their cabins are seldom a protection against the weather ... a bed or a blanket is a rare luxury ... and... in all their pig and a manure heap constitute their only property." They went on to conclude that they "could not adequately express their strong sense of the patient endurance which the labouring classes have exhibited under sufferings greater, we believe, than the people of any other country in Europe..."

James died in 1825. By then, Johannes was in his mid-thirties, with a fourteen-year-old son of his own. The baton had been passed on and now it was his turn to keep the mill going.

His father's landlord had been David LaTouche — the latest in a long line of Huguenots who'd fled from France in the previous century. Three years before La Touche died, his estates had been sold to the Beresford family, whom Johannes knew little about.

Johannes could only pray to St. Mullins that like La Touche Beresford would be a reasonable landlord. In the meantime, almost one-third of the Irish population had become dependent on the potato. In extremely poor regions like Mayo, it was the only food they ate. As Irish tenant farmers struggled to survive, landlords were pulling out rents of £6,000,000 (£975mn) a year without investing a single penny back.

It was a disaster waiting to happen.

CHAPTER FOUR

The mystery of the mill

The first time I remember being taken to Ireland was when I was around five. I have dim memories of lush green fields filled with haystacks, cattle, and sheep; earthy smells; and an old house — but that's about it.

In the late sixties, the trips became more regular. Each year around August, my father would pick my grandparents up from their terrace in Sparkhill, heave their overloaded suitcases onto the roof rack, and drive us up to the docks in Holyhead.

My father had a Ford Capri — essentially a two-seater sports car — and getting all five of us in was a struggle. The drive through Wales was long and uncomfortable, and the ferry was worse. I don't think they had stabilisers in those days, and if they did, they didn't work for me. I just remember six hours of Hell, bouncing over the Irish Sea and feeling as if I were going to throw up. The ferry sailed to a place called Dún Laoghaire on the outskirts of Dublin. Jack told me that in his day it was called Kingstown — in honour of a visit from George IV back in the 1820s.

To keep costs down, we usually left Holyhead at some ungodly hour in the morning. Invariably the ferry was packed. Most of the passengers preferred to party than sleep. I assume they were on their way home to visit friends and relatives and their collective excitement was palpable. As for the rest of us, it was impossible to take a nap with all the shouting and singing going on. By the time we arrived, almost everyone on board was drunk.

The stress levels in the Capri hit ten almost as soon as we disembarked. Invariably, we would get lost. Dublin was big, complicated, busy, and unknown — at least to my father. Josie would sit in the front, complaining about his driving and sense of direction. Jack as usual was his laid-back self — not saying much. Those days, there was no air con and there were too many traffic lights. As we circled the high stone walls of Mountjoy for the fourth or fifth time, tempers frayed until Jack leaned forward and quietly directed my father to some obscure bridge that crossed the Liffey and headed south.

For those first few years, we stayed at Josie's brother's house in Clomoney, a small village just outside Gorsebridge. Although it was only seventy miles from Dublin, it took us three or four hours to get there. Jack told me that this was because Irish miles were longer than English ones. He was joking, of course, but only half. I subsequently read that back in Elizabethan times, four Irish miles were equivalent to five English ones. There was still confusion about the length of an Irish mile until the Free State sorted it out in 1926. As it happened, the real reason it took us so long to get there was that the roads were poor, my father's driving slow, and Josie invariably insisted on stopping off for cake and tea on the way.

Her brother was called Pat and the house had been left to him by their mother. She was long gone by then and it fell to his wife, Rita, and their three daughters to host us.

It couldn't have been easy for them. Their squat, badly-rendered cottage was just a two-up, two-down. On the ground floor was a small living room and a scullery. Upstairs, a small bedroom and an even smaller box room. When we turned up, Pat's family moved into the box room while my parents, grandparents, and I were given the bedroom.

Pat earned his living from farming — on a very small scale. He kept a few sheep in a two-acre field at the back of his house. Rita kept chickens and the ones she didn't eat or sell provided the family with fresh eggs. Pat also had a couple of cows. His eldest daughter, Bernadette, milked them in the morning and Pat would pour the milk into large metal cans and take it to the creamery in Gorsebridge in his Morris Minor Traveller.

My yearly trips to Ireland were an eye-opener. Used to my food coming from Tesco, it seemed odd to eat eggs straight from a chicken. Experiencing the tart taste of unprocessed milk on my cornflakes was also strange. What surprised me, though, was the sanitation. Essentially, there wasn't any. No toilets inside or out, just chamber pots under the bed which Bernadette would empty after she'd milked the cows. As she was roughly the same age as me, I found the thought of her having to empty my waste embarrassing and I wondered why life in rural Ireland seemed at least thirty years behind the times.

The upside was the freedom. Rita lent me her bike and I was able to follow Bernadette at breakneck speed through the fields and around the practically empty lanes. We cycled everywhere — up to a big Celtic cross at the top of her road and down to the old battlefield of Kilcumney. She told me the cross marked the spot where some priest had been mysteriously murdered back in the day. When I read the inscription, it said: *Kindly pray for the soul of Rev. John Walsh C.C., Borris, whose dead body was found at this spot on July 31st 1835 and who according to a verdict of a coroner's jury was killed by a person or persons unknown.*

Sometimes we cycled into Gorsebridge. It was an odd sort of place, unlike anywhere I'd seen before. There was a stark Orwellian look about it. A one-horse town with grey, featureless buildings, a town square, and seemingly no inhabitants. To get to it we had to cross a bridge over a fast, wild river. Not the Gore, as I initially guessed, but according to Bernadette, the Barrow.

Gore, she told me, had been the name of an English officer who'd been gifted the land in the eighteenth century. She also added that the bridge had been the site of the Battle of Gorsebridge when some rebels fleeing from a defeat at Vinegar Hill attacked it.

Josie had been born in Pat's house and I assumed Gorsebridge was her go-to town growing up. Jack told me his had been Borris. From the road signs, I could see it was only a couple of miles away, but as I'd been firmly instructed not to cycle on the main roads, I had to decline Bernadette's offer to go.

A few days later, Josie asked my father if he'd take her and Jack there in the car. I was bundled in the back and our first port of call was their old house in Ballinagree — just a half a mile out of town.

Like Pat's place, their house was also a two up, two down. But instead of the external walls being rendered, it was still possible to see the old granite stone. My mother told me that when she was young, Josie had it looking beautiful. It was hard to believe. To my eyes, it looked like nothing more than a glorified hovel in a state of dereliction. So many slates had fallen into the front garden that you could see the rafters. Ivy had smothered the walls, and virtually all the glass had been smashed out of the windows.

I'd heard they'd moved there in the 30s from a coastal resort in Wexford called Carrick on Bannow. My mother would have been seven or eight at the time and when they arrived the house was being used as a cattle shed. Not only had it been filthy, but there was also no running water, power, sanitation, or glass in the windows. She'd nearly died from pneumonia a few years before and it wasn't surprising that during the first cold winter in the new house, she contracted it again. She didn't remember her father being around, but she remembered how kind the neighbours had been — how they came around to replace the glass free of charge and help Josie make the place liveable.

Her memories of living there seemed happy ones. Attending the local school in Borris with her sister, playing with their dog in the fields behind the house, and helping her mother sow potatoes and feed the pigs and chickens.

As Jack and Josie disappeared inside, I remained in the garden with my parents. Apparently, it had once been possible to see Mount Leinster on the horizon. Josie could even tell what the weather was going to be like from how close it appeared. Now the garden was overgrown with nettles, bushes, and weeds. Tall trees had pushed their way into the sky, blocking out the light, and if there had been views of the mountain they were long gone.

Once my grandparents finished their inspection, it was time to lock up. The house had been broken into the previous year and Jack wanted to booby-trap it by running live electric wires to the doors and windows. I must have been eight or nine at the time, and even then I wondered if that was a good idea. Fortunately, Josie managed to persuade him it wasn't.

We headed back across a railway bridge to a T-junction a few hundred yards on. The road to the right led to Pat's place. The road to the left, to Borris. Straight ahead was a gated entrance to what Jack told me was the Kavanagh estate.

Borris House

We took a left and headed down the hill into town. Directly ahead I could see a mountain looming up from the horizon — presumably the Mount Leinster my mother said she could see from her old house in Ballinagree. On the right was a high stone wall. A few hundred yards along it was broken by a narrow but official-looking mock-Tudor portcullis gate, which Jack told me led to Borris House.

On the left was a row of single-story workers' cottages, then a lane called Station Lane — which I assumed led to the station. Further down there were two pubs almost side by side, Shea's and Joyce's. Then a road to the left signposted to Fenagh. According to Jack, it led to Kilcloney and that's where I was told we were heading, to meet up with his sister, Nell, and her two sons.

It was what I'd been waiting for: a chance to see the mysterious Kilcloney he'd told me so much about. Before my father could turn, however, Jack asked him to keep going. There was something else he wanted to show me.

Art's viaduct

We carried on past a shop called Nolan's, the Sacred Heart Catholic Church, then the bank. At the end of the town, there was another road to the left, the ruins of an old building and a high stone viaduct which seemed totally out of place.

According to Jack, the ruins used to be Scorteen Corn Mill. A tough competitor for Kilcloney until his grandfather added blanket weaving and wool dying to his offering. As for the viaduct, it had carried the Great Southern and Western Railway from Wexford to Bagnalstown and it was built by the man who owned Borris House — Art MacMurrough Kavanagh.

Art had been born without arms or legs. Josie maintained this was because his pregnant mother had inadvertently dropped a statue of the Blessed Virgin and broken off its limbs. Jack didn't comment but said he'd been quite a character. He told us how his footmen used to strap him to his horse so he could hunt. In his youth, he got so many local girls pregnant his mother had to send him away. When he eventually returned, she discovered he'd been living in a harem in Turkey.

While the others waited in the car, my father and I took a stroll up to the viaduct. There were no safety barriers — just a sheer drop on either side of what I guessed was a twelve-foot-wide track. The views were striking. Almost a 360 degree panorama from Mount Leinster to Borris. We stayed for a few minutes and then returned to the car. When everyone was on board, we headed back into town. Just past Nolan's, we swung right onto the Fenagh road and carried on a couple of miles until we reached a crossroads. This, Jack told us, was Kilcloney Cross and on the right was the mill I'd heard so much about. From how he'd described it back in Sparkhill, I assumed it would be sort of manorial Mandalay. Instead, it was just a low, grey, two-storey house with some of the stones around the door and windows picked out in red.

As we pulled into the yard, he asked my father to honk the horn. Three people appeared as we helped Josie out of the car. A man in his late twenties, a slightly younger man with blond hair, and an old woman — probably in her seventies, thin as a rake, and with her back bent double, presumably a consequence of hard work and osteoporosis.

The old woman greeted us, then stooped down and took my hand. She asked how my journey had been. I smiled and said it was fine. She smiled back and invited us in. This, I guessed. was Jack's sister, Nell; they looked remarkably similar. The two men were her sons, Larry and Michael. and as I would soon discover, it was they who provided the muscle to keep the place going. The door from the yard led into the kitchen, and as we entered, I could see that a large wooden table had been laid. Nell invited us to take a seat and within a few minutes she and the boys were serving us large plates of ham and floury potatoes.

Kilcloney Mill from Fenagh Road

I'd been to Ireland a few times, but this was the first time I'd met her. Like an anatomical DaVinci drawing, I was fascinated by how her muscles and sinews pulsed beneath her thin translucent flesh. Her neck and face were bleach white, her skin as wrinkled as a leather purse. She wore some sort of extra thick-lensed glasses, and she had a way about her that oozed the same devil-may-care confidence as her brother.

She'd made some attempt to rouge her lips, but the inaccuracy of its application and the fact she looked so uncomfortable in her long flowery dress gave me the impression this wasn't how she'd usually appear on a normal working day.

When we'd eaten, she and Jack withdrew to the fireplace and spoke in hushed whispers. Then, he returned and, presumably with her permission, told me he was going to give me a tour.

While she sat back with the others, he took me outside. The first thing he showed me was the spout. A thin stone funnel jutting out of a field wall at the crossroads. This, he told me, had provided the cool spring water he drank as a boy. He showed me how to cup my hand to collect it and asked for my opinion. It didn't seem to taste any different than the water back in Sparkhill. Still, I didn't want to spoil his enthusiasm. He was adamant it was purer, cooler, and fresher than any water I'd drunk before, and I found myself agreeing with his assessment. Besides, I couldn't think of anything better than being here with him on a warm summer's evening with the gentle gurgle of the river and Mount Leinster, purple and brown, behind us on the horizon.

When we finished taking the water, he led me back to the yard. Opposite the entrance to the kitchen was what looked like stables. The doors were closed, but through gaps in the timber I could see what looked like the remains of an old car. Without explanation, he continued up a flight of steps. At the top, he turned right and led the way into a shed.

It was filled with archaic machinery, like wooden looms and broken belts. Straps and pulleys hung from hooks in the ceiling, while others lay scattered across the floor. Stacked in the corner were giant spools of white wool. It reminded me of one of those living museums but without the commentary from talking mannequins in tailcoats and top hats. This, he explained, was the remains of the carding factory where his father and grandfather made a variety of woollen products. Three men used to work there in his day and their blankets had been especially popular. The dying process was complicated, and it was done in another shed, but in the corner he pointed out some old bottles. Those, he told me, were the "piss bottles."

The yard at Kilcloney Mill

He saw the look on my face and grinned. The ammonia in urine, he explained, was a strong bleach. It was also used to bond dye to cloth and brighten up the colours. The bottles were given to the neighbours and when they were full, one of his father's men would go around to collect them.

It sounded disgusting — but also fascinating. As I took a closer look around, he began tinkering with a loom. I suspect if I hadn't been there, he might have continued to fiddle with it for hours. After a few minutes, however, he noticed me again, gave that shrug of his, and led the way out.

Behind the carding shed was another building. This, he explained, was the wheelhouse. The wheel itself had been hung on the wall furthest away from the main house and it was half submerged in a sludge of green water. Like the house, it was much smaller than I had imagined. It also looked in a bad way. The metal buckets were rusty or broken and the whole thing leant to one side. I assumed the mill race must have been sluiced off years ago to stop it from rotating, but even so it occasionally clicked and moaned like a frail old man struggling to get out of bed.

Jack told me how it had been shipped over from Manchester to replace an earlier wooden one. The update happened well before his time, but he remembered his father describing how it had been ferried to Dublin, then loaded onto the new railway line and taken by steam train to Borris. He'd also heard how hundreds of locals had lined the route to Kilcloney to watch it being hauled by traction engine to its new home.

By the time we returned to the kitchen, it was getting dark. Someone had lit a fire and I couldn't help noticing how Dickensian it all looked. Two metal hooks hung above a Victorian iron stove and what looked like a witch's cauldron on the hearth beneath. Next to the fire was a low wooden bench, which Nell was sitting on. As Jack went across to chat with her, I decided to conduct my own unofficial tour.

My first port of call was the room leading off to the right. This, I would find out later, was the parlour. It was an old-fashioned word that conjured up Jane Austin and Mr. Darcy — and it lived up to its promise.

Essentially, it was a lounge, but one that looked like it had been mothballed for a hundred years. It was much smaller than the kitchen but far more opulent. Two fuzzy green landscapes hung on the overtly flowery wallpaper and to my astonishment, what looked like a clavichord had been tucked beneath the bay window.

When I asked Jack about it later, he told me his father played it when he was a boy. Being a budding musician myself, I thought I'd give it a go, but when I lifted the lid I could see that it hadn't been loved for quite some time. Half the keys were missing, and the rest looked like they'd been broken up with a hammer.

On a large wooden table next to it was a gramophone, complete with a handle and a big brass horn. Still sitting on the felt turntable was an old 78rpm Bakelite record, a Vitaphone recording of the famous Irish tenor, John McCormack.

Sneaking out of the parlour, I made my way past the chatting adults to the other side of the kitchen. There I found another smaller room that looked empty and unused. What it was for, I had no idea, but later Jack explained that it had been the dairy — presumably where his mother stored the milk, made butter, cheese, that sort of thing.

In the kitchen itself, opposite the door to the yard and in front of a window that looked out on a mesh of overgrown weeds and bushes, was a steep staircase. I followed it up to a hallway and a front door. It seemed odd to find a front door upstairs until I realised that the house had been built into a slope. At a guess, I reckoned this level was a good ten feet higher than the yard downstairs.

A flight of narrow, much steeper steps led to what I guessed was the loft. Before I could climb them, I was called down for tea. I didn't have a chance to explore again, but I reckoned there had to be at least three bedrooms up there — presumably one each for Nell, Larry, and Michael.

Over the next few years, Kilcloney became one of our regular ports of call when we stayed in Ireland. Nell and her lads were always welcoming — particularly Michael, who began to build up a firm friendship with my father. Unfortunately, there was something dark and mysterious about the place that I couldn't quite put my finger on. To add to my sense of unease, the house had no electricity. Whenever we found ourselves there at night, the only light came from a paraffin lamp and the open fire. Sitting at the edge of the room with the flickering shadows of the flames and the occasional clank of the water wheel, I seriously wondered if the place might be haunted. Michael's ghost stories didn't help. A priest carrying a lantern who dwelt in the mist by the crossroad. A dead soldier who marched for eternity along the road to Wexford.

My mother told me she'd also felt uneasy when she stayed there thirty years before. Put to bed without a nightlight, she and her sister would lie awake in the dark listening to the clack of the water wheel and the occasional strange sounds that came from down the landing. Back then her grandmother Biddy, with a back as bent as Nell's, spent most of her time in the bedroom next to hers. At least she knew her grandmother. What she didn't know was who was in the third bedroom. She was told never to go in there, but sometimes she could hear the creak of a bed and someone moaning like a wounded animal.

Fortunately, I never had to sleep over at Kilcloney — but after a few years with Pat, Nell offered to put us up. Not at the mill but in a house she'd recently bought in a place called Currane.

It was a good-looking Georgian property with four bedrooms and, like Kilcloney, it had an exceptionally large kitchen. It smelt of mould and our clothes would be damp almost as soon as we took them out of the suitcase. It hadn't been lived in for a few years and it took a while for Josie and my mother to clean the place from top to bottom and for Jack and my father to clear the garden.

The graveyard at St. Mullins

There was a barn opposite the house and next to that a shed. It was the days of factory farming, and the shed, with its metal doors and corrugated iron roof, was packed with unhappy, sweating pigs. Michael would come early every morning to feed them, mixing up their swill with water from the outside tap and pouring buckets of it into their troughs. As soon as he flung the doors open, the stench was indescribable. It filled the house and left its taste in everything we ate. As a city boy, I thought factory farming a cruel and appalling idea, but that was the zeitgeist and to compete with his fellow pork producers, Michael had no choice but to follow suit. When I complained about the smell to my father, he told me it was a country smell — inferring by implication that it was good for me.

As I grew into a teenager, my cycling took me further afield. Now, without Bernadette and with the blessing of my parents, I cycled everywhere. Down to New Ross, across to Enniscorthy, and over the mountains to Bunclody. Around the same time, my father started bringing over his metal detector. Michael had told him about a battle that had taken place in nearby Kilcumney, and he was determined to find one of the many pikes or swords supposedly buried there.

We also started to visit St. Mullins, an ancient, picturesque graveyard up on a windswept hill. It was surrounded by low mountains and bordered by the ubiquitous River Barrow. My grandmother would always insist my father help her down the stairway of the uneven stone steps that led to the holy well. At the bottom, she would pray for a while, then fill an empty Coke bottle with half a pint of its miraculous healing power.

According to Jack, St. Mullins was where his ancestors had been interred for centuries. He showed me the Kiely tombstone and when he saw I wasn't listening, he upped his game by telling me that other far more interesting people were buried there. Rebels from Cromwell's time. Kings of Ireland, like Dermot MacMurrough Kavanagh — a relative of the limbless Art who built the viaduct — and dozens, if not hundreds, of pikemen from the '98 uprising.

Just outside the cemetery wall was a small hill. My father was certain that it was a Viking burial mound that most probably contained gold — or maybe a longboat. We often spoke about driving there in the dead of night and digging into it to see what we could find. Later, to my disappointment, I discovered it had been built by the Normans as a motte — the foundation of a tower that helped them keep watch over the Barrow.

Apart from manically running up and down it with other young teenagers who had the same idea, my only other interest in St. Mullins was fishing. Josie wasn't keen on me going anywhere near the river. She said it was dangerous. My father assured her he'd look after me and although neither of us had any idea how to fish, we spent many happy hours chatting at the bank and catching nothing.

Jack and my father at Currane

Despite the all-pervasive smell of pigs, we enjoyed staying at Nell's house. It was a lot bigger than Pat's little cottage and we had the place to ourselves. There'd be constant visitors. Pat and Josie's other brother, Mick, Bernadette and her sisters. Then there were Jack's old comrades, and his relatives from Ballymurphy and St Mullins, who'd always be up for a drink and a song.

We must have holidayed there for two or three years, until one morning for no apparent reason, Nell decided we needed another table. Michael and Larry brought it over on the roof of their car. It turned out to be the big wooden one with tri-corner legs I'd seen in the parlour.

Jack recognised it immediately. He told us it had belonged to his grandfather — and when Michael and Larry left, he told us it also had a secret compartment.

This was exciting *Famous Five* stuff, and after a few minutes fiddling around he managed to click some sort of button and swing the top open. Inside were sheafs of letters with what I recognised as penny red and penny black stamps on the envelopes. There was a poster for the mill with the headline "Woollen mill at Kilcloney" which was dated 1858 and there was correspondence from another Larry — a Laurence Keily who was writing to my great-great-great-grandfather, James from Wheeling, Virginia. One of his letters was dated 1865 — a few days after the end of the American Civil War — and it was full of pathos, asking his uncle how the mill was going and waxing lyrical about the old country and how he missed his mother, who must have just died.

Jack hadn't known Laurence, of course, but he knew of him. He was one of his father's cousins. One of many, he told me, who'd had to go to America. As an ignorant fifteen-year-old, I wondered why his letters were so sad and poignant, and why, if he'd loved Ireland so much, he'd gone to America in the first place.

Someone made the mistake of telling Nell what we'd found, and the following morning Michael and Larry returned to retrieve the table. That day a treasure trove of priceless family letters and heirlooms disappeared. What Nell did with them, I never found out, but Jack had managed to hide away the poster and a couple of the American letters. Just before the top was brought down for the last time, I also noted another letter, signed off by someone called Jas. It was dated 1936 with the words Mountjoy gaol stamped in red ink across the front.

CHAPTER FIVE

Widow McCormack's cabbage patch

By the mid 1830s, Johannes was in his late forties. His son James — Jack's grandfather — was hitting thirty. Still a bachelor, he'd spent his entire life helping his father run the mill. Now, as Johannes was slowing down, it was left to him and his brothers to sharpen the grinding stones, lug heavy bags of wheat in and out of the factory, and generally take care of business.

As a boy, he'd been told about the rebellion of '98, how it had so brutally been put down, and how so many of their neighbours had been murdered by Asgill's rampaging Redcoats. He knew the stories about Cromwell and, not surprisingly, his view of the British wasn't favourable. To make matters worse, the Act of Union had taken away any chance of independence and left tenants totally at the mercy of their landlords.

Fortunately, their landlord was Lord Beresford. Since he'd bought the township from LaTouche, there'd been no trouble. Johannes and James had been careful not to raise their heads above the parapet and Beresford had been noticeable by his absence. Things had been going well, but when his son Henry, inherited the estate, alarm bells started to ring.

Lord Henry, the third marquess of Waterford, was the same age as James, but that's where the similarity ended. His reputation was poor, to say the least. Two years earlier, he and his friends had been heavily drinking at the Croxton races. On their way home via the Thorpe End tollgate in

Melton Mowbray, the tollkeeper asked for payment. The drunken Beresford took exception. There were some brushes and pots of red paint left nearby and he thought it would be a laugh to paint the tollkeeper red. When he finished, he started on a policeman who'd tried to intervene.

Lord Henry Beresford

After nailing up the tollhouse and painting that red as well, he and his friends began rampaging through the marketplace like latter-day football hooligans. They painted the Old Swan Inn, then vandalised the post office and the Leicestershire Banking Company. At the ironically named Red Lion, they ripped the sign down and threw it into the canal. When more police officers tried to stop them, they were beaten up and painted red, too.

The expression "painting the town red" was coined from Beresford's vandalism that day. When he finally sobered up, he paid for the damage, but being one of the landed gentry, there was no custodial sentence — just a fine he could easily afford.

Henry was young, volatile, and aggressive. He lacked respect for authority and empathy for anyone lower down the food chain. He believed he had total impunity to do whatever he liked to whomever he liked. Unfortunately, with the Victorian social system as it was, he wasn't far wrong. One of the first things he did after inheriting his estates was to throw out his Catholic tenants in Ballyellin. He replaced them with loyal Orangemen, and as tensions rose, John Walsh, the Parish priest in Borris, decided to head off to London. He intended to complain to the House of Commons about how landlords like Henry systematically terrorised and intimidated their tenants. He was due to speak on the 31st of July 1835. The day before, he was pulled off his horse at the lonely crossroads at Kilgrany and murdered.

One of Beresford's new Orange tenants, Archibald Sly, was arrested. In the end, the evidence against him failed to stack up. Sly was released and the magistrate concluded that Walsh had been murdered by a person or persons unknown.

The priest's murder was the talk of the town and a great deal of anger bubbled beneath the surface. James hoped he could keep well below young Henry'ss radar. Then five years later, his worst fears came true.

Henry was a keen fox hunter and Kilcloney was a place he loved hunting. Riding through the townland in the spring of 1840, he noticed that his hounds were more interested in his tenant's sheep than the fox. Annoyed that his sport was being spoiled, he confided to his friend, Robert Uniacke, that he was minded having the sheep shot. Uniacke, understanding the legal ramifications of such an action, advised against it, and suggested that the smart thing to do would be to evict the tenants instead.

Beresford did just that. The Bailiffs were called and eighty-six Kilcloney tenants, including elderly women and children, were thrown out of their homes. Many of them had lived there for over a hundred years. They'd spent their blood, sweat, and tears improving their land and houses and now, on the whim of one man, they'd lost everything.

An article in the Freeman's journal summed up the feeling across the country:

> The unfortunate people of Kilcloney, consisting of seventeen families, were ejected on Tuesday last. It is impossible to describe the misery and desolation that has taken place there within the last few days. Some of them gave up possession and threw down their houses, for which they received from thirty shillings to three pounds (£65-391) each. Others kept their possessions until they were put out by the sheriff, and these are to be stigmatized as conspirators against the rights of property and will be recorded as such.

According to the Dublin Register of 21st April 1840, the evicted tenants included:

> John Kealy, his wife, brother, and two children. Edward Kealy, who was 92, along with his wife, 84. Their two sons and a daughter-in-law — and a widow Kealy who was struggling to bring up five children.

The "Kealys of the spout," as James' family had become known, escaped eviction by the skin of their teeth. The Kealys listed in the Dublin Register lived nearer to Currane, less than a mile up the road. They were relatives, of course — uncles, aunts, and cousins — descendants of the Kealy diaspora who'd migrated from St. Mullins fifty years before.

The evictions caused a lot of anger and resentment as yet another example of an English landlord throwing his weight around without any care for his tenants. There were protests in Borris, but Beresford stuck to his guns. The law was firmly in his favour and when push came to shove, there was no redress for the people he'd made homeless.

Two years later, at the age of thirty-one, James married his childhood sweetheart, Mary Hayes from St. Mullins. She must have known he was a good catch. Classed as a "farmer" in the 1841 census, he was defined as a "person who had a comfortable standard of living, could participate in local and national politics, arrange beneficial marriages, and provide leadership for other tenants." Farmers were also allowed to be landlords in their own right — as he would soon become to his younger brother, Edward.

Despite the title, James wasn't really a farmer. His income derived mainly from the mill. Although business had been patchy over the last few years, he wasn't as vulnerable as many of his smaller neighbours, who relied on agriculture to make a living. In the main, they fed their family on potatoes, but with rents going up and more land needing to be put aside for crops that paid the rent, it was becoming increasingly difficult to find enough space to grow them. The worst times were the summer or "meal months" when the old crop had been eaten. Not surprisingly, this was the time merchants ramped up the price of meal — the only viable dietary substitute. Most people couldn't afford it, and for most of the summer they waited in a half-starved zombie state for the new batch of potatoes to arrive in August.

This feast-to-famine existence had been the case in Ireland for over a hundred years and James was used to the annual pilgrimage of hungry children begging for flour at the kitchen door.

In 1845, however, things took a turn for the worse. Initially, the crop looked one of the best for years. Then the first disquieting news came from an unexpected quarter. Tory PM Robert Peel received a letter from the Isle of Wight. Renowned for its market gardens, the news was that a disease had appeared in the potato crop. A week or so later a severe blight was reported in Kent. Then in September, Dr. Lindley — the man who built Kew Gardens —declared it had reached Ireland.

At the time no one knew what had caused it. Static electricity from the new railway lines was blamed, along with vapours rising from the centre of the earth. In reality, the disease originated in Mexico in the form of a fungus called *Phytophthora infestans*.

Within less than a year, Ireland's entire supply of potatoes was decimated. The irony was that while there were plenty of vegetables, grain, and butter in the country, hard-pressed farmers had to sell them to pay their rent. In desperation, they resorted to eating rotten potatoes and entire villages started coming down with cholera and typhus. Before long, things had got so bad that rats, cats, and dogs were on the menu.

In the end, many had no option but to eat the crops that paid the rent. Landlords quickly moved in to evict defaulting tenants and James looked on horrified as the ditches along the road into Carlow began to fill with starving families struggling to survive in makeshift hovels. To make matters worse, 1845 was one of the coldest and wettest years in living memory. As well as disease and malnutrition, people started to die from pneumonia and hypothermia. Those who managed to find a place in the Carlow Workhouse weren't much better off. Typhus and cholera were rife. Many couldn't bear the stigma of having their hair cut short or of being dressed like convicts and there was no medical care. Families were split up and often the only way to get food was to fight for it.

Crime began to rise, and as the workhouses filled up. Claims on the meagre benefit system of the day — the Poor Law — shot through the roof. The cost to the exchequer was getting out of hand and landlords were seeing a sharp fall in rental income.

Before long, Peel was forced to step in. Before taking on the Premiership, he'd been Chief Secretary of Ireland. During his tenure, he'd consistently opposed motions for Catholic emancipation and enquiries into the state of Ireland. The Duke of Leinster recalled that in his youth Peel frequently rose after dinner and stood on a chair with one foot on the table to propose a toast to the "pious, glorious, and immortal memory of William III."

His anti-Catholic stance earned him the nickname "Orange" Peel. Having said that, it seemed that since his "Orange" toasting days his attitude to the Irish had softened. In 1843, he'd appointed the Devon commission to look into the land lease situation. He'd also trebled the annual grant to the Catholic seminary at Maynooth.

His first attempt to relieve the famine was to buy American maize for £100,000 (£13mn) and ship it to Ireland. It seemed like a good idea, but it hadn't been thought through. The maize turned up as unground, dried kernels, nicknamed "Peel's brimstone." Effectively, it was inedible unless put through a long, complicated milling process and then cooked again. Those unfortunate enough to try it found themselves suffering from severe bowel problems.

He then turned his attention to the Corn Laws. They'd been Introduced after the Napoleonic Wars to levy tariffs on cheap foreign corn. Their impact was to keep prices high — and maintain huge margins for the suppliers, invariably the big, Tory landowners. Not surprisingly, when he suggested they be repealed, there was uproar in the House.

Initially, the landowning aristocracy insisted on keeping the laws in place. After a few months, they began to waiver. Whilst they didn't want to see corn prices drop, dead or starving people couldn't work — and if they couldn't work, they couldn't pay rent.

Eventually, with the help of the Whig opposition, the laws were repealed, but by then it was too late. Even with cheaper corn, tenants who'd lost their land and income couldn't afford it.

Peel concluded that the only solution was to get more money into the hands of the starving — not with some sort of COVID subsidy, but by making them work for it.

This pound-of-flesh mentality appeased his supporters and huge public works projects were set up across the country. In Carlow alone, over three thousand people flocked to them. Most of the work was soul-destroying and pointless, like breaking rocks or flattening hills. To increase the inequity, landlords received grants to employ labourers, which they used to improve their vast estates. The upshot was that exhausted men, women, and children toiled away for less than sixpence (£4) a week, often dying before collecting their wages.

While all this was happening, bountiful supplies of food were still leaving the country and James was appalled to see his neighbours trying to survive on next to nothing while their vegetables and crops were being loaded onto carts bound for British ships.

In the same year, his first child, Bridie, was born — named after her maternal grandmother Bridie Ryan. A year later, Jack's grandfather John arrived — named after Johannes, who was still very much alive. Johannes was delighted that James had an heir, especially when another grandson, James the Spare, arrived a year later.

Even so, things were almost as difficult as they had been in '98, possibly worse. By May 1846, the price of potatoes had tripled. By the end of the year, when the crop completely failed, there were none in the entire County. In Borris, unemployment soared to 80%. With mass evictions and deaths, business hit rock bottom.

As James watched his cousins take refuge in the workhouse or flee to America from New Ross harbour, the Whigs under Lord John Russell came to power. Repealing the Corn Laws had been the death knell for Peel and James hoped Russell would sort out the mess. He'd always felt the Whigs were more empathetic when it came to Ireland — but this time he was to be proved wrong.

Russell was determined to get costs down. Charles Trevelyan, his new assistant secretary to the treasury, was put in charge of dealing with the famine and gave a flavour of what his approach might be when he said, "If the Irish once find out that there are any circumstances in which they can get free government grants, we shall have a system of mendicancy [begging] such as the world never knew."

Trevelyan's sympathy — or lack of it — was evident from the word go. Charles Darwin's *On the Origin of the Species* wouldn't be published for another year, but in terms of "natural selection," Trevelyn was ahead of the curve. In a letter to his friend Lord Monteagle, he suggested the famine was an "effective mechanism for reducing surplus population."

Immediately, he brought Peel's public works program to a halt. Then he attempted to shift costs from the exchequer to the landlords by introducing a new Poor Law Act. This forced them to pay a subsidy for tenants whose rent was less than £4 (£520) a year. These subsidies were then to be used to fund a new relief program.

Unfortunately, like Peel's American maize idea, it hadn't been thought through. To maximise their return, most landlords had divided their land into the smallest plots possible. Now they found they had hundreds of tenants who fell under Trevelyan's £4 (£520) limit.

Faced with the prospect of huge bills, they decided to change their business model. Their solution was to evict smaller tenants and create larger plots. They could then rent these out for more than £4 (£520) and avoid paying the subsidy.

As thousands more became homeless, another of Russell's men, Sir William Gregory, poured oil on the fire. Gregory, who'd inherited a large fortune from his grandfather and blown most of it on the racetrack, added a new clause to the Act called, appropriately enough, "The Gregory clause."

It proposed that tenants who rented more than ¼ acre wouldn't be entitled to Poor Law relief unless they surrendered the balance of their land to their landlord. Someone renting an acre, for example, and on the verge of starvation, couldn't apply for any sort of benefit unless they handed over — for nothing — their remaining ¾ acre.

Most tenants in such an insidious position preferred to starve. Often, their land had been in their families for generations, and besides, entitlement to relief was no guarantee they'd get it. Where Gregory's Act morphed from cruel to ridiculous was when they had no other choice but to accept it. Once reduced to renting just ¼ acre, their landlord again became responsible for paying the government subsidy. As a result, despite doing everything required of them such tenants found themselves still served with eviction notices. To ensure they didn't come back, the landlord's bailiffs often burnt their homes to the ground — usually while they were at the workhouse, trying to claim relief.

In 1847, Dan O'Connell, the first Irish MP to be elected after the Act of Union, died. He'd been of the opinion that the English could only be shown the error of their ways by peaceful protest. Younger members of his Irish Parliamentary party weren't so sure. Once he'd gone, they formed a movement called "Young Irelanders." Their goal was to achieve an Irish national Parliament with full legislative and executive powers — nothing more, nothing less — and while they didn't openly advocate violence, they made it clear they were prepared to use any means necessary and "consistent with honour, morality, and reason."

James was fully behind them. The newspapers were full of revolution. Louis Phillipe had just been thrown out of

France and similar regime changes were happening in Berlin, Vienna, Rome, Prague, and Budapest. Why not Ireland?

Billy O'Brien, a Protestant MP from Limerick, started the ball rolling. He began marching through the country to gather recruits and throw out the big landlords. It was bad timing. Most people were more concerned with feeding their families than an insurrection. Undeterred, he kept going. When he reached Tipperary, he tried to give a speech. As the police moved in to arrest him, a small crowd who wanted to hear what he had to say turned on them. Outnumbered, the police retreated to a nearby cabin belonging to a Mrs. Margaret McCormack. She wasn't at home at the time, but her four children were. For the next few hours, they were held hostage while a baying mob gathered outside. Eventually, the police let them go. Then O'Brien demanded they hand over their weapons. When they refused, the crowd began throwing bricks through the windows until the police were forced to fire back.

The newspapers dubbed it the "Battle of Widow McCormack's Cabbage Patch." After reinforcements arrived, the crowd melted away and O'Brien was arrested. To James, it seemed like a ridiculous skirmish that should have amounted to nothing. After all, half of Ireland was starving, and surely the authorities had better things to worry about. Despite the comedic headline, however, O'Brien was sent to Tasmania, and the Young Irelanders movement collapsed overnight.

That same year, Thomas Kavanagh's son, the limbless Art, saw an opportunity. Thanks to the famine, the people of Borris were desperate for work. Using skills he'd gained in India as a draughtsman, he used their cheap labour to construct a sawmill at the bottom of the town. The British

Empire's requirement for lumber was enormous and before long he was turning a profit. To maximise his return, he rebuilt the town in stone, renting out the new Georgian-style properties to tenants he considered financially robust.

Then he turned his attention to the railway system. The Great Southern & Western Line had just reached Bagnalstown. To improve his transport logistics, he wanted a station in Borris. Using his position as a major landowner and MP, he persuaded the rail company to extend the line and fund a sixteen-arch viaduct to get it over the River Black.

As well as hundreds of locals, masons, carpenters, and navvies were brought in from across the country to construct it. Stone was carved on site, dressed, then winched up by a steam crane and pulley and positioned in place. The pillars were made from local limestone and the parapets, string courses, and keystones were dressed in the best granite.

The workmanship was top quality and every Sunday, after Mass, James would take his wife and young family down to check its progress. By now he had five children: Bridie, seven; John, six; James, five; Kitty, four; and baby Nell. Art's viaduct was the talk of the town, and the inseparable John and James were fascinated watching the men high up on the wooden scaffolds, piecing everything together.

By the time the worst of the famine was over, Art had won the admiration and thanks of the Borris community; he'd also made himself another fortune.

Other big landowners weren't so lucky. Hit by government subsidies, the cost of bailiff evictions, and loss of rent, many had to file for bankruptcy. The famine should have ended Ireland's oppressive landlord-and-tenant system, but when the Encumbered Estates Act was introduced, things got worse.

The Act allowed creditors to petition for insolvent estates to be auctioned off so they could get their money back. Often, they were sold for far less than their market value and wealthy speculators snapped them up.

Unlike their gentrified predecessors, these speculators weren't content to be passive rent collectors. They'd bought their estates to make money and they had a much sharper focus on the bottom line. Inevitably, they racked up rents, and over the next few years another 50,000 families joined the homeless.

During the famine, at least a million people died from hunger, typhus, and dysentery. Another two million emigrated to countries like Britain and America. Half the population of Borris disappeared, and in Kilcloney the famine, along with Beresford's evictions, left the township almost empty.

Irish potato famine

It was one of the greatest exoduses in history, an unparalleled humanitarian disaster. If the Irish expected sympathy from the British, however, they needed to think again. An article in the London Times concluded: "Thanks to a bountiful Providence, the Irishman on the banks of the Shannon will soon be as rare a sight as the Red Indian on the banks of the Hudson."

Three years later, James expanded the wool-making side of the business. It was an attempt to hedge against the vagaries of wheat and corn production. On 12th May 1858, he produced a poster with the headline, *Woollen mill at Kilcloney.*

Underneath it ran:

> *James Keily most respectfully announces to the public that in addition to his other machinery of carding wool, he has got up a way of spinning weaving colouring tucking and dressing.*

By 1860, the mill was back on its feet. Young John was now sixteen and working hard with his father and grandfather. The family had been fortunate enough to have weathered the storm. Even so, the Rusell government's incompetence and insensitivity had left them angry. The mill had been on the verge of bankruptcy. Many of their relatives had been evicted or fled to America and they'd seen neighbours dying on the streets of Borris.

John Mitchel, the Young Ireland leader who'd been transported to Van Diemen's Land for opposing shipments of harvests to Britain, summed up their thoughts and the thoughts of many when he said.

The Almighty, indeed, sent the potato blight, but the English created the famine.

CHAPTER SIX

The winning ticket

By the early seventies, I'd stopped staying with my grandparents on Saturdays. I was old enough to look after myself and I also had "O" levels to revise for. When I did pay a visit, I often found Jack hunched over a table with pencil and paper. He'd taken it into his head to knock down his old house in Ballinagree and build a new one. I watched him pore for hours over Daily Mail books of house plans until he lighted on one he liked. It was a bungalow, of course, as were most new Irish homes springing up like mushrooms that decade. A few months later, he packed up his tools and enough clothes for a year and headed off to catch the boat.

We joined him as usual for the summer holidays. He was getting on well and, with the help of Michael and Larry, had already laid the foundations. At the weekends, he'd take some time off and while I cycled around the lanes and my father tried to catch that elusive fish, he'd pay a visit to his old comrades. Sometimes he'd take me with him, and when he did I always found it interesting.

They were all friendly and very fond of Jack. They'd meet in various places — sometimes Nell's house in Currane or in Joyce's or Shea's, where they'd invariably buy me an ice cream or a lemonade.

Apart from being old, the other thing I noticed about them was that they were all poor. Jack seemed to have been the only one who'd made it to England and accumulated a modicum of wealth. Whilst they'd cycle to meet him in dusty patched jackets and flat caps, he always made a point of keeping up appearances by wearing his best suit and tie.

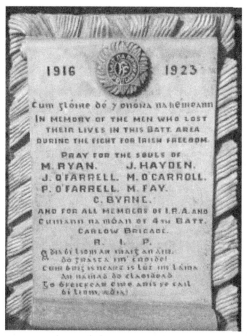

Memorial at Ballymurphy

It was fascinating to hear them talk about the old days. A man called John Hynes had been one of their leaders. So had a Dr. Dundon. From what I could gather, Dundon had been the commanding officer of Jack's brigade. He'd pointed his house out to me. A picturesque ivy-covered old stone building on Borris High Street. He said Dundon's granddaughter was Olivia O'Leary, one of the presenters on BBC's *Newsnight*, a program he and Josie were invariably glued to when they were in England.

I found one of his friends, Jack Ryan, particularly fascinating. He made model steam engines in his shed in Gorsebridge. They were perfect in every detail, and he took great delight in showing me how all the moving parts, like pistons and regulators, came together to make them work. To watch his traction engines moving around and pushing out steam was a delight and I often wondered where he'd built up his expertise. Luke Dwyer was rougher and ready. He smoked a pipe and always had a story to tell. One that stuck in my mind was about a house owned by a family called Marley. Michael had already told me that the place was haunted and that if the gates to the yard were ever closed, evil spirits would wreak havoc until they were opened again. Luke repeated the same tale, and later that night, when we were back in Currane, Jack added a further twist. He said that back in his IRA days, he, Luke, and some of the others had been on the run and, as the place was empty, they decided to hole up there. One of the Brigade had foolishly closed the gates and that night, when they were sleeping in one of the bedrooms, they heard footsteps approaching down the hall landing.

Jack said he picked up a rifle and crept towards the door. He waited until the footsteps stopped just outside. Then he kicked it open, only to find no one there. I wasn't sure whether to believe him or not, but he assured me it was true. My father suggested we should check it out for ourselves by driving up there and closing the gates for ourselves. Josie told him not to be so silly and to take the supernatural more seriously. Jack just sat back in his armchair and grinned mischievously.

Luke also told me about the tower of Currane, an old ruin near Ballymartin where Art Kavanagh — or the "crippled Kavanagh" as he inappropriately called him — ordered a torch to be lit to guide him home from his occasional trips to Wexford. Danny Foley, another of Jack's friends, told me a story about a King of Leinster who'd been buried on

Mount Leinster somewhere — possibly with a hoard of gold — and that if I spent my holiday searching, I might find it.

The other tale they told was less frivolous. They spoke about it in hushed tones and with an odd mix of anger and sorrow. It was about Peter and James Farrell. They showed me a monument to them in Ballymurphy churchyard, just down the road from where Danny Foley lived. They told me that back in the 1920s, the brothers had been out ploughing their father's field when they were attacked and murdered by a contingent of "Black and Tans."

At the time, I had no idea who or what Black and Tans were, but as the conversation fell away and their eyes started to redden, I did my best to reflect their mood and look as sombre as possible.

As usual, we spent our holidays at Nell's house in Currane — minus the table. When Jack's friends came around, Josie and my mother would always make sure they were well fed and watered – and by watered, I mean plied with alcohol until their speech became slurred, beads of sweat broke out on their foreheads, and any songs they sang took twice as long.

One of the most enjoyable days in the holiday calendar was the 15th of August. This was the day of the Borris fair, when farmers and traders from all over the County bought and sold their livestock. Most of the sheep and cattle were penned at the lower end of the town whilst the horse traders used the area at the top, outside the old barracks. Invariably, there'd be a lot of drinking and often a lot of fighting. Josie's younger brother, Mick, would often meet us there and take us into Joyce's. He'd buy me a lemonade and I'd watch him smoke his pipe and tell his stories and wish that someday I could be like him. Afterwards, Josie would head downtown to see what the Travellers had for sale, while the rest of us stayed chatting in the pub.

The 15th of course had a religious significance. In the Catholic calendar, it was the day the Virgin Mary was assumed body and soul into heaven. Even back then, I was dubious. My mother, as a firm Catholic, believed in its literal truth. My father wasn't so convinced. Years before, when I asked him why I had to go to church every Sunday, he thought for a while and replied that it was good exercise. It got me up in the morning, and all that standing up, sitting down, and kneeling was good for me. When I asked Jack if there was a God, he also thought for a bit and then told me he didn't know — but he went to church, just in case.

Years later, I discovered that the 15th of August was when the sun blocked out the Virgo constellation in the night sky. Perhaps the astronomic origin of the Christian assumption story, and a piece of trivia I never failed to bring up whenever I had the opportunity.

One year, my father took me to New Ross to see where the coffin ships had set sail to places like America. He told me they were called coffin ships because the chances of ever seeing anyone who sailed off on one again were practically zero. It was as poignant to him as Jack. Even though he was an out-and-out Brummy, somewhere on his mother's side there was an Irish connection. Later I was to find out it was the O'Malley's and the McCormack's and that one had their roots in Roscommon, the other in Mayo.

They'd come to England at the height of the famine, and it struck me that life had probably been a lot tougher for them than the Kealys. The famine must have been bad. The idea of being burnt out of your house seemed cruel beyond belief. The idea of having to watch the food you'd grown being carted off while you and your family starved to death was even worse.

I don't know what it was like for most of the immigrants who had to leave Ireland, but my father told me his fellow Brummies didn't exactly welcome them with open arms. Understandably, I suppose they feared for their livelihoods and, as a result, the Irish wound up doing jobs no one else would do for a wage no one else would accept.

A Royal Commission summed up the sort of work they did as "usually of the roughest, coarsest, and most repulsive description, and requiring the least skill and practice."

The only housing they could afford were places like the dingy back-to-backs near the city centre. Chronically overcrowded, they had a small yard, a toilet shared by five or six families, a night barrel to dump excrement, and a shed to wash clothes. I discovered years later that although most of them had been pulled down, one remained: 15 Inge Street in the city centre. It had been preserved by the National Trust and, bizarrely, it was one of the many properties my father's ancestors rented when they came over from Ireland.

Every year that we holidayed in Ireland, I learned a little more about the Kiely family. I already knew Jack had been brought up in Kilcloney along with his three sisters, Mary, Nell, and Bridie. What I hadn't known was that he also had a brother. It was something I picked up on a visit to St. Mullins. In previous years, I'd been too busy running up and down the Norman Motte to take much notice, but that year I caught his name on the headstone. *"James Kiely, 1898 – 1947."*

If I'd given it enough thought, I could have predicted his existence from the traditional Irish naming system. The first-born son named after his grandfather, the second, after his father. Jack shared the same name as his father, and therefore there had to be a James.

Why Jack never mentioned him to me was a bit of a mystery. Perhaps they didn't get on — perhaps it was too painful to talk about. Years before, I remember him having a gallstone operation in the QE in Birmingham. When he was waking up after the anaesthetic, he kept muttering "Jas" under his breath. I wasn't sure what he meant at the time, but now it made sense. He'd been calling out for his big brother.

When I asked my mother about him, all she knew was that he'd been bedridden for years. He'd died just after Jack had taken them to England, and she couldn't remember having met him. Thinking back on it, she wondered if it might have been him she'd heard moaning in that Kilcloney bedroom. With her memory jogged, she recalled Nell's daughter, Nancy, taking meals up there. When she came down, she'd be carrying blood-stained bandages that she'd wrap in newspaper and burn in the field above the yard.

While Jas was named after his grandfather, Mary, the eldest girl, was named after her grandmother. Nell as the second sister should have been named Bridie after her mother. Instead, her younger sister was named Bridie and I guessed that somewhere along the line, Nell had an older sister, Bridie who died a couple of years after she was born.

Why she'd wound up owning the mill was another mystery. I would have thought that Jack as the second son would have taken it over when his brother died. All I knew about it was that there'd been some sort of falling out between Nell and Mary. How that affected Jack's inheritance, I didn't know. As for Mary, I only met her once, and that was on one of my rides to Bunclody.

Jack told me she lived at the foot of Mount Leinster, and although he had no intention of seeing her himself, he subtly encouraged me to do so. On his instruction, I knocked on the door of her little cottage and was welcomed by a short woman in her late seventies with a red face and a bun of grey hair pulled tight behind her head. Dressed in a long blue coat and wellies, she looked like a poor man's Queen Victoria. When I told her who I was, she invited me in for a cup of tea and a cake. I wasn't expecting such a warm welcome, and after she asked me how I was doing at school, she asked after Jack. When I returned to Currane with news of how she was, he seemed pleased.

If there was some sort of unfinished business going on between them, I didn't know what it was. However, it revived a memory of a strange tale Michael had told me years before. We were in the kitchen at Kilcloney, and he pointed out a dent in the plaster above the fire. He told me it was a bullet hole left from when his mother took a potshot at Mary using one of Jack's revolvers.

I dismissed it as one of his tall stories, but now I wasn't so sure. What I did know was that the enthusiastic reception Mary had given me when I went around seemed to provide him with the ideal opportunity to bite the bullet and pay her a visit — but as far as I know, he never did.

Jack returned to England in September. The new bungalow was progressing well, but he had to stop for the winter. As the nights drew in, he and Josie returned to watching Olivia on *Newsnight*.

Things were hotting up in Northern Ireland. After Austin Currie's squat-in, a group of Catholics formed a civil rights movement. Their idea was to persuade Unionists that they deserved some sort of equality — not only in housing but jobs, education, and life in general.

Jack's sister Mary

Their first move was to hold a peace march, but Like Martin Luther King's effort at the Edmund Pettus Bridge a few years earlier, it didn't go well. Halfway through, Loyalists began attacking them. To make matters worse, the Royal Ulster Constabulary joined in.

It seemed anathema to me that the police would do such a thing but, as Jack explained, the RUC were recruited solely from Unionists, so it was easy to see where their loyalties lay.

Unfortunately for the RUC, the march was televised, and pictures of officers joining the attackers and wading in with batons didn't look good. Like Alabama's governor, George

Wallace, the government decided it was better all-around if peace marches were banned.

When the peace movement ignored the ban and held another march, the government sent in the heavy guns. Like Wallace's state troops in Alabama, the RUC were given carte blanche to do whatever was needed to break it up. Without provocation, they began throwing tear gas and using excessive physical force to clear the marchers away. Over a hundred people were injured, including a few politicians, and again the TV crews were there to record the RUC's heavy-handedness.

There was more public outrage and a few days later, Belfast's Protestant and Catholic students came together to create their own non-partisan civil rights movement. It was called People's Democracy and, hoping for a better outcome, they began a four-day march from Belfast to Derry. They were attacked, too. This time by over two hundred Loyalists, including off-duty RUC men armed with iron bars, bricks, and bottles. Many students were severely injured and when they eventually reached Derry, they were attacked again — this time by mobs aided and abetted by uniformed police.

Back in England, BBC News reported marches had been banned for a good reason. Basically, to calm things down and avoid civil unrest. Jack's gripe with that was that unlike Simon Cowell, the BBC hadn't given us the full back story. To add insult to injury, the government gave a special dispensation for the Loyalist Apprentice Boys of Derry to hold their usual 12th July Orange Day parade just a stone's throw from an embittered Catholic Bogside.

The following summer, I returned to Ireland. Jack had been there since the spring and his bungalow was now at roof level. It was of huge interest to passers-by, who slowed to gawp and check his progress as they drove by.

Jack building his bungalow.

By now he was seventy-two and it's only as I approach a similar age that I fully appreciate how dogged and determined he must have been. Whenever I cycled around to see him, he was always in the middle of something — balancing on a rafter or cementing in another breezeblock, and I rarely saw him tired. On one occasion I found him at the bottom of the garden, standing over the old well. He was holding a wooden box filled with dozens of old black and white photographs. I asked him what he was doing, and he told me that he was throwing them away. It wasn't just photographs. There were gold watches, chains, old letters, and a host of other oddities in that box. He must have seen the consternation on my face, and he gave me a look that seemed to say, "You didn't want any of this, did you?"

For a moment he hesitated, then fished into the box and pulled out a photograph. "Do you know who that is?" he asked. It was a good-looking young woman in a cloche hat. I suspected it might be my grandmother, but I wasn't sure.

I told him I didn't, and he smiled. He took a gold watch and chain from the box gave it to me and threw the photograph and whatever else was in the box down the well.

That was the thing with Jack — he lived for the moment, and he never seemed to dwell on the past. He told me later that he'd won the chain for cross country running and I could make out the letters *GAA* and the date *1916* engraved on the face.

Three months later, he finished his bungalow. It stood on almost the exact site of the old house, and it comprised three bedrooms, a lounge, and a kitchen. He was immensely proud of it: "The house that Jack built," he liked to tell me. He wanted to move in straight away, but Josie wasn't keen. They would have no way of getting into town, she said, and most of their friends had moved away long ago. Besides, they would hardly ever see me and my cousins, and the nearest Marks & Spencer was in Dublin.

To his disappointment, she insisted they continue living in Birmingham — at least for the time being. The good news was that for the first time, we had a permanent base for our summer holidays.

It was the year of the moon landing. While I was glued to the TV watching Neil Armstrong take his first "small step for man," Josie and Jack were becoming increasingly horrified at what was happening in Northern Ireland.

Every night, Olivia reported riots and RUC atrocities. To try and stop peace marches, the Unionist government decided to equip the RUC with armoured cars and Browning submachine guns. Most of the world was appalled with this "sledgehammer to crack a nut" policy and pressure to de-escalate the tension began to pour in from Europe and

America. In Ireland, De Valera asked the British to send in a UN peacekeeping force.

Jack and Josie thought it a sensible idea, but PM Harold Wilson decided to mobilise the British army instead.

Their brief was to keep the peace and, initially, they were welcomed by the Nationalists. At the same time, the findings of the Hunt Committee were reported. They vindicated everything Jack had told me about the RUC. Effectively that the RUC, and their armed comrades the B-Specials, were partisan and out of control.

Hunt recommended they be disbanded, and that night the paramilitary Ulster Volunteer Force took to the streets. Later that week, they began bombing targets in the Republic.

Since the end of the Second World War, the IRA had been practically non-existent. Now, with Unionist violence and so many Catholics becoming disaffected. hundreds of new recruits were queuing to sign up. The problem for the IRA was that they'd undergone a split.

On one hand, there were the "Officials" — sometimes called "Stickies" because they sold Easter lilies with a peel-off sticky back. They believed Ireland couldn't be unified until the Protestant and Catholic communities were at peace. The "Provos" — called the "Pinnies" as their lilies had to be pinned on — weren't so compromising. Their stance was that Britain should hand back the six counties to the Republic with no ifs or buts — and right now.

As Jack bemoaned that Republicans couldn't agree on anything, twenty-six Catholic men on a civil rights march were shot at by the British army. Fourteen of them died. The incident became known as "Bloody Sunday" and BBC

News reported that the troops had responded to IRA fire from within the crowd. They also reported that someone had lobbed a bomb in their direction. The inevitable conclusion across the British media was that the army's response had been one of restrained self-defence.

Fr. Edward Daly, Bloody Sunday

Jack was firmly of the opinion that it was a whitewash. He said he'd seen fake news put out by the British government many times, and this was just another example.

Certainly, TV pictures of Father Edward Daly waving a blood-stained handkerchief while trying to escort the mortally wounded Jackie Duddy to safety were highly emotive. All the same, it seemed unlikely that my government would stoop to telling lies. I concluded, therefore — as many of my friends did — that if the British army said they were attacked, then attacked they were.

I had to wait forty years until I discovered Jack was right. The Saville Enquiry of 2010 concluded that the killings were "unjustified" and "unjustifiable." That all those shot were unarmed, none were posing a serious threat, no bombs were thrown, and that soldiers "knowingly put forward false accounts" to justify their firing. What's more, many of the victims were shot while running away, some were even shot helping the wounded, and two were deliberately mown down by army vehicles.

Jack said the same sort of thing had happened back in the 20s when the Black and Tans fired on the crowds in Croke Park. I knew nothing about that, but while I put the blame for Bloody Sunday squarely on the IRA, the locals knew the real score. Not surprisingly, many began flocking into the arms of the much more radical "pinny" Provos.

I was only sixteen at the time and still wet behind the ears. When I could be bothered turning my attention from T-Rex to *Newsnight*, I seriously wondered why people were fighting over something as esoteric as religion. After all, the opposing sides were clearly labelled. Catholics believed Orangemen to be Royalist anti-Christs. Protestants believed Catholics to be idolatry-worshipping papists. Surely, I conjectured, if both sides believed in the same God and the same Christ, a little mutual give and take could readily sort things out.

When I put this to Jack one Saturday, he smiled. It was a patronising smile, and I could feel my hackles rise. He must have seen how I felt and quickly adjusted his expression to one of interest. He let me rattle on for a while, and when I'd finished, he sat me down and offered me a cup of tea. It took him a few minutes to boil up the kettle in the kitchen, and when he returned, he sat down in his usual armchair and told me point blank that the conflict in the North had nothing to do with religion. By way of explanation, he asked me to imagine I'd bought a front-row ticket for the Railway Cup hurling championship. When I asked him what that was, he changed the analogy to the FA Cup final. As I take my seat, someone comes over and shows me their ticket. It's identical to mine. So, he asked. What do you do?

That's all he said. At that point, Josie came in from her shopping trip and we both got up and helped her carry her bags into the kitchen.

Jack had an annoying way of answering a question with a question, and this one had got me stumped. He also wasn't the sort of person you'd quiz twice. It wasn't that he was daunting or threatening — just that when he finished a topic, it was finished. Fait accompli, nothing more to say.

It wasn't until a year later that I think I figured out what he was getting at.

Nationalists and some Unionists had gotten together with the British and Irish governments to negotiate a peace settlement. They came up with the Sunningdale Agreement that, amongst other things, suggested a power-sharing arrangement. The instrument would be a "Council of Ireland" made up of ministers from both sides of the border.

On the whole, Unionists weren't keen. Their real red line, however, was the "Council of Ireland" — or what they perceived as an all-Ireland parliament-in-waiting. Despite a real attempt by politicians on both sides, the Agreement was eventually brought down by strikes organised by Loyalist paramilitaries and Unionist workers.

It was a tragedy, but the idea of those at the top of the food chain not wanting to share power with those at the bottom was a universal theme. Somewhere I read a quote from Martin Luther King:

"We know through painful experience that freedom is never voluntarily given by the oppressor; it must be demanded by the oppressed."

It's interesting that the attack on his civil rights march across the Edmund Pettus Bridge in 1965 was also called Bloody Sunday. In that case, the all-white state troopers felt that the black population should know and accept their place at the bottom of the pile. In South Africa, when thousands of children in Soweto began a peaceful protest against having to learn Afrikaans at school, the mainly white police force began shooting them with tear gas and bullets.

All these responses were totally over the top because they weren't about the right to march — they weren't even about colour or being Catholic — they were about maintaining the superiority of one group over another.

And that got me thinking about Jack's FA Cup final ticket. If you found yourself in the best seat in the house, how likely would you be to give it up without a fight?

It was a good point. If I'd been one of those landlords during the famine, would I have reduced my rents and lost money? If I were a Unionist, would I want to give up the advantages I had in the job and housing market? If I were living in 1960s Alabama, would I want to give up my position of white superiority?

It raised the question of how Unionists had got the best seats in the first place, and as usual I asked Jack to fill me in.

He began by explaining that three hundred years ago, the protestant William of Orange and his wife Mary had been invited to seize the throne of England from the Catholic James II. Orange deriving from *Oranghien* — the place where William was born.

A dislike of Catholicism at the time was understandable. Their track record from the Crusades to the Inquisition was appalling. Besides, it wasn't that long before that Guy Fawkes had tried to blow up the King's grandfather — along with his court.

Having said that, James felt it was time to forgive and forget. Catholicism, at least in England, had been mainly neutered and his idea was to allow the free practice of all Christian religions. In 1687, his Declaration of Indulgence was specifically drafted to do just that. From a moral perspective, it seemed eminently reasonable, but there was a political consideration that threw a spanner in the works.

Since the time of Henry VIII, the power of the Catholic upper classes had been eroded. Lands had been confiscated and dynasties quashed. With James' new law, there was now the possibility that they might try and make a comeback.

Not surprisingly, William's supporters were worried. They had the best seats and they wanted to keep them.

Ironically, it was James's grandfather, the Protestant James I, who'd handed out those seats in the first place. It came about when he concluded that the predominantly Catholic population in Ulster were barbaric and dangerous. They were constantly rebelling and to tighten control, it seemed like a good idea to replace them with sympathetic Protestants. He began a process of forced eviction and for every 3000 acres he transferred to his rich friends, he required them to settle at least twenty families — all of whom had to be English-speaking and Protestant. These "planters" were explicitly banned from taking on Irish tenants and could only import workers from England and Scotland. Moreover, he made it illegal for them to sell their land to anyone Irish or Catholic.

It was the descendants of these "planters" who supported William, and their resounding victory against James at the battle of the Boyne on 12th July 1689 made sure Protestant supremacy wasn't going away anytime soon.

The upshot was that three hundred years later, Orangemen still felt obliged to remind their Catholic neighbours that not only had they been firmly thrashed at the Boyne, but that their position in the social hierarchy was still bottom of the heap.

After the Sunningdale Agreement collapsed, Nationalists became disillusioned. They felt that enough hadn't been done to break the Unionist strikes. In desperation, the government pushed through emergency measures to suspend the Unionist-controlled Stormont parliament and bring in direct rule.

This upset both communities and tit-for-tat reprisals escalated. In 1974, an IRA bomb went off in a coach, killing twelve people. A year later, a cabaret band was ambushed by the UVF and three of the band members were shot — two were Catholics and one was Protestant.

In the same year, two bombs exploded in Birmingham city centre. I was lucky not to have been a victim myself. That night I'd arranged to meet my friends in the Tavern in the Town — a regular haunt for us. Fortunately, for a reason that I can't remember, we changed venues at the last minute.

Jack was a firm supporter of the Nationalist cause, but these indiscriminate killings didn't sit well with him. When I asked what he thought about the Birmingham bombings, he was uncharacteristically quiet. I suspected he didn't want to criticise what he saw as the struggle for a united Ireland. On the other hand, I had the feeling he wasn't happy with the way things were going.

It was a frightening time for many in the Irish community who wanted to keep out of politics. I remember my mother being worried about travelling on a bus or being at work and someone hearing her accent. My aunt and uncle, who used to dance at the Irish Centre in Digbeth, stopped going. Even Josie took to carrying a stick when she went shopping.

A year later, as Eamon De Valera was attending a meeting of the John McCormack Society in O'Connell Street, he was taken ill. He died a month or two later at the age of ninety-two. It was a big blow for Jack and Josie. They'd always maintained what a great man he was, and for as long as I could remember they'd supported his Fianna Fail party. As to why they didn't support the more obviously IRA-biased Sinn Féin party, I didn't quite understand.

From then on, the violence continued. Lord Mountbatten's boat was blown up in Sligo, there was a spate of hunger strikes at the Maize, and the IRA tried to assassinate Margaret Thatcher at the Grand Hotel in Brighton.

By then, my trips to Ireland had become more infrequent. I got married in 1981, two children came along in '85 and '88, and Josie died in '92. A year after that, my third child was born. During those years I had better things to do than to worry about Northern Ireland. I had a family to raise and a business to run. Besides, like many people, I'd become desensitised to the continual drone of hunger strikes, murder, and mayhem.

By the mid-nineties, any interest I'd had in Irish nationalism, the IRA, and what Jack might have got up to had all but left me.

Then in the summer of '96, my wife and I decided to take the family over to the bungalow. By now, things were a lot different. A year earlier, my parents had sold up in Birmingham and moved there permanently. Without Josie, Jack was lost, and my mother decided he needed to end his days in the Borris nursing home.

He wasn't happy about it. A few days after we arrived, I visited him and enquired how he was doing. He just smiled a Mona Lisa smile and shrugged. There was nothing more he could say. His time had come, and he knew it. I asked him about the food and the nurses. Was he being looked after alright? He assured me he was, and I asked him if he fancied a spin in the car.

After three months inside, he was only too keen, and with the permission of the staff, I took him for a whistle-stop tour through Borris, up to Kilcloney, and on to St. Mullins. When we got back, I helped him into his armchair and asked him if he'd enjoyed himself. He took my hand and told me he had. I kissed him on the cheek and told him I'd come back in a couple of days and maybe we'd go on another trip.

I was about to leave when I remembered something I wanted to tell him. I asked him if he'd heard of Liam Neeson. He shook his head. I told him he was a relatively new actor and that he was starring in a film about the Anglo-Irish War. Jack looked vaguely interested, so I told him the title —*Michael Collins* — and asked if he'd like to see it.

His reaction took me by surprise. He stood up and clenched his fists. "I would not set foot outside that door to see that man," he spat.

It took a good minute or so before he calmed down. As far as I knew, Collins was an IRA leader back in the '20s. In fact,

I'd read in the publicity blurb that he was the man who'd won the guerrilla war. There was a picture of him looking quite dapper in a green captain's cap outside the GPO and I thought that being involved himself, Jack might want to see it — obviously, I was wrong.

I changed the subject, and we chatted a little while longer. When he began to close his eyes again, I covered him with a blanket. By the time I tip-toed out of his room, he was snoring like a foghorn.

CHAPTER SEVEN

Fenian Guy Fawkes

After the famine, the general feeling in Ireland was one of distrust and hatred for the British. What's more, it was now glaringly obvious they viewed the Irish as an inferior subspecies not worthy of help or empathy.

Back in the eighteenth century, Thomas Jefferson — ironically the man who penned "All Men are Created equal" — said that "blacks, whether originally a distinct race, or made distinct by time and circumstances, are inferior to whites in the endowments both of body and mind." Other philosophers like Christoph Meiners went a stage further, concluding that people of colour "felt little pain, lacked emotions and possessed no human and barely any animal, feeling."

James could only conclude the British felt the same way about the Irish. When Darwin published his *On the Origin of the Species* in 1859, its central proposal was that "species compete to survive and only the strongest survive." Scientists like Francis Galton — Darwin's distant cousin — extrapolated to suggest that humans could be divided into breeds competing for the top spot. Not surprisingly. he concluded that the noble white races — particularly the British — were top of the food chain.

The major exception was the Irish. Afro-Americans were often referred to as "smoked Irish" and it was seriously suggested that Irish people were black people in white skin — or, more colloquially, "blacks turned inside out."

During the famine, immigration records didn't record the Irish as "Europeans" as they did for every other white race, but as "Irish" – a technically separate and distinct category.

Irishmen were standardly caricatured in British newspapers as grotesque, red-faced gargoyles carrying cudgels. Common adjectives used to describe them included "apish, incestuous, alcoholic, and barbaric."

A Mr. J Redfield, a friend of Darwin, published a book called *Comparative Physiognomy*. In it, he helpfully compared the facial structure of an Irishman with a dog. The similarities, he said, were quite striking and he concluded that the Irish were animalistic, cruel, and cowardly. He continued, "The commonality takes to dirt-digging more naturally than to anything else. They are dirty in their persons and admit pigs into their mud-cabins which they themselves occupy. They are good servants if you deal harshly with them, as a master does with his dog; but the moment you are disposed to be familiar with them they are all over you, jumping against you and laying their dirty paws upon your clean clothes, as if you were no better than they."

In 1864, two of James' children, Jim and Nell, succumbed to Tuberculosis. At the time it was called "Consumption" – sometimes darkly referred to as "the robber of youth." The *mycobacterium tuberculosis* bacteria wouldn't be discovered for another thirty years and no one knew where the disease came from or how it could be cured. Young Jim would have been nineteen and Nell fifteen. To lose children of any age is devastating, but two teenagers at the prime of life, possibly more so. They may have contracted it from a neighbour. It was equally possible they'd picked it up in Borris or the streets of Carlow. Either way, James blamed the British. After all, it was they who'd been responsible for the famine and the slum- overcrowding, poverty, and malnutrition that encouraged its spread. Not surprisingly, when the Young Irelanders created a new movement called the Fenians, he was in full support. Effectively it was a liaison between the Irish Republican Brotherhood (IRB) in Dublin and the Fenian Brotherhood in America. Their aim was nothing less than to establish an independent Irish Republic by force of arms.

The American Civil War ended in May 1865. A few months later, James received a letter from his nephew, Larry, in Tennessee:

> *Excuse mistakes and errors also, bad writing*
>
> *To oblige, your nephew.*
>
> *United States of America, Nashville Tennessee*
>
> *Tuesday evening*
>
> *August 1st, 1865*
>
> *Dear Uncles and Aunt and cousins,*
>
> *With pleasure, I acknowledge the receipt of your very kind highly interesting and affectionate epistle of the 2nd of July which came to hand yesterday. Let me assure you I have no words to express how gratified I was to learn the good news and glad tidings of all of my relatives being in good health and prospering in life. And also, to know that you have not forgotten me...*

Larry was saying how much he missed his mother and the old country. He was also boasting how great life was in the States compared to what it would have been in Ireland. He had plenty of food and good prospects and had risen to the rank of sergeant in Company E of the 15th Kentucky infantry.

He and his brother, John, had been taken to America as boys to escape the famine. Now their future looked bright. As James filed the letter away in the secret drawer of his newly purchased Georgian table, the Fenians began preparing for rebellion. Their idea was that battle-hardened veterans like Larry and John would join up with local Volunteers and drive out the British.

Many Irish Americans had brought their resentment with them to the New World and the Fenians soon found they weren't short of recruits. Within months, fifty thousand men signed up to fight.

Like the United Irishmen's uprising fifty years earlier, the British soon got wind of what was happening. In September, they began making arrests. They closed the Fenian newspaper, *The Irish People*, and suspended Habeas Corpus.

The suppression of the *People* was a bitter blow. An even greater blow was the introduction of the new Protection of Public Property Act. This banned public protest, imposed curfews across the country, and effectively created an environment where political campaigning was nigh on impossible.

Ironically, British public opinion at the time was very much on the side of the Irish. It had been shocked by graphic reports of the famine and appalled by the greed of the big landowners. Demonstrations in favour of Home Rule were being held across the country and the feeling on the Clapham omnibus was that something had to be done to help Ireland — and done quickly.

That was about to change.

In 1867, two American Fenian leaders were arrested in Manchester. As they were being transferred from the courthouse to Belle Vue gaol, the police van they were in was ambushed. The police fled and once the attackers established control of the road, they tried prising open the doors with crowbars. When that didn't work, they shot the lock off. In the process, they accidentally killed a policeman who was sitting inside.

The killing changed British public opinion overnight. The newspapers demanded revenge. One conservative periodical announced that it was, "one of the most audacious outrages that has occurred in this country for many years." The *Times* added, "There is but one way of meeting unlawful terrorism. It must be repelled by lawful terrorism."

Over the next week, the police made a full sweep of the Irish ghettos in Manchester. Thirty people were arrested, of whom five were eventually condemned to death.

In the same month, two other Fenians were arrested in London. They'd been buying guns in Birmingham and charged with treason. Both were in Clerkenwell awaiting trial when their co-conspirators rolled a barrel of gunpowder against the prison wall and set it off.

The explosion demolished a sixty-foot section of the wall. It also destroyed several houses, killing twelve people and leaving a hundred and twenty maimed and injured.

The bombing, later described as "the most infamous action carried out by the Fenians in the nineteenth century," enraged public opinion even further. Charles Bradlaugh, an otherwise "Irish-friendly" MP, condemned the act as "calculated to destroy all sympathy, and to evoke the opposition of all classes."

Fenian Guy Fawkes

Karl Marx, who was living in London at the time, observed:

> *"The London masses, who have shown great sympathy towards Ireland, will be made wild and driven into the arms of a reactionary government. One cannot expect the London proletarians to allow themselves to be blown up in honour of Fenian emissaries."*

The Fenians had shot themselves in the foot. A cartoon published in *Punch* on 28th December showed a Fenian Guy Fawkes sitting on a barrel of gunpowder with a lighted match, surrounded by innocent women and children.

As James pondered what might happen next, Johannes died. He'd been ill for a long time and finally succumbed at the age of seventy-nine. Kilcloney was officially his, but three years later, at the age of fifty-eight, he also passed away.

John was thirty-seven and now it was his turn to pick up the baton. His mother, Mary, was in her fifties, still very much alive and still very much in charge. Under her watchful eye, the business continued to run as it always had, with him and his brother, Edward, providing the muscle.

By now, the family name was settled at Kiely — sometimes Keily. John insisted the family keep to the new spelling so as not to be confused with distant Kealy relatives who lived nearby. He was slim, laid back, and athletic. Sometime around his twenties, he had had a photograph taken of himself which he hung in the kitchen beside his grandfather's old cavalry sword.

He loved music and he taught himself to play the concertina — mainly reels and jigs for the occasional dances his mother allowed him to hold in the kitchen. He had his eye on a couple of local girls in St. Mullins, but like most Irish mothers, she discouraged him from getting too attached.

The mill was making money — perhaps more money than it ever had. There were also rents coming in from a street of houses in Dublin he'd inherited from his Uncle Edward. Then, two years later, the greatest financial disaster to date hit the world economy. John knew it as the Great Depression, but after the Great Depression of 1929, historians revised the name to the Long Depression. No one knew what had triggered it. It may have been the Franco-Prussian war and the huge reparations France had to pay when it lost, or the US government tightening up on monetary supply after the Civil War. Either way, Britain and Ireland were particularly badly hit. Grain started flooding in from America at a fraction of the cost it could be produced at home. New advances in refrigeration led to cheap meat from as far afield as New Zealand swamped the markets.

Portrait of John Kiely

If that wasn't bad enough, the potato blight appeared again. A year after, there was a severe drought.

Faced with poor yields and cheap imports, John's neighbours started to experience the same misery their grandparents had. Many faced hunger — more found it impossible to pay their rent.

Big Landlords with deep pockets like Lord Lucan started another round of mass evictions. Others with fewer resources offered rent reductions; after all, a lower rent was better than no rent at all.

As in the 1840s, evicted tenants started to fall back on poor law relief. The government tried to persuade landlords to contribute to the costs, but their pleas fell on deaf ears. The big five refused to contribute anything at all despite collecting more than £80,000 (£12.5m) that year in rent.

In response to the evictions, Michael Davitt, one of the founders of the IRB, called for the liberation of Ireland from "the land robbers who seized it." His idea was to protect tenants by forming a Land League to ensure rents were fair, tenancies were of a reasonable length, and there was a mechanism to allow renters to buy their land. John saw it described in the papers as the three Fs: "Fair rent, fixity of tenure, and free sale."

At its first meetings, Charles Stewart Parnell was elected president. As leader of the Irish Parliamentary Party, he held the balance of power between the Whigs and Tories and was in the ideal position to put pressure on the government.

As a result, William Gladstone introduced The Land Law Ireland Act, designed to give greater rights to tenant farmers under what was called a dual-ownership scheme.

Unfortunately, it didn't have enough clout to halt the evictions and Parnell and his supporters complained so forcibly in the House that Gladstone had them thrown in prison. When they were released, Parnell launched a new organisation, The Irish National League.

The idea this time was that tenants would offer what they thought was a fair rent to their landlord. If it was refused, they could pay it into a fund instead. The fund would be held by a responsible person — usually the parish priest — and it would stay there until the tenant and Landlord agreed.

The low-hanging fruit for the League were landlords who were highly geared and underfinanced. While they had little choice but to compromise, others with deeper pockets refused, complaining that Parnell's proposal was nothing more than "anti-landlord agitation." Some, like Lord Lucan, continued with the evictions despite the impact on their bottom line. Alluding to parish priests holding rents in escrow, Lucan proclaimed that "he would not breed paupers to pay priests."

Most landlords had little time for the League. They took badly to having their God-like powers curbed by ignorant Irish peasants. Unfortunately for John, one of them was his own landlord, Viscount Dennis Robert Pack Beresford.

Dennis was a distant relative of the famous fox-hunting, painting-the-town-red Marquess of Waterford, and he'd inherited the land at Kilcloney just a year or so previously. In his twenties, with dark eyes, a receding hairline, and a weak chin. the studious Dennis lived in his ancestor's imposing Fenagh House three miles down the road. He considered himself an intellectual — an expert on woodlice and wasps. His provenance was impeccable: the eldest son of nine children, an ex- pupil of Rugby school, and a graduate of Christ Church Oxford.

Thanks to the Marquess, the Beresfords already had a bad reputation, and it seemed young Dennis had little interest in improving it.

Like his father, John had always been careful to keep on the right side of his landlord. In many ways, he was the ideal tenant — quiet, well-behaved, and able to afford the rent. His brother-in-law and neighbour, Mike Watters, didn't fit that mould. He was a Fenian, a political activist, and one of the league's strongest supporters. He'd married John's sister, Joanne, a few years earlier, and at 6' 4", stubborn and belligerent, he wasn't the sort of man you'd want to mess with.

Along with his mother, Annie, he owned a large sixty-acre farm nearby, and in 1884, they turned to the land court to fix a fair rent with Beresford. After some haggling, they agreed to a £5 (£770) a year reduction. This rankled with Dennis. He wasn't keen on the Land League; he wasn't keen on Mike and he certainly wasn't keen on the reduction. Rents were traditionally paid every six months, but the next time the Watters rent came up, he invoked what was called a "hanging gale."

Even at the time, a hanging gale was a historical curiosity. Theoretically, it was a six-month suspension of rent granted by a landlord to a new tenant to help them out until their first crop was sold. Over the years the suspension had been hard-wired into the standard landlord-tenant agreement as an expectation rather than a favour — a small print clause which was rarely exercised.

Instead of requesting the usual six months in advance, Beresford told them they needed to pay twelve, which included the payment of the hanging gale.

The cruelty of it was that the gale had been granted over a hundred and fifty years earlier, and it was obvious that this was his way of telling Mike he didn't approve of his politics. He also rubbed more salt in the wound by giving him just six days to pay.

Mike contacted the Land League, but they told him nothing could be done. Frustrated, he felt he should make some sort of protest and refused to pay right until the last minute. When the bailiffs were about to remove his final items of furniture, he reluctantly opened his wallet and paid Beresford's demand — along with the Bailiff's legal costs.

Dennis Pack-Beresford

Local people like John were disgusted. A crowd of them turned up at a meeting in Borris where the local priest railed against the Beresford family and proclaimed that from that day forth, Dennis should be known as "Hanging Gale Beresford."

It's unlikely this bothered him, as he continued to live in his ivory tower at Fenagh house and study woodlice. A year later he sent, a demand to the Watters for a full year's rent in advance. This time, with the state of the economy and the bad harvests, Mike couldn't afford to pay. Another meeting was held in Borris and addressed by the parish priest. It had been fifty years since a hanging gale had been invoked by any landlord in the country, he claimed, and Beresford's actions were not only immoral, they were punitive, merely a way to demonstrate power over his tenants and evict the Watters. He then went on to urge his fellow tenants to withhold their rents until he backed down.

By now, the Tories had regained power from the Whigs, and their new leader, Lord Salisbury, had the Land League in his sights. He instructed his nephew, Arthur Balfour, to do something about it, and as a result, a new act was passed called The Irish Coercion Act. This effectively made intimidation, meetings about, and conspiracies against the payment of rents illegal. It also made it illegal to boycott anyone contracted by the Landlord to crack down on non-payers.

Hundreds of people were imprisoned. Trial by jury was abolished and the National League was declared illegal. Sending armed police and soldiers in to help evict tenants became the norm, and it wasn't unusual for them to use battering rams to gain access.

The optics weren't good. Newspapers around the world started to condemn the policy, and in Britain, there was mounting sympathy for those evicted.

One of the men who fell afoul of Balfour's Act was Edward Kiely — John's younger brother. The local sheriff in Borris had attempted to use strong-armed tactics to seize the Watters's cattle to pay towards the defaulted rent. He claimed in court that when he went to make the seizure, Kiely was one of the men who stopped him by standing in the way, blowing a horn, and generally making it impossible for him to round up the animals.

Because of lack of evidence — and probably the unwillingness of local magistrates to help Beresford — the action was dropped. Even so, with the weight of the law against him, Mike eventually gave up. After a long fight, he and his mother were evicted in 1892.

Beresford became a hated figure not only in the local community but much further afield. Reports of his actions even reached the Houses of Parliament. During a debate on the Evicted Tenants Bill, Tim Healy, an MP for the Irish Parliamentary Party, said his tenants were "defrauded of their rights by legal chicanery, their improvements confiscated, and the groundwork laid for increased rent." A fellow MP praised him for the speech and said that Healy's "... exposure of the action of Mr. Pack Beresford against his tenant Mr. Watters of Kilcloney was very effective."

For years after, temporary caretaker tenants were installed on the Watters farm. Flying in the face of Balfour's anti-coercion laws, they were made to feel very unwelcome. At one point, John's neighbours even set up a checkpoint on the Fenagh road to prevent food and supplies from getting through.

A year later, Mary died. She was seventy-three and had seen three generations of Kealy's run the mill through thick and thin. Less than three months later, John married Biddy Farrell from Ballymurphy.

He was forty-eight and she was just twenty-eight. Such a large age gap wasn't unusual at a time when money was scarce, and it was expected that a man should establish himself before committing to marriage. Having said that, he'd taken an inordinately long time to take the plunge. He'd inherited the mill back in 1871 as a successful business. Yet, despite his wealth, he'd remained a bachelor for a further twenty-two years. Perhaps — as was usual in Irish households — his mother had made it clear she wouldn't share her home with another woman, someone who might tell her what to do or disagree as to what was best for her son. It may also have been that when he no longer had anyone to darn his socks, he felt the need to find a replacement.

In 1895, their first child, Mary, was born. Three years later came Jas. Two years after that, Jack, then a year later, Nell.

Mike Watters died in 1903, a broken man. Ironically, it was the year the Wyndham Land Purchase Act came into force. This encouraged estates like Beresford's to be broken up. If landlords were willing to sell, their tenants could make them an offer, and the government would grant them a mortgage for the difference.

A few years later came the Birrell Act. This went a stage further. If tenants wanted to buy, landlords were legally obliged to sell. As a result, Mike's children were able to return home to Kilcloney — and John was finally able to buy out the mill.

Reassured that investment in the business couldn't be lost at the whim of a landlord, he had a new water wheel shipped in from Manchester. Biddy also wanted some changes. First, a new extension for a parlour — and next some furniture to put in it. John had already inherited a clavichord and an oak table from his Uncle Edward in Dublin. Now he added a few works of art and a state-of-the-art phonograph.

By the time the First World War began in 1914, business was as good as it had ever been. Biddy had taken on a maid. Young Jas was helping his Uncle Edward on the farm. Jack, still at school, was learning how the mill worked. Mary, to Nell's annoyance, had started making socks for the troops in France.

A year later, Biddy decided that fourteen-year-old Jack should learn a trade. After all, Jas would inherit the mill and he'd need a way of earning a living when that day came. Her idea was that he should find work in Dublin — it was the capital, after all, with lots of opportunities and plenty to interest a young man. She also hoped it might get him away from her husband's bad influence. He'd been filling the boys' heads with politics, and she didn't want Jack doing anything that might get him hurt.

With John's help, she found him an apprenticeship at Sinnott's in Temple Bar. His digs were to be in Patrick Street and his pay was £3 (£333) a year — not much, even back then. John bought him a new suitcase and a new suit and with Biddy and his big sister, Mary, waving him off, an excited Jack boarded the Borris train to Kingsbridge Station in Dublin.

Biddy missed him but she was pleased he was learning a trade. Then the papers reported a coup. On Easter Monday 1916, over a thousand members of the Irish Volunteers and Irish Citizen Army had taken over key locations in the city. Citizens had been evacuated and the police forcibly removed or taken prisoner. Windows and doors were barricaded, food and supplies secured, and first aid posts set up. A few hours later, four hundred Volunteers marched to the GPO on O'Connell Street and hoisted two Republican flags. Later that day, as Jack looked on in awe, Padraig Pearce proclaimed Ireland independent.

CHAPTER EIGHT

The historian

John Nolan and his sister ran a shop in Borris. I never really knew what it was supposed to sell. Josie said everything and nothing, as there seemed no rhyme or reason for what they put in the windows. No one seemed to buy it, anyway.

Jack had introduced me to John in the 80s. He told me he'd been friends with his father. We hit it off straight away and from then on, whether Jack was with me or not, I made it a point to call in to see John whenever I was over on holiday.

Since I had some time on my hands after visiting Jack, I thought I'd make my usual annual pilgrimage before heading back to the bungalow for dinner.

I picked up the car from the nursing home car park, threw my coat into the back, and drove down the hill into town. It was a Tuesday, and even though for the rest of the world it was rush hour, here, as usual, there was hardly anyone about. I parked up outside Joyce's and made my way the few yards to the shop.

It occupied the ground floor of a grey, two-story Georgian house at the junction of Main Street and Fenagh Road. As I got closer, I could see the windows had been boarded up, and I suddenly remembered my mother telling me John's sister died the year before.

It took him a good three minutes to answer my knock and when he finally appeared, I was surprised at how pale he looked. He'd always taken pride in his appearance, but today he was uncharacteristically unshaven, his eyes sunk, his fingernails long and dirty, his skin almost translucent, as if it hadn't seen the light of day for years.

"Raymond." His spirits seemed to lift when he saw me. "How are you? How's Jack?"

"I'm fine," I said. "He's in the nursing home now."

"So I hear."

He held the clapper of the spring bell above the door to stop it clanging and ushered me in. "I'm sorry about your loss," I said as he locked up behind us.

He shook his head and thanked me. She was bad at the end, he said — it was more a blessing.

John must have been in his sixties, tall, with thick grey hair and a way of shuffling around as if someone had tied his ankles together. I was told that in his younger days he'd been a great runner and had played trumpet for the Borris band. Whatever his previous manifestations, he now seemed to regard himself as the font of all knowledge — at least local knowledge. Nothing that happened or had happened in Borris seemed to have escaped him and even when I first met him, it was obvious that he took a particular interest in Jack.

It was as if he considered him a pivotal point around which the early twentieth-century history of Borris revolved. When Jack wasn't in earshot, he'd ask countless questions about him and quiz me on names and places I'd never heard of. Sometimes he'd tell me stories that seemed to have nothing to do with Jack, but then somehow wove invariably back. John had an insatiable interest in Jack, but over the years I got the feeling there was something he wanted to tell me. He seemed close to it many times but always pulled back at the last minute. In the early days, I thought he might be playing some sort of game, deriving a perverse pleasure from holding out the promise of some great reveal, then pulling it away. As time went by, I began to change my mind. From his body language and the guarded way he spoke, it struck me that he was just being wary. That while Jack was still around, he felt it prudent to keep any secrets he had about him to himself.

"Have a pew," he offered as we walked into the shop. He pulled a handkerchief from his trouser pocket and wiped a layer of dust from a faded wooden chair in front of the counter. As I sat down, I reflected that the place had always been an oddity. The old pound, shilling, and pence cash till, the nail on the counter with a sheaf of receipts pinned through it. The gnarled oak floorboards and the Avery weighing machine. It wasn't an accident it looked that way — it was his attempt to preserve an Ireland that everywhere else had disappeared years ago.

He shuffled around to the other side of the counter and climbed onto a high stool. "How's the family?"

"Very well, thanks."

"And Jack...how's he getting on?"

"I've just been to see him. He seems OK. I was told he wasn't keen at first — but I think he's accepted it now."

He tapped a finger to his head. "And he's still all there?"

"Seems to be."

"Good, good."

Seemingly satisfied with my answers, John settled back on his stool and gave me an update on what had been happening in Borris. In return, I told him about the birth of my new son, how I was about to sell my advertising business, and how my mom and dad were getting used to living in the bungalow. The politics of the day looked good, too. Thatcher was out and John Major had just been elected PM. The Unionists and the IRA had both declared ceasefires, and Bill Clinton was about to visit Ireland to discuss a peace deal.

"So, what's new on the history front?" I asked.

He smiled and swivelled around on the stool. He opened a drawer behind him and took out what looked like a newspaper clipping. "Take a look at this."

It was a black and white photograph of a young man, quite good-looking, with an Irish smile and big ears. It had obviously been taken a long time ago — I guessed around the 20s.

"I don't suppose you know who that is?"

I shook my head. "Not a clue."

He looked disappointed. "Did you ever hear Jack talk about a man called Jimmy Lillis?"

"No, who is he?"

"An old comrade of his."

"Has he died or something?"

John gave a long sigh. "He was involved in an ambush up in Graney. They caught him with a rifle and some ammunition. Collins' lot executed him up in Carlow. He was only sixteen."

"Michael Collins?"

He nodded, took the clipping back, and carefully folded it up. As he replaced it in the drawer, I thought I'd lighten the mood by telling him how Jack had reacted to my suggestion that he should see the film *Michael Collins*. I expected him to crack a smile. Instead, he frowned and sat back on his stool. "You know who he was, I suppose?"

"Yes. He was the leader of the 1916 uprising." I was pretty sure of my ground, but John sighed again.

"Would you like a little history lesson?"

John always took great delight in putting me right on Irish history, and I had plenty of time on my hands. "Sure," I said. "Fire away."

"Well," he began. "You've obviously heard of the Easter Rising."

Eamon De Valera

I had. When I was a child in Birmingham, men with long grey coats and shabby hats rattled tins and sold little paper badges outside our church on Easter Sunday. My grandmother told me they were Easter lilies and for years I thought they had to do with Christ rising from the dead. Years later I learned that they commemorated a different rising — the 1916 rising in Dublin — with sale proceeds going to the IRA.

"Well," he continued, "it was a washout. The whole thing fizzled out in less than a week. The Volunteers, as they called themselves, were arrested, and most of the leaders were shot. Things died down for a couple of years until the Germans started making advances in France. That's when the British threatened to bring in conscription and the trouble really started. A lot of local lads did take the King's shilling, but most didn't want to fight for the British. There were strikes across the country and huge anti-conscription rallies. There was even one here in Borris. The RIC tried to break it up, but the local lads — including Jack — kept them out of the way until the speeches were given."

"So where does Michael Collins fit in?"

"You've heard of Eamon De Valera?"

I nodded.

"During the Rising, he'd been put in charge of defending a building called Boland's Mill. When the Brits pulled him out, he was one of the lucky leaders who wasn't shot. Later, he became head of Sinn Féin. Michael Collins fought in the rising as well — but only as a foot soldier. He also joined Sinn Féin and became an MP. When the party won a landslide victory at the end of the war, De Valera declared Ireland independent and made Mick Minister of Finance. Soon after that, he became the brains behind the guerrilla war."

"So why does Jack hate him so much?"

He smiled. "That's where the story takes a twist. The war with the English dragged on for three years. Then Lloyd George invited Dev across to London to discuss a peace deal. He'd met the PM before, and everyone thought he'd go himself. Instead, he sent a group of what he called "plenipotentiaries" to do the negotiations. One of them was Mick Collins. Now, depending on who you talk to, that was either the right or the wrong thing to do. It was certainly odd. At the time, the only thing the English knew about the "Big Fella" was that he was this shadowy figure behind the guerrilla war. They had no idea of who he was or what he looked like, and to most of the Irish parliament it seemed a good idea to keep it that way. Dev was also much better at arguing the point than most people, so why he didn't go over himself is a bit of a mystery."

Michael Collins

John stood up from his stool, lay the palms of his hands on the counter, and looked down at me like a schoolteacher. "I'm not boring you, am I?"

"Not at all."

He was obviously on a roll, and it would have been churlish to stop him. Staring up at the damp, patchy ceiling for inspiration, he drew a deep breath and continued.

"Now, some of Mick's friends warned that he was being set up as a scapegoat, but loyal to Dev, he ignored them. The negotiations took over two months and when he came back with the signed treaty there was trouble. To be honest, I can't remember everything that was on it, but it included Ireland being granted Free State status, a bit like Canada. The Irish parliament would be totally independent — although the King would still be a sort of titular head. The British army would be pulled out and their weapons and bases handed over to the new government. The new Free State would include all the island of Ireland — but with the proviso that the North could vote itself out after a year — which of course it did. And what upset a lot of people: Irish ministers had to give an oath of allegiance to the King before they could sit in Parliament."

He sat back down and folded his fingers together. "So as an Englishman yourself, what do you make of that?"

"Half English," I corrected. "Well, an oath means nothing, really, does it?" And personally, after seven hundred years of occupation, I would have jumped at it.

John nodded. "A lot of people thought the same way. Especially when Mick said Lloyd George had threatened "immediate and terrible war" if he and the others didn't stop dragging their heels and sign. He said the threat hadn't frightened him per se, but he didn't think it was right to commit Ireland to another war — one he was convinced most people didn't want. Dev didn't see it that way. When he got back, he accused him of selling out. Mick argued that if he'd felt so strongly, he should have gone himself. Besides, Dev had called them plenipotentiaries. Do you know what a plenipotentiary is?"

"A negotiator"?

"More than that. According to your *Oxford English Dictionary,* a plenipotentiary has total freedom to act on behalf of whoever appointed them. That's why some people say Mick and the rest of the delegation had every right to negotiate that treaty as they saw fit. Others, like Jack, would disagree."

Years earlier, I remember listening to Jack debate the treaty with one of his neighbours. They both would have been in their seventies, and although I didn't know the ins and outs of it at the time, I remember the argument getting so heated I thought they might come to blows. Fortunately, Josie intervened and insisted that if there was any more talk of politics, one or other of them would be thrown out.

It's a shame she wasn't in the Dial in 1921. John went on to explain that after an equally heated debate, the treaty was finally ratified by a vote of 64 to 57. It might have been reasonable to assume that a self-proclaimed democratic politician like De Valera would have sucked it up and accepted the vote, but he didn't. Instead, he walked out in a huff. Not long after, the country was thrown into civil war.

Jack had taken the anti-treaty side and John's history lesson had clarified in no uncertain terms why he'd so fervently refused to "set foot outside the door" to see Mr. Collins. In terms of who was right or wrong, I had no strong opinions.

As a pragmatist, I probably would have taken Collins's side and accepted the treaty. No one wants a continual war, and what was offered, although not ideal, seemed reasonable enough. Having said that, I wasn't Jack. I hadn't lived his life and I hadn't had his experiences. I'd only known him in his later years. What went on during his youth, why he felt so passionate about the sort of Ireland the treaty obviously didn't deliver on, I had no idea.

One thing I did know. If I were having a dinner party and had to choose between inviting Collins or De Valera, it'd be Collins every time. From the film trailers I'd seen, he was a handsome, charming, slap on the back bon viveur. De Valera, with his schoolteacher glasses and huffy expression, looked dour, boring, and officious. He reminded me of Charles De Gaulle — tall, arrogant, pompous, and absolutely no fun. Of course, looks were no reason to invite someone to a dinner party — or for that matter, vote for them — but as per JFK vs. Nixon or Blair vs. Major, it certainly seemed to have a part to play.

I would have liked to have asked John a few more questions, but suddenly he glanced across the room at a big wooden clock on the far wall. It must have stopped years ago, but that didn't seem to matter. "I'm sorry, Raymond," he said. "I've just remembered. Dennis is coming to pick me up in a minute. He's got to take me to the doctor. I need another prescription for this old back of mine."

Dennis was John's son, and it seemed that our meeting was at an end. I stood up and held out a hand. "It's been good seeing you again," I said. "And you're looking well."

He knew I was lying, but he smiled anyway. He came out from behind the counter as I stood up. "How long are you here for?"

"Just a few days"

"Well, have a good holiday — say hello to your mam for me."

I told him I would, and he held the bell again as he unlocked the door. As I walked out, he put a hand on my shoulder. "I don't suppose Jack will be coming out of that Nursing Home?"

"I doubt it."

His voice dropped to a whisper. "Then find out about T'mon."

"T'mon?" I repeated.

I thought he might offer some explanation, but instead he glanced up and down the street to make sure no one had overheard. "T'mon," he whispered again and closed the door firmly behind him.

CHAPTER NINE
"Remember 3 months earlier"

As the Volunteers raised their flags over the GPO, Jas Kealy was approaching eighteen. His father, John, was in his seventies and in bad health, while his mother, Biddy, was still in her late forties. With Jack up in Dublin, it was effectively her, his Uncle Edward, and himself who were keeping things ticking over.

Commercially, things were good. Kilcloney's business model had moved from grinding corn to weaving wool, and there was no shortage of people who wanted blankets, coats, and socks. On top of that, his father now owned the mill outright. Jas should have been pleased, but it wasn't enough.

Although it wasn't taught in schools, he'd learned the history of British oppression at his father's knee. John had told him stories passed down from his father and grandfather. Stories that ranged from the cruelty of Cromwell to the horrors of the famine. He'd seen how his Uncle Mike had been treated by Beresford and how his neighbours still struggled to pay their rent. He saw firsthand how the anglicised Protestant landowners still owned the biggest houses and pulled out thousands in rent for land they should never have owned in the first place. The English still had the upper hand. They'd banned the Irish language, their rights, and their culture, and like his father he was determined to do something about it.

Parnell had introduced the first Home Rule Bill back in 1886. Not surprisingly, it was decisively defeated. He tried again in 1893. That time it passed through the Commons, but was rejected by the Lords. Twenty years later, his successor, John Redmond, tried again. This time, the bill was supported by the Whig Prime minister, Asquith, and looked like it might get through.

The stumbling block was the Ulster Unionists. They didn't like the idea of being lumped in with the south and ruled by a Catholic government. In 1913, the two big Unionist beasts of the north, Carson and Craig, formed the Ulster Volunteer Fighters — a paramilitary group dedicated to making sure Ireland continued to be ruled direct from Westminster — by force if necessary.

This gave Asquith a problem. He needed the backing of the military if things turned nasty. They should have been impartial, but it soon became apparent where their loyalties lay. Key British officers told him that they would resign en masse if he commanded them to take any action against the UVF.

With Asquith stuck between a rock and a hard place, the Nationalists in the north created their own paramilitary group — the Irish Volunteers. While the UVF had the blessing of the British military and the good sense to import their state-of-the-art weaponry in secret, the Volunteers weren't so circumspect. One of their main arms suppliers was ex-Unionist Erskin Childers, the famous Anglo-Irish writer. With little thought of discretion, he bought a consignment of outdated nineteenth-century rifles in Holland and sailed them to Ireland in his private yacht, the Asgard.

Seeming to lack any common sense, he landed them in a public dock in Dublin in the middle of the day. Not surprisingly, he was soon spotted by a small group of British troops. Initially, they tried to stop the weapons from being offloaded, but, surrounded by a mob, they backed away. Later, when the guns were ashore, the mob started mocking them. In retaliation, they fired into the crowd. The result was the death of three unarmed civilians.

Jas read about it in the newspapers. The deaths went down badly. Not only in Ireland, but the rest of the world — particularly America. By 1914, with mounting friction between Protestant Ulster and the Catholic south, Ireland seemed on the brink of civil war. Yet Redmond's Home Rule Act was passed.

The reason was more expedient than altruistic. Asquith was trying to hang onto power, and the only way he could do that was to get into bed with Redmond's Irish Nationalist party. In addition, an act had recently been passed to limit the power of the Lords. Now they could no longer defeat a bill — merely delay it. As most of them were rich aristocratic landowners with a vested interest in opposing Home Rule, this removed a massive hurdle in getting it through.

It was everything Jas and his father had hoped for. The idea of Home Rule had been thrown around for years, and it had finally happened. Admittedly, Ireland wouldn't be independent, but at least it would have a major say in its own destiny.

How the Unionist UVF would have reacted, they never got to find out. A few months later, when war looked to be breaking out with Germany, the government moved into emergency mode. One of their first actions was to pass the Suspensory Act. The upshot was that until things settled down in Europe, home rule would be suspended for at least a year.

Jas had been shown the winning post and had it snatched away. Like thousands of like-minded men and women across the country, he felt that enough was enough. The English had been making promises for the last fifty years, and this was the final straw.

Sir Roger Casement

Redmond promised immediate implementation when the war was finished and urged his supporters to fight alongside Britain against Germany. Thousands took the King's shilling, but Jas wasn't one of them.

Along with a large minority of angry and frustrated young men, he joined one of the many Volunteer groups springing up across the country — essentially a branch of the Fenians known as the Irish Republican Brotherhood (IRB).

His local group was in nearby Ballymurphy. He had to pay a subscription of 3 pence- a week and the local priest, Father

John Lawlor, spurred them on with tales of famine and the '98 rising. An ex-British soldier called Synott volunteered to train them up, and to the amusement of the locals, he had them marching around the countryside with wooden rifles sloped across their shoulders.

The idea was to prepare for an insurrection. The hope was that it wouldn't be needed. Home rule had been delayed for just a year, and with luck and a following wind, it would soon be implemented. As it turned out, it wasn't to happen. A year later, another order was made. Home rule would be suspended again — this time until at least March 1916.

The volunteer groups stepped up their training, and as war raged on in Europe, there were increasing calls for rebellion — but that's all they were. To Jas' frustration, nothing concrete seemed to be on the horizon. What he didn't know was that the Supreme Council of the IRB had been planning an uprising since the start of the war. Their idea, as always, was to hit Britain while it was otherwise engaged. 1916 was when Britain was most stretched, and as in '98, the rebels had no problem with getting into bed with the enemy.

The man chosen to seek out German help was the Anglo-Irish Roger Casement. In 1905, he was honoured for his report on the abuses in the Congo and knighted in 1911 for his investigations of human rights violations in the rubber industry of Peru.

He'd been appalled by the British atrocities he'd witnessed during the Boer War — particularly their use of concentration camps — and he was firmly of the opinion that the Irish had been treated pretty badly. The first thing he did was try to convince the Germans to openly announce their support for Irish independence. The second was to push them to release Irish POWs. His third, and most contentious, proposal was that they should invade Ireland while the British were distracted by an uprising in Dublin.

The Germans weren't keen on his invasion idea, but like the Napoleonic French a hundred and thirty years earlier, they agreed to supply him with arms.

In May 1915, a Military Committee was set up to organise the rebellion. Padraig Pearse was elected Director of Operations and around January of the following year, he set the date as 24th April — Easter Monday.

Pearce was an Irish teacher. He was also a barrister who'd famously defended Neil McBride — a poet and songwriter who'd been fined for having his name displayed in "illegible" writing on his donkey cart. By illegible, the British authorities meant Irish, and although Pearce lost the case, it became a cause celebre for those who wanted to see change.

In early March, Enniscorthy held its annual "Emmett" commemoration and Pearce was due to give a speech. Robert Emmet had been one of the leaders of an ill-fated coup in Dublin a few years after the imposition of the Act of Union. He'd been executed for his efforts and it must have crossed Pearce's mind that if his revolution went pear-shaped, something equally bad might happen to him.

After the meeting, he shook hands with the crowd. When most of the attendees had left, he was introduced to Seamus Doyle, a member of the local IRB, and the real reason for his attendance. In a private meeting, he told Doyle that he was planning an insurrection and that Enniscorthy should be ready. He then gave him a secret code to let him know when to send his men into action.

A month later, Doyle received the message he'd been waiting for:

"Browne and Noland's tell me they will have the books you require on 23rd July next. Remember 3 months earlier."

The code was simple. Pearce told him that the date of the rising would be exactly three months earlier than the date the books would be ready — and in case Doyle forgot the code, he repeated the instruction — Remember 3 months earlier — in his letter.

In the meantime, the German navy was keeping their end of the bargain. They despatched the SS Libau to Kerry under a Norwegian flag with the name Aud. On board were 20,000 rifles and a million rounds of ammunition. Casement was in Germany, and he left for Ireland around the same time on a submarine called the U-19.

Padraigh Pearce

Both vessels landed on 21 April, but due to a mix-up, no one was there to meet them. It was the same sort of error the '98 rebels made when they should have been picking up Napoleon's guns in Bantry Bay. To make matters worse, the Royal Navy knew they were coming. Seeing the writing on the wall, the German captain scuttled his ship. It was too late for Casement. As he waded onto the Banna Strand, he was arrested for treason and brought under escort to Dublin.

This threw Pearce and the other leaders into confusion. Should they proceed, or should they not? Conflicting messages were being communicated across the country, and in Enniscorthy, Doyle received one of his own. It was from GHQ in Dublin and told him quite clearly that the uprising was off.

Dr. Edward Dundon's house, Borris

He was frustrated and confused. His men were ready — he was ready — and he couldn't see any reason why the uprising shouldn't go ahead as planned. Pearce himself had told him it would start the day after next and there was a possibility these new orders were either incorrect or fake. The last thing he wanted was for fighting to start and for him not to be ready. Unsure which way to turn, he decided to catch the train to Dublin, seek out Pearce, and find out exactly what was happening.

As soon as he alighted at Kingsbridge, he headed to Tom Clarke's shop on Parnell Street. Clarke was another one of the leaders, but because it was a bank holiday, his shop was closed. The Volunteer HQ in Dawson Street couldn't shed much light on what was happening either. Eventually, he wound up in the Freedom Office in D'Olier Street where he was told another order had already been sent to Enniscorthy telling him it was all back on — this time for Easter Sunday.

Heaving a sigh of relief, he caught the train home, and by the following day, he and his men were ready. Pearce often used newspapers to communicate coded messages. In the unlikely event there'd been another change of plan, Doyle bought a copy of the *Sunday Independent* to check. To his bewilderment, it appeared the uprising was off again.

A man called O'Connell was Doyle's commanding officer. Later that morning, he and Edward Dundon unexpectedly turned up at Doyle's house. Dundon was the Kiely's family doctor in Borris. He'd also been at Trinity with some of the ringleaders, including Pearce, and had the inside track as to what was happening. After a long discussion, the three men decided the best thing to do was hang fire. Later that evening, when O'Connell and Dundon left, Doyle received another message from Pearce. It confirmed the uprising was off.

It seemed they'd made the right call and Doyle thought it best to cycle to Borris and let them know. As he entered

Dundon's front room, he found them talking to an attractive young woman. Nancy Wyse Power was in her mid-twenties and a leading member of the Cumann na mBan. She'd travelled down from Dublin earlier that day to give Dundon a message. It was from Pearce, and it said that the uprising was still on after all. This time for the following day – Easter Monday.

O'Connell was furious. He told Nancy he was out, and that Pearce couldn't expect any help from him. Doyle, loyal as ever, decided to cycle back to Enniscorthy and prepare his men to make a stand.

British troops, Dublin 1916

The next day, as Nancy had said, the uprising began. Pearce and the other leaders knew the landing of arms had been a total disaster. They knew that Volunteers across the country were confused as to what was happening. They knew most of the population would be against them — especially friends and relatives of men fighting on the Somme. They knew they were outgunned, outmatched. They knew they'd lost German support — but they also knew they had to do something.

Roughly 1,200 Volunteers and Citizen Army members took over strongpoints in the city centre. James Connolly, a staunch communist union leader had been elected the overall military commander and he and four other members of the Military Council, including Pearce, moved their HQ into the GPO. Once in place, they hoisted up two Republican flags and Pearse read out what he called the Proclamation of the Republic.

"Irishmen and Irish women. In the name of God and of the dead generations from which she receives her old tradition of nationhood, Ireland, through us, summons her children to her flag and strikes for her freedom...."

Fourteen-year-old Jack, who was enjoying a break from work over the bank-holiday weekend, was enthralled. The revolution his father and big brother promised was finally happening. That night a foreman at Sinnott's suggested he might want to become a "Fianna" or boy scout for the IRB. He didn't need much persuading. Over the next few days, he found a way of secretly leaving his digs in Patrick Street through a cellar tunnel into Hanover Lane. From there, he began delivering despatches to the rebels in strongholds like Boland's Mill, Jacob's Factory, and the G.P.O.

At first, the British were taken off guard, but by the 29th, they'd brought in reinforcements.

Biddy was beside herself. The newspapers described the fighting as savage, and Jack was in the middle of it. By the end of the week, she read that 17,000 British troops had been mobilised into Dublin, equipped with the type of machine guns and 18lb field artillery canons they were using in Mons. She begged John to get Jack out of there and bring him back home as soon as possible.

British troops with captured rebel flag

John sent their eldest, Mary, to find him, but the search wasn't easy. Dublin was in ruins and there were soldiers and checkpoints across the city. The staff in Sinnotts said they hadn't seen him. Fearing the worst, Mary made her way around every barracks and police station, checking in with hospitals, following up every lead his friends gave her. When she returned to Kilcloney empty-handed, Biddy was distraught. All she could do was beg the local RIC to keep her in the loop if news of him came to light — and say a prayer to St. Anthony every night to bring him home safely.

In the meantime, Pearce was forced to surrender. On hearing the news, local uprisings like Doyle's in Enniscorthy were also forced to throw in the towel.

The majority of those killed and wounded were civilians and most were caused by the artillery, incendiary shells, gunboats, and heavy machine guns the military used to dislodge the rebels. There were also numerous reports of British atrocities, such as the North King Street Massacre, where fifteen unarmed civilians were robbed and murdered at Portobello Barracks.

The battle-hardened and much decorated General-in-Chief of British armed forces, John Grenfell Maxwell, quickly signalled his intention "to arrest all dangerous "Sinn Féiners" — a label that was technically incorrect, as at the time the small Sinn Féin party was neither militant nor Republican and had absolutely nothing to do with the rising.

3,430 men and 79 women were arrested and 187 court marshalled, most of them at Richmond Barracks. Contentiously, even to the prosecutors, Maxwell ruled the trials should be held in secret and the accused not allowed to submit a defence. Ninety men were sentenced to death and fourteen were executed by firing squad, including the seriously wounded Connolly, who had to be shot while tied to a chair.

The most prominent leader to escape execution was Eamon De Valera. He'd commanded the 3rd Battalion at Boland's Mill, one of the strongholds to which Jack had delivered despatches.

The day after the arrests, Redmond observed that "happily" the Rising seemed to be over. "It has been dealt with firmness," he said, "which was not only right but was the duty of the Government…"

He then urged Asquith "not to show undue hardship or severity to the great masses of those who are implicated."

The PM appeared not to have listened. As he continued to sanction executions, Redmond pleaded with him again to stop, warning that if more took place, "the position will become impossible for any constitutional party." His deputy added, "thousands of people who ten days ago were

136

bitterly opposed to the whole of the Sinn Féin movement and the rebellion, are now becoming infuriated against the Government on account of these executions. it is not murderers who are being executed; it is insurgents who have fought a clean fight, a brave fight, however misguided."

Even Unionist leader Edward Carson agreed, and finally Asquith phoned Maxwell at Dublin Castle expressing his concern that "a large number of executions would sow the seeds of lasting trouble in Ireland."

Connolly's chair execution was particularly badly received, and following Asquith's call for restraint, Maxwell decided to commute the remaining death sentences to imprisonment. Most of the remaining rebels were then sent to internment camps like Frongoch in Wales. Among them was Michael Collins.

Around the same time, Biddy's prayers were answered. Jack appeared on the doorstep, his shoes hanging off his feet, his new suit dusty and torn as if, in her own words, he'd been pulled through a hedge backwards. She took his suitcase from him as he hung his cap on the peg in the kitchen. It was difficult to know whether to give him a hug or a scolding. She considered the latter but as she knew it would do her no good, she opted for the former.

He was pleasant enough — as he always was — smiling and cracking a few jokes, but she noticed a change. He would just shrug whenever she asked him where he'd been or what he'd been doing, and in the end she gave up. To her relief, John assured her that he wouldn't have to go back to Dublin and that he could return to working at the Mill.

A few months later, the government, under huge public pressure, declared amnesty. Most prisoners were released, and many decided politics had to be the way forward — at least for the time being. The tiny Sinn Féin party that had been mistakenly blamed for the uprising ironically became their focus. On his release, De Valera joined them, and not long afterwards was elected MP for Clare. A year after that, and mainly because the other big beasts of the uprising were dead, he was voted in as President.

In Borris, news of the trials and executions further incensed the already incensed Jas. He'd also been talking to his brother, and whatever they discussed seemed to radicalise him even further.

A few months later, the Carlow 4th Brigade of the Irish Republican Army was created and both Jas and Jack joined up. Dr. Dundon was voted in as commanding officer. Jas' friend, James Lennon, was elected Captain, with a man named John Hynes as his first lieutenant. Their objective was to make sure De Valera 's Sinn Féin won the next general election —whatever it took. Within a few months, Lennon stepped down to run as MP for Carlow. To help him get elected, Jas and the rest of the Battalion used their manpower to organise public meetings, distribute literature, put up posters, and canvass votes.

It wasn't easy. Sinn Féin was small and Redmond's Irish Parliamentary Party was big. Sinn Féin's focus was narrow — essentially the attainment of an independent Ireland — which appealed to a minority of radicals and die-hard Republicans.

The breakthrough came in April 1918, when Lloyd George introduced a conscription bill for Ireland. His quid pro quo was that he'd make sure Home Rule was immediately implemented.

For people like Jas, the idea of being forced to fight for a country that had bled them dry for the last seven hundred years was an anathema. It also sat badly with almost everyone else, including the Catholic Church.

Lloyd George soon abandoned the idea, but the damage was done. Taking advantage of his faux pas, De Valera cleverly hid Sinn Féin's independent Ireland manifesto inside an anti-conscription one. So pervasive was the anti-conscription feeling that before long he had a Sinn Féin branch in every parish.

The historian A. J. P. Taylor later remarked that the day the conscription bill was introduced was "the day England lost Ireland."

One of Jack and Jas' first tasks as members of the new IRA was to make sure an anti-conscription rally held in Borris ran smoothly. Practically everyone in the county turned out to see Sinn Féin representatives Milroy and Mahoney speak. The RIC had been mobilised in the town square to keep numbers down, but after a brief skirmish, the IRA pushed them out so they could be heard.

The strength of feeling in the country was reflected in the December election. Thanks to the highly unpopular executions of the 1916 leaders and the threat of conscription, Sinn Féin won a resounding victory. A month later, on 21st January 1919, De Valera, like Pearce two years earlier, declared Ireland independent.

CHAPTER TEN

The discovery

As I started to walk back to the car, I wondered what John meant. T'mon? Was it an Irish word or someone's name? Had I misheard him? Did it matter? Perhaps it had something to do with that James Lillis he'd just told me about or maybe one of his old favourites, "Fin the spy." Years earlier, when Jack and his old comrades showed me that memorial to James and Peter Farrell in the Ballymurphy churchyard, I hadn't known they'd been shot. Since then, John told me, someone nicknamed "Fin" had betrayed the Carlow flying squad to the Black and Tans, which subsequently led to the brother's murder.

My car was parked outside Joyce's, and I decided I might as well pop in for a drink. Over the years, it hadn't changed a bit. Like John Nolan, Mr. Joyce had gone out of his way to preserve the place just as it might have looked in the twenties — a meat slicer on the bar, rat traps hanging from the ceiling, bottles of stout stacked on the shelves, and the long, dark wooden bar itself. The only thing I missed from my childhood days was the heavy smell of tobacco from my Great Uncle Mick's pipe.

The pub itself might have been preserved for posterity, but it hadn't stopped the progress of the Joyce empire. A few years earlier, an extension had been built at the side to offer a Wake service. In 1992, my grandmother was one of their customers. It was an odd experience. As she lay in her open coffin, women I didn't know knelt around her reciting The

Rosary, Bless me, Fathers, and Hail Marys over and over in a mumbled drone that sounded like a Muslim Tajweed.

What's always struck me is the matter-of-fact way the Irish deal with death. In England, I was used to a closed casket and a sombre treading-on-eggshells deference. Over here I watched, horrified, as children played with her hair and adults clutching pint glasses gathered around her coffin to discuss Kilkenny's performance in the final. I saw strangers call in out of sheer curiosity, just to see who was dead. One man with a red face and big farmer's hands asked me who she was. When I replied that she was my grandmother, he asked how she died. I told him she just went off her food and slipped away. He shook my hand and, with no sense of insincerity, looked into my eyes and told me that he'd had a sheep "just like that."

The bar was crowded, and I ordered a Guinness, like most tourists. Once I thought it was the cool thing to do — partake of the quintessential drink of the Irishman. Years later I discovered the stout of choice in Ireland was Murphys — and that most modern Irishmen didn't drink stout at all.

A hurling match was being shown on the small, grainy TV above the bar and the men — there were no women — were huddled in front of it, sighing or roaring with approval depending on who'd scored.

As I had nothing to contribute about missed penalties or erroneous offsides, I chose a table at the back of the room, pulled out a chair, and sat there nursing my glass for a half hour or so. Even though I hadn't enjoyed the Guinness or spoken to anyone, I decided to stay for another. There was something about the accents, the atmosphere, and the camaraderie, even the gruff monosyllabic grunts that reminded me of my childhood. Back then, my grandmother's brothers would come over from Ireland or up from London to her house in Sparkhill — and when they did there'd be a party. All of them would drink, most would have a bet on the horses, and in the evenings, they'd sing their party piece song. For Jack it was "The battle of Ashtown Road," and he would sing it with such sentiment that when he finished, he'd be rewarded with a round of enthusiastic applause and more than a few "Well done, Jacks."

I hadn't taken much notice of the song as a child. It was usually me next and while he was singing, I was mentally preparing for my own performance.

Years later, I decided to listen to it more closely.

"T'was a cold December day, when a lorry ploughed its way, midst bullets splash and play in Ashtown road. In that car a living tool of Britain's hated rule, there was began a duel on Ashtown road."

The "living tool" referred to was Lord French, the former commander in chief of British forces. In 1919, he'd been appointed Lord Lieutenant of Ireland and sent to Dublin. After disembarking the boat from Liverpool, he caught the 11.40 train to Ashtown station. From there, he was picked up in an armoured car to be driven to the Vice-Regal Lodge and take up his post. It wasn't to go quite as planned. As his convoy drove through the park gates, a group of IRA men appeared. They concentrated their fire on the second car, in which they thought French was travelling. As it turned out, he was in the first and while he escaped injury, a young Volunteer named Martin Savage was shot dead.

Why Jack was so keen on that song, I never found out. Maybe he liked the words, maybe it just suited his voice. My

Uncle Tommy, the youngest of my grandmother's brothers, had "Noreen Bawn" as his go-to song. In its unabridged version, Noreen had over ten verses — and when he sang it with drink stops at every verse, it seemed twice as long. It wasn't a rebel song, but a song about emigration. As a child, I didn't fully appreciate the emotion Tommy put into that song — how tears would flow down his face as he reached the end. Admittedly, the drink had something to do with it, but so did the sentiment. How could I understand what it meant to people like him and Noreen to have to leave their homes and families in search of a better life?

My mother had dinner on when I got back — a hot roast followed her version of my grandmother's signature sherry trifle. We spoke about Josie, as we often did. She'd only been gone a couple of years and the bungalow seemed empty without her. Every Christmas and summer holiday, she'd been there with Jack, holding court. Their old friends would come wandering over, dropping in without invitation, always with some gossip or a story to tell. Now, few of them were left, and the ones that were either couldn't get about anymore or felt it inappropriate to drop in on the new owners.

I'd heard that in her youth, Josie had been a bit of a head-turner. There'd been those photographs, of course, the ones Jack had thrown into the well. I remembered only fleeting images from them — but there was also that one my mother found of her standing with two friends outside the Salutation Hotel in Scotland. We reckoned she must have been nineteen or twenty. That would date the photograph to around 1921 or 1922 — exactly when the Civil War was in full swing. My mother remembered being told that Josie and her sister had been in service back then, and a postcard she found in her belongings of nearby Glebe House seems to suggest that's where she was.

Certainly, I'd never seen her like that. I'd only known her from her mid-sixties on. My recollection of her centred more around her personality. She was proud without being arrogant, someone who could horse-trade with the best of them, someone who held her family together, and someone as passionate as Jack about politics. Almost every night they'd watch Robin Day on Newsnight, grilling Thatcher or sometimes representatives of Sin Féin who had their voices dubbed in by actors. Their favourite man to hate when the news turned to the conflict in Northern Ireland was, of course, Ian Paisley. It was an interesting dynamic: Paisley's rhetoric would get them wound up, but there was so much of the pantomime villain about him that I suspect they perversely enjoyed watching his tirades. I once asked Jack why the IRA hadn't taken him out. "Why would they do that?" he grinned. "He's our best asset."

To anyone looking into their little world, Jack appeared to be the one wearing the trousers. You only needed to dig a little beneath the surface to see that it wasn't the case. He might have been the driving force, the one with the energy and the ideas, but Josie was the moderator. She kept him under control. I imagine it must have been a lot easier for her in his later years.

Like a mischievous fourteen-year-old boy, he'd have a go at anything. While his 1930s neighbours were still using paraffin lamps, he erected a wind turbine in the garden, storing DC current in various car batteries to light up the house. He made shoes, built his own donkey carts, dug his own well, reconstructed his house in Sparkhill, and eventually built the bungalow in Borris.

By the time he was in his eighties, his DIY days were over. I often heard Josie tell him that a job needed to be done in the house and they should get someone in to do it. He would invariably poo-poo the idea and assure her that she should leave it to him. That man would move mountains sitting on that chair she would tell my mother. Yet she never contradicted him — just waited until he'd forgotten about it and got a man to do it anyway.

I didn't realise the full dynamic of the relationship until after she died. My mother told me she'd been caring for him behind the scenes for years — and the stress of that as well as running the house had taken its toll. Basic biology seemed to dictate that Jack would pass first, but it turned out to be the other way around. When she died in Birmingham, my mother had her body flown over to Dublin and then brought down by hearse to Borris. After the Wake, she was buried in the new cemetery at the top of the town. Jack, then ninety-two, but as determined as ever, insisted on walking behind the hearse the mile or so up the hill to her final resting place.

Josie's coffin was draped with the Irish tricolour. It was an honour bestowed by the government for having served in an organisation called the Cumann na mBan — literally The Women's Council. It was created in 1913, and as the name suggests, it was an all-female organisation ostensibly set up to help the IRA deliver messages, dress wounds — that sort of thing. But some of the women weren't so ladylike. One of the most fearsome fighters in the 1916 rebellion was the gun-toting suffragette Constance Markievicz, who became their leader and, ironically, the first woman elected to the Westminster parliament.

I assume Josie must have played some useful role in the Anglo-Irish conflict because as well as being allowed the tricolour on her coffin, she was also awarded an IRA medal. As with my grandfather, I knew very little about her history — except for one incident. I'd heard the story as a child, both from my mother and another relative. It happened at Joyce's — ironically the very place I was sitting and where she'd made her last stopover. Until 1923, it had been a hotel known as Flood's. She was working behind the bar one night when a group of Black and Tans burst in and arrested someone they suspected of a terrorist offence — or maybe had just taken a dislike to. They dragged him outside and tied him to the back of a Crossley Tender. Their idea was to drag him along the road when Josie, armed with the knife she'd been using to slice ham in the kitchen, ran out and cut his ropes.

It was a ballsy thing to do. She risked putting herself in the firing line and there must have been consequences. Other things my mother told me about her confirmed she was a strong woman. During the flu epidemic of 1919, she'd go around to the houses of infected relatives and neighbours, delivering soup and offering care and occasional medication. And it was dangerous — thirteen people alone died from flu in Bagnalstown that year. Later, when her children were born, she'd rear pigs, sell eggs, take my mother and her sister to school every morning, do the washing — and according to my mother would regularly cycle off to God knows where in the early morning, to return exhausted in the small hours.

When I got back to the bungalow, we had tea and put the children to bed. I told my parents that I'd been to see Jack and that he seemed OK. I told them how he reacted when I asked him if he wanted to see *Michael Collins*, which raised a laugh. I also told them I'd popped in to see John. Whilst I remembered, I asked my mother if she'd heard of "T'mon."

"What is it?" she asked.

I told her I didn't know. For a while, the four of us discussed it, taking guesses at what it might mean, and then gradually the conversation turned to Eastenders and whether Blair had been right to send British forces across to Sarajevo.

I'm not sure how long I would have maintained an interest in John's clue. Not only did it not make sense, it wasn't beyond the bounds of possibility that he'd said something else entirely.

I'm convinced that by the next day I would have forgotten all about "T'mon," but as luck would have it, my mother's neighbour, Maura, paid a visit that evening. Still fresh in my mind, I asked her if she had any idea what it meant.

"T'mon," she repeated, "is a small town in Wexford."

It was a revelation. The next morning, I borrowed my father's road atlas and looked it up. Not T'mon but Taghmon. As Maura said, it was a small town in Wexford, about thirty miles away with, as far as I knew, no connection to my grandparents. It was certainly not a place I ever heard them mention. It meant nothing to my mother either.

We had only planned to be in Ireland for another week and I seriously deliberated whether it was fair for my family to pursue Taghmon any further. My kids wanted to visit the Leprechaun Museum in Dublin, my wife wanted to do some clothes shopping, and I was quite keen on going to the Guinness factory. Needless to say, curiosity got the better of me. Selfishly, I decided Dublin would have to wait. Just one day, I promised myself. I'd spend just one more day looking into this and no more.

I wasn't quite sure where to start. My father told me there was a newspaper archive in Wexford, and maybe if I looked up *Fin* or *Kiely* or *Taghmon*, I might find something. After that, he suggested I could take the slow route back to the bungalow and swing into Taghmon itself.

It sounded like a plan. The next morning, I got up early. Only Rupert, my eldest, was up before me, lying on his belly in the kitchen, head propped on his hands, watching *Fireman Sam* on the TV. I gave him a kiss, wolfed down a couple of slices of toast, and left him to it.

By the time I reached the archive, I had pretty much decided that my focus should be to research the local newspapers between 1919 to 1921, the years of the Anglo-Irish War. If that yielded nothing, I could maybe keep looking up to the end of the Civil War in 1923.

Caught up in a weird mix of excitement and trepidation, I found myself at a desk, told the archivist what I wanted, and waited until she brought out a large A1 leather-bound folder of newspapers labelled 1919-1920. Without knowing what I was looking for, I began leafing through.

When that yielded nothing, I tried the next year. There was a short paragraph about the mill being raided in 1921, but no further details. When I reached 1923, I was ready to stop. It looked like John had sent me on a wild goose chase, and I felt annoyed. I was on the brink of leaving — getting back with maybe just enough time to take the kids to the cinema in Carlow — when I had a last-minute change of heart. I'd driven all the way here and I might as well keep looking for another half hour or so.

I asked the archivist for the next year and then the next. There was another paragraph in June 1925 about the mill being raided again.

"Sargent Taffy, accompanied by a party of military searched the house of John Kiely of Kilcloney Borris where it is alleged, they found a Still in full swing. John Kiely was taken into custody and charged before Mr. Millet's P.C., Bagnalstown, who remanded him in custody to the next district court at Borris. He was later conveyed under escort to Mountjoy."

I assumed the still must have been for making poteen. It was highly illegal at the time, but all the same, it seemed a bit overkill to cart someone off to prison for fermenting a few potatoes. I also wondered if the John mentioned was Jack or his father. Then I remembered his father had died a year earlier. I also remembered Jack showing me his still in the garden shed in Sparkhill, so it was pretty evident he was the guilty party. All the same, this was mild stuff, and again I was tempted to call a halt to my search. A glance at the clock told me I had fifteen minutes until the archive closed. It wasn't long and I decided I would hang on until then. Absent-mindedly, I leafed through another few pages until I hit the beginning of 1926. The clock had reached four and I was about to hand back the folder when I spotted another short paragraph. A Jack Kiely had been arrested in connection with a bank robbery in Bunclody.

CHAPTER ELEVEN

Who killed Kennedy?

After declaring Ireland independent, De Valera headed off to America, ostensibly to raise money for the cause. When he checked into the Waldorf-Astoria in New York, he gave himself a new title when signing the ledger: "President of the Irish Republic."

As he left, two RIC officers were ambushed and killed in Soloheadbeg, Tipperary. It was January 1919, and that violence kicked off the Anglo-Irish War. Almost immediately, the IRA began capturing weapons and freeing Republican prisoners. In September, the British outlawed De Valera's Dáil, and in response, the IRA started to ambush RIC and British Army patrols.

De Valera had told Collins he preferred to conduct the war as a conventional man-on-man confrontation. It seemed the upright, fair thing to do. Besides, the optics would look better to anyone looking in — particularly the Americans. Collins, who at the time was wearing multiple hats as Minister for Finance, Commandant General of the IRA, head of the Irish Republican Brotherhood, and Director of Intelligence, disagreed. He was convinced a head-to-head with the British — an empire with the largest standing army in the world — would be suicide. He proposed that the IRA should adopt the same guerilla tactics as the Boers had used fifteen years earlier. He reasoned that his men were outnumbered, outgunned, and poorly trained. The only way they could win, or at least get to the negotiating table, was to conduct the war on their terms.

While De Valera continued his tour of America, Collins began organising his resources. Guerrilla warfare had been used successfully for centuries, and he adopted it as his own. His maxims were that an IRA attack had to have the element of surprise. They, not the British, should choose the time and place. They should be familiar with the terrain, and they should strike from left field, degrading the morale of the enemy and leaving them in constant fear of attack. They'd have no uniforms so that they could blend seamlessly back into the civilian population — and they should be aware that success depended on the unwavering support of the community.

Sitting alongside guerrilla flexibility, his model was based along traditional military lines. At the top were brigades — in Jack's case the Carlow Brigade. Beneath brigades were battalions and beneath battalions, companies.

Because of his experience running despatches during the Rising, Jack was appointed 2nd lieutenant of G company — the area that covered Borris. G company had, at least in theory, a hundred-and fifty-foot soldiers, and within six months Jack was promoted to 1st lieutenant. Jas soon rose to the same rank in F company.

To make the County ungovernable, they began attacking infrastructure. Over the following months, Jack found himself blowing up bridges and raiding houses for arms and ammunition. With guerilla activity coordinated across the country, it wasn't long before the railways were brought to a standstill and the British military found it impossible to move. When the RIC were forced to retreat, the brigades began burning out their barracks so they couldn't return.

There were also attempts to burn out the big houses. "Hanging gale" Beresford's pile at Fenagh was one such target. When an attack there failed, Jack picked up a can of paraffin and told Hynes he was off to burn Borris house. The owner at the time, sixty-six-year-old Walter Kavanagh, had been the high sheriff of Borris and was now the local MP. His son, Arthur, had been in the Queen's Hussars. Yet, despite their "Englishness," the family were careful to give the appearance of neutrality, carefully sitting on the fence until they saw which way the dust would settle.

As it happened, De Valera was against burning "The Big Houses." Famously he said, "Terroristic methods may silence those of our opponents who are cowards, but many of them are very far from being cowards and attempts at terrorism will only stiffen the bold men amongst them."

Kellistown cottage

Jack was ordered to stand down, but a branch of his landlord's family wasn't so lucky. A servant for Dennis

Beresford's sister, Elizabeth, told Dundon that Elizabeth had been passing information to the British. She lived in Kellistown cottage — not so much a cottage as a small but grand Georgian house a few miles north of Fenagh. As a consequence, a group of IRA men, including Jas, broke in and forced her and her sister, Annette, outside. As they set fire to the house, they told them to leave the country. If they came back, they'd be shot.

By the mid-1920s, the IRA controlled most local councils. In nearby Thomastown, they'd established a court and policing system recognised not only by the local Catholics, but also by the big Protestant landowners. So many banks had been robbed that the country's economy was in meltdown. The Inland Revenue had ceased to operate. Rents were difficult, if not impossible, to collect, and rate payments were making their way directly to Republican coffers.

Jack was appointed quartermaster for the brigade — responsible for hiding away their arsenal of weapons. Along with his old friend Luke Dwyer, he then became part of a specialised sub-group of IRA men who raised money for arms and ammunition by robbing mail trains, post offices, and banks.

For most of that time, he and Jas were on the run and sleeping rough. Biddy was worried sick. She couldn't count the number of times the military had forced their way into the mill looking for them. Business wasn't good either. The war in Europe had ended, but with so many men still away or dead, there'd been a sharp decline in the demand for woollen goods. Cheap cotton imports were also pouring in from America, and with the country going through yet another round of economic collapse, no one had any money.

With John ill and the boys away, Biddy found it was down to her and the girls to keep things going. As she struggled to make ends meet, IRA ambushes intensified. Hundreds of RIC officers decided to resign, and the British began recruiting war veterans to take their place. With the promise of high pay and a good pension, thousands applied. Most were battle-hardened, unemployed, single Protestant men — and of those, many had been severely traumatised from their experience in the war.

Because of a shortage of RIC uniforms, the recruits were issued with a mixture of dark RIC tunics and Khaki army trousers. The Irish called them "Black and Tans," and they were given carte blanche to shoot first and ask questions later.

As the economy continued to plummet, the first unit of Tans arrived in March 1920. By October, there were over a thousand in the country. As they continued to flood in, RIC men began to hand in their resignations. Many were sympathetic to the uprising and didn't relish working with the Tans. Famously, Jeremiah Mee, a long-serving RIC officer, staged a mutiny when he was commanded to hand over his barracks. He said he'd joined up "with characters second to none" and that he "refused to co-operate or work in any capacity with the British military, men of low moral character who frequented bad houses, kept the company of prostitutes, and were generally unsuitable and undesirable characters."

With the arrival of the Tans, concerns about rape and sexual assault escalated. In India, a company of Connaught Rangers stationed at Jullundur laid down their arms in protest at British military activity in Ireland, insisting their action was prompted by the way their "mothers and sisters had been treated by the Black and Tans."

As well as a reputation for immorality, they soon gained another for brutality. From the summer of 1920, they responded to IRA attacks by carrying out the arbitrary murder of civilians. As well as individuals, many villages and towns were subject to mass reprisals. Tralee was one. In response to the killing of two RIC men, they closed local businesses, allowed no food in for a week, and murdered three innocent people.

After an ambush on an Auxiliary patrol in Cork, they reduced the city to flames with firebombs. As well as looting the town, they terrorised civilians and carried out incalculable beatings, shootings, and robberies. As local firefighters attempted to put out the blaze, they took potshots at them. If they persisted, they were arrested, killed, or had their hoses slashed. By the time the fire burnt itself out, Cork City Hall, the library, and three hundred and fifty homes and businesses had been razed to the ground.

Black and Tan atrocities across the country left thousands homeless, jobless, and traumatized, yet the attacks were fully supported by both the heads of the RIC and the British government. Bloody reprisals had won the war against the Boer guerrillas, and it seemed reasonable to assume they'd do the same in Ireland.

One of the most notorious occurred on 21st November 1920.

That morning, Collins had ordered the killing of the Cairo gang — a notorious group of British spies in Dublin. Fourteen were shot dead, and that afternoon there was a football game at Croke Park between Dublin and Tipperary. The army commander, Nevil Macready, thought it likely that some of the assassins had come up from Tipperary and instructed that the crowd be searched for weapons as they left the game.

About fifteen thousand people were at the match and the military contingent was made up of Auxiliaries, the RIC, and the Tans — all under separate leadership.

Black and Tan hold-up

According to the initial, official British reports, IRA elements in the crowd fired first. That wasn't supported by eyewitnesses or many of the British officers who were there. Major Mills of the Auxiliaries told an inquest that it was:

A rotten show, the worst I've ever seen. The regular RIC from Phoenix Park and the Black and Tans arrived in lorries and opened fire into the crowd without reason. They killed about a dozen and wounded many more. I eventually stopped them firing.

According to Mills, some of the Tans wanted to execute the entire Tipperary team. As it happened, they shot just one — Michael Hogan. The rest of the fourteen fatalities were civilians, including two children. Another sixty or so were wounded.

The claim that the police were fired on first was eventually dismissed by the British authorities. Like the "Bloody Sunday" of 1972, they concluded that the shooting was "unprovoked, indiscriminate, and excessive."

Whatever sympathy the British might have gained from Collin's attack that morning, it had melted away by the evening. World condemnation — particularly from America — was harsh. Buoyed up by popular opinion, Republicans in Mountjoy began demanding that they should receive political rather than criminal status.

Hundreds of Dubliners gathered outside the prison walls in support. In Borris, Dundon felt the town should also show its solidarity and ordered businesses to close.

Every shopkeeper obeyed the call — except one. Forty-four-year-old Bill Kennedy, a larger-than-life pharmacist with several commercial interests in the town, including a chemist shop, hackney carriage company, hardware store, and hotel.

Kennedy was Marmite. Jack found him pleasant enough. He'd been a friend of the family for years and his father often called in to see him for medical advice and a bottle of opium. He was pig-headed, but a strong nationalist. Only a few months earlier, he'd sheltered a poacher wanted by the RIC for stealing game from the Kavanagh estate. Others weren't so keen. His commercial success had stirred up a lot of jealousy among his rivals. Ed Hogan was one of them. His family owned another cab company in the town and if that wasn't reason enough for bad blood, Kennedy had recently dated his sister. When it all ended in tears, Ed and his family weren't happy. As to whether Kennedy supported the prisoners in Mountjoy, that was neither here nor there. His gripe was that he had no intention of kowtowing to a group of young whippersnappers telling him what to do — especially when they had a personal axe to grind. That nuance was lost on Dundon He ordered the Brigade to picket Kennedy's shops. Not to be outdone, Kennedy instructed his friend and solicitor Mick O 'Dempsey to sue Dundon, Hogan, and a few of their friends for loss of earnings.

Kennedy's house and pharmacy, Borris

For a while it was stalemate. Then, a few months later, G company robbed the mail train from Borris. It was standard IRA procedure — to intercept intelligence, discover secret police cyphers, and track down informants. This time the robbery yielded an additional haul. Letters O'Dempsey had posted off to Kings Council in Dublin, pursuing the legal case against Dundon.

Jack wasn't sure if the gripe against Kennedy fell under the heading of official IRA business. Dundon was adamant it did. To make it impossible for Kennedy to proceed with the case, he ordered Hynes and his men to break into O' Dempsey's office and steal the rest of the paperwork.

Sacred Heart church, Borris

As Hynes set to work, Terence MacSwiney, the Lord mayor of Cork, died after a seventy-four-day hunger strike. He'd been demanding the release of sixty-five men held without trial in Cork City prison. Dundon had been replaced by then, but his successor had the same idea. Local shops should close to show support. Again, Kennedy refused. Not only that, but he began canvassing his fellow retailers to do the same.

Kennedy might have had the financial upper hand, but Dundon and Hogan had the political one. They complained to GHQ about his anti-IRA activities. Inevitably, orders came down that they should make an example of him.

In February, a group of nine Volunteers took over Bolger's house opposite Dundon's. The idea was to ambush Kennedy when he turned up to harass him. The attack failed abysmally when they failed to take the safety catches off their revolvers.

A month later, Hynes got word that Kennedy, O'Dempsey, and two of their friends would be going to a party at the top of the town. He picked twelve of his best men and divided them into three units. One was to hide in the church grounds. Another would cover Maloney's Lane a few yards up the road, and the third, including himself and Jack, would climb into the Kavanagh estate and wait behind the old stone wall overlooking his house.

Jack was no stranger to action. He'd helped burn out the barracks a few months earlier, and he'd taken out a Tan called Franey when the force first arrived in Borris. He'd also been involved in countless raids to collect arms from unwilling farmers — one of which he'd carried out on his own.

Site of Maloney's lane, Borris

He shouldn't have been hesitant, but he was. He was unhappy about the whole idea. Kennedy might have been stubborn and arrogant, but he wasn't the enemy. Besides, he had cohones. He'd stand up to anyone about anything, and it was a trait Jack admired.

Hynes didn't share his admiration. Kennedy was a confirmed atheist who continually poked fun at the clergy. On one occasion, he cleared out his pharmacy window to put up two signs — *men* and *women* — a jibe at how the congregation was segregated during confession.

As far as Hynes was concerned, Kennedy had not only overstepped the mark commercially and politically, but his mockery was a direct affront to God. There was no doubt he had to go.

Around nine pm, Jack trudged his way through the Kavanagh estate to join Hynes. The brigade leader was already in place behind the wall and, as it started to rain, Jack pulled down his cap and checked for the umpteenth time that his revolver was loaded. Hynes asked if he was alright. Jack shrugged and nodded that he was. The truth was that being asked to take out a fellow Irishman, someone he knew well, and at such close quarters, sat badly with his conscience.

Less than three minutes later, Kennedy and O'Dempsey emerged through Kennedy's front door. Street lamps wouldn't be introduced to Borris for another forty years and only the pale light from an overcast crescent moon lit the street.

Both men were laughing. O'Dempsey was carrying a bottle, presumably for the party. It seemed their friends must have left earlier and now the unit had only two targets to deal with.

The wall from where Kennedy was shot.

As soon as they started walking up the road, Hynes blew a whistle. The unit he'd stationed at the church began firing. Everyone knew that Kennedy's eyesight was particularly bad, but even so, he managed to pump back a few rounds. For a few seconds, he and O'Dempsey sheltered behind the steps to the church. When they emerged, Hynes' units started firing again. Within seconds, both men fell to the ground. Kennedy was dead. O'Dempsey was wounded — but fatally so.

As he lay gasping for breath, the wife of one of Kennedy's business rivals crossed the street and kicked him in the ribs. When Hynes wanted to hang a placard around their necks with the usual "Spies beware" warning, no one seemed to have the appetite for it. As O'Dempsey succumbed, the assassins melted away.

Up until then, Borris had escaped the worst of Tan atrocities. A month later, that changed. The Carlow flying column was planning to join up with the 4th battalion and attack the barracks in Bagnalstown. Somehow, the Tans were tipped off and the attack had to be postponed.

Disappointed, the column moved north to Ballymurphy and made camp in a derelict house. A day or two later, they were conducting exercises in a nearby field when a military patrol pulled up in two Crossley Tenders. Before the column knew what was happening, six soldiers and seven Black-and-Tans jumped out and started firing. The column were about two hundred yards away. As they started running, the military split into two and gave chase.

Six of the columns were caught. Three others were shot dead.

In the subsequent inquest, the Tans maintained that the three killed were taken out cleanly by shotgun. That didn't tally with the evidence of the IRA commander, who claimed that at least one of his men had been bayonetted to death while lying wounded on the ground.

The military also killed three innocent bystanders. Sixty-two-year-old Michael Ryan, who was shot in the face while fetching water from his well, and brothers James and Peter Farrell, both in their early twenties. According to initial Tan evidence, the Farrells had been out sewing corn and were accidentally caught in the crossfire. Further examination revealed they'd been savagely bayonetted while begging for their lives.

The next morning, hundreds of British troops were sent to Ballymurphy. Orders had been given for the bodies of the dead to remain unburied until an inquest was held. The angry families decided to ignore the order and at 11 am, they brought them into the church for a funeral service. John and Biddy Kiely were there. So were Jas and Jack. While Biddy comforted the boys' parents, the military burst in, forced their way through the congregation with guns and bloodhounds, and prised open the coffins.

Old Barracks, Borris

The insensitive brutality of the intrusion caused an upsurge of huge sympathy, not only locally, but across the country. A month later, a Black and Tan ironically also named Farrell was ambushed at the top of Borris. He'd been on GHQ's 'blacklist' for some time and was generally suspected to be part of a gang who, masked up and anonymous, had been involved in reprisal atrocities.

It was a Sunday morning, and again the chosen place of ambush was from behind the wall of the Kavanagh estate. As he came into sight, Hyne's unit began shooting. Farrell fired back and retreated towards the temporary barracks at the Protestant school. When his comrades realised what was happening, they managed to pull him in — wounded but still very much alive.

The fact that the column failed to kill the Black and Tan rankled with Jack. This was one of the men who'd murdered the Farrell brothers. As it happened, they were Jack's first cousins.

CHAPTER TWELVE

"Fin" the spy

I really should have read the sign on the archive door. Closed on Wednesdays. I'd got there at 10 am, notebook in hand and ready to go — and it was all a waste of time. I gave a long sigh. I'd let the kids down yet again to satisfy my crazy quest for the grail. Maybe if I got home early enough, I could make it up to them.

As I drove back, I wondered if I should take them to see the Michael Collins film. Probably not. My wife would probably find a historical drama as boring as they would. I'd noticed that *James and the Giant Peach* was on in Carlow, and I resigned myself that although not a great Roald fan, I'd have to bite the bullet and go to that.

Tomorrow, I promised myself I would return to the archive.

Jack's secret appeared to be that he'd robbed a bank in Bunclody, and I could understand why he wouldn't want the family to know. All his IRA stuff had been for a cause — robbing a bank obviously wasn't. Still, I couldn't see Jack as a bank robber. It didn't seem his sort of thing — but then, who can tell? All sorts of ideas flashed through my mind. Was Bunclody the only bank he'd ever robbed? Did he get away with it? And what happened to the money? Maybe that's how he could afford the house in Sparkhill, although my mother told me he and Josie had saved for years to raise the deposit. Certainly, Taghmon seemed to be a red herring. I must have misheard what John said — or perhaps he'd got mixed up somehow. Either way, as I passed a signpost to it, I decided not to drop in.

As for Bunclody, I remember it being a postcard village with a ridiculously wide main road and an equally wide gushing river. I also remember being sick as a dog when I rode there one time. It was my own fault. I'd bought a block of pipe tobacco from Joyce's and, not being allowed to smoke it, I thought I'd chew it like a "spittoon spitting" cowboy.

It was my pathetic attempt to imitate my pipe-smoking Uncle Mick and it backfired. Anytime I've smelt a pipe since then I've felt decidedly ill — and I'm not too good with cigarettes either.

When I returned home hot and sweaty, I saw Jack suited and booted and on his way out. He said he was off to meet a friend and asked if I wanted to come along. I was still feeling bad, but, intrigued as always, I said I would.

His friend turned out to be a woman, probably in her fifties. It looked like she lived alone above the chemist shop in Borris, or at least somewhere near it. Her name was Kennedy. I remember because it was just before JFK was assassinated — in fact, I think they discussed his recent visit to Ireland and how he'd been to New Ross Harbour to see where his ancestors left for America.

Thinking back on it, I wondered if she'd been related to the Bill Kennedy that John Nolan was always on about. It must have been twenty years later when John first showed me the letter. It was handwritten in dark blue ink, and he seemed very proud of it. As he lay it on the counter, I could see that it had been torn from something like a school exercise book.

While his sister fetched the tea, he asked if remembered the story. I assured him I did. Back in the day, Kennedy had been the local pharmacist. He'd refused to close his shop when someone important died on hunger strike. John seemed happy enough with my answer and handed me the letter. As I opened it up, I could see that it had been written in old person, flowery, embellished script, and at the bottom it was signed "IRA."

John leaned forward. "It's a warning note," he told me. "It was pinned to the back of an old dresser. Someone found it when they were throwing it out.

On closer inspection, I could see it was addressed to a Mick O'Dempsey. From what John told me, O'Dempsey had been Kennedy's lawyer. When he refused to shut up shop, the IRA — essentially the local village lads — threatened to boycott it. Kennedy, knowing who they were, instructed O'Dempsey to issue them with an injunction. The lads tried to scare O'Dempsey off, but when he ignored them, he was kidnapped and the case files stolen. They let him go just before Christmas, and it looked like nothing more would come of it. Then, in March, he and Kennedy were shot.

"Where did you get it?" I asked.

He tapped his nose. "Isn't that a find though?"

It was. A real piece of local history. It belonged in a museum, but I suspected he'd squirrel it away in his collection, along with the countless other historical oddities he'd picked up over the years.

"So why did they kill him?"

John took the letter back, folded it carefully, and put it back in his favourite drawer. "I read the military report Hynes submitted in the fifties. It makes interesting reading."

I wasn't sure of an appropriate response, so I just raised a quizzical eyebrow.

"He said Kennedy would go out at night with a revolver and flashlight, firing at anyone who looked like a Volunteer. Then he took to parking outside Dundon's house with his Tan friends, blowing his horn and firing shots through the windows. Hynes also said that he and the Tans forced Ed Hogan to his knees and made him sign a declaration to stop boycotting his shops."

"Seems pretty damning."

"It does, doesn't it?"

Somehow, I got the feeling he didn't buy it.

"Did Jack ever tell you anything about Kennedy?"

I shook my head. He hadn't. At least not directly — but years before there'd been a family reunion at Kilcloney. While everyone remained in the kitchen playing cards, he and Nell retired to the parlour. I was under that big Georgian table playing with some toy cars, and they seemed not to notice me. As they sat chatting, I remember the subject of Kennedy coming up. It was grown-up talk, and I wouldn't have remembered it if it hadn't been for one thing. It was the first and only time I saw Jack cry. His words to Nell stuck with me. "It should never have happened."

Maybe I should have told John, but bearing in mind what Hynes said in his report, it didn't make sense. If Kennedy had been in bed with the Tans, why had Jack felt so bad about him being taken out? Perhaps John felt Hynes's report had been "sexed-up" to justify his murder. I had no idea why Hynes might want to do that but either way, I decided to keep what I thought I'd heard to myself.

My journey home from the Archives took about an hour. The route took me through New Ross and past St. Mullins.

A half mile further on, I saw signs for Ballymurphy, and it reminded me of John's other big story.

It was about the Farrell brothers. I'd heard the how they'd been killed a thousand times, but one year John added an extra piece to the puzzle.

The morning before the attack, a local man had been seen talking to the RIC. For years, the old IRA men only referred to him as "Fin" and the story went that he'd taken a large bung to tell them where the Brigade was hiding out. I knew all this already, but that year John told me that he'd discovered who Fin was.

How accurate his information was, I didn't know, but he told me his real name was Michael Hackett and that he was from Bagnalstown.

Apparently, as soon as Jack's brigade heard about the conversation, they decided he needed to be questioned. A few days later, as he was riding to a hurling match in Fenagh, they pulled alongside him in a car, forced him to the side of the road, and went through his pockets. They found £100 (£6000). In an Ireland where almost everyone was on the breadline, it seemed reasonable to assume it was payment for the tip-off.

They left his bike in the ditch, covered his head with a blanket, and threw him onto the back seat. Not sure what to do with him, they locked him up in an old house in nearby Ballinree. That night, while they were debating their plan of action, he managed to escape, but early next morning they caught him again as he tried to reach the barracks in Borris.

That night, he was tried by an IRA court and found guilty of treason. Around 10 pm he was dragged out of the house, forced onto his knees, and told to make an Act of Contrition. Then someone put a bullet in his head.

Although John didn't say as much, I was convinced he thought it was Jack. He'd told me the Farrells had been his cousins, so I suppose it wasn't beyond the bounds of possibility. If nothing else, I imagine he would have been invited to pull the trigger.

When I arrived back at the bungalow, I noticed my wife's car had gone. My mother told me the kids had got bored and she'd decided to take them out herself. I asked her if she was annoyed. She shook her head in a way that meant "yes" and asked me if I wanted a cup of tea.

I told her I was OK and began helping with the washing up. I assumed my father was up in the lounge reading the Dennis Wheatley novel I'd brought him from England. I hadn't had a chance to talk to her properly yesterday, so as we were on our own, I thought I'd bring her up to speed.

"I found something in the Archives yesterday," I said. "About grandad."

I expected her to reply with "I thought you might" or even "So, you found out at last," but instead, she put down the plate she was washing, turned on the tap, and began filling the kettle.

"Would you like to know what?" I queried.

She lowered the kettle onto the hob and lit the gas. "As long as it's nothing bad."

I could see by the way she was chewing her lip that she was bracing herself.

"It's OK," I lied. "It's just that I think he might have robbed a bank. The one in Bunclody."

Ray Knowles | A Seam of Emerald

I wasn't sure what reaction to expect. Certainly not the stone-faced look of disbelief I got.

"Didn't you know?" I asked.

"No."

"You must have."

"No." Her answer was emphatic. She slumped down into her armchair and thought for a minute. "When?"

"1926."

"Two years before I was born."

That was true — but it was hard to believe that over the years someone hadn't told her something. I asked her to cast her mind back. Was there anything she remembered that seemed strange, or out of place?

She frowned in concentration. Then a slight flicker as a memory bubbled to the surface. "I must have been eight or nine," she began. "Mum told me dad was in hospital. That he was extremely ill. That he might die."

The timeline was at least ten years out — but I'd never heard her talk about this before. She remembered travelling a long way to see him — maybe by train, maybe in a taxi. Then climbing a long flight of wrought iron stairs, looking down through the gaps as her mother grasped her hand. At the top, they were taken into a large, grey room with metal framed beds, white linen sheets, and bars on the windows. Her father was on one — emaciated, his eyes sunk into his head, and his tongue... she distinctly remembered his tongue: white, furry, dry, distended.

She had no idea what hospital it could have been or what he might have been suffering from — just that his face had been drawn and haggard. She also told me that it had been so long since she'd seen him that he had looked like a stranger — and that made her scared.

I asked her if it might have been a prison, but she shook her head. "More like a hospital, but I don't know."

The only time I'd seen Jack in hospital was that time he'd been admitted to the QE in Birmingham with gallstones.

As the kettle started to boil, I stood up to make the tea. There were some Garibaldi biscuits in the cupboard, and I put one on the side of my mother's saucer as I handed her the cup. Then she told me another oddity I hadn't heard before.

She'd been born in 1928, but not in Ireland. According to her birth certificate, it had been Armagh, in the north. She remembered her parents had run some sort of shop — and they must have been reasonably well-off, as a seamstress came in from time to time to make her dresses. Then one day, they left.

That was all she could remember. In fairness, she would have only been a toddler. It probably had something to do with them being Catholics in a Protestant area, but that begged the question, why? From what I'd read, raising a Catholic family in 1920s Protestant Belfast wasn't a great idea. I could only assume Jack must have had a good reason for going there.

I quizzed her a bit longer, hoping she'd remember something else. She couldn't — but she did tell me something just as intriguing.

Years later idea, her cousin Maisie, the daughter of Jack's youngest sister, Bridie, rang to say they needed to talk. Bridie had just died, and my mother assumed she'd found something in her mother's belongings she wanted to tell her about. Maisie lived in Manchester and said she couldn't go into it on the phone, but she would come down to Birmingham to meet her.

My mother rang Josie to tell her about the call and immediately she got on her high horse. She told her in no uncertain terms that Bridie was a gossip and tittle tattle, and nothing she said could be believed. The same obviously went for Maisie. As a result, my mother declined the invitation.

Back then, she had no reason to believe that her parents had led anything other than a vanilla life. Maisie did manage to tell her one thing, though. My mother hadn't been baptised Kiely. She'd been baptised "Doyle." At the time, it seemed patently ridiculous and, reinforced by her conversation with Josie, she'd put it out of her mind. Now she wasn't so sure.

We sat talking for the next couple of hours. Then we joined my father in the lounge. *To the Devil a Daughter* seemed to have gone down well, and he was anxious to tell me what he thought of it. Two hours later, my kids came running in, followed by my disgruntled wife. She dismissed my apology with a wave of the hand. "Not to worry," she said. "We had a great time without you anyway." When I asked where they'd been, she told me to the cinema. Predictably, to see *James and the Giant Peach*.

While she and my mother disappeared into the kitchen to prepare dinner, I took out the Jenga set and made up for lost time by playing with the kids.

Then we settled down to steak — the best Irish, my mum told me, bought from Charlie Nolan's in Borris. When it was time for bedtime, I dug out Rupert's favourite book, *The*

Hungry Caterpillar, took the kids to their bedroom, and read them off to sleep.

As I returned to the kitchen, it struck me that the only person who really knew what any of this was about was Jack. My problem was that putting him under the spotlight would make me feel incredibly bad. After all, wasn't digging into a past he'd tried to keep secret for seventy years an act of betrayal? I loved him way too much to want to be accused of that.

The problem was that now I was more curious than ever. He was becoming an addiction, and although it didn't seem fair, I knew I couldn't stop. To make myself feel better, I decided that if I left him in blissful ignorance, that would be OK. What he didn't know wouldn't hurt him.

In the meantime, no matter how unpopular it would make me with my family, I decided I would have to head back to Wexford in the morning and find out what this Bunclody business was all about.

CHAPTER THIRTEEN

Escape to the North

For Jack and the men of the 4th battalion, the attack on Sergeant Farrell was the last skirmish of the Anglo-Irish war.

Over the previous two years, practically the entire country had mobilised against the British. Dublin dockers had refused to offload their weapons, and the Irish Transport and General Workers union had banned railway drivers from carrying their military. With the country in total disarray — and practically ungovernable — the conflict had reached a stalemate.

The British were worried that the IRA's guerrilla campaign could continue indefinitely. They were also concerned about increasing criticism from home and abroad. The Irish — in particular Michael Collins — feared their men were running out of steam. There seemed to be an endless flow of troops coming into the country, and they were dangerously short of arms and ammunition.

Ironically, the breakthrough came from George V. His negative feelings about the Black and Tans were well known, and in a speech in Belfast he called on

> "all Irishmen to pause, to stretch out the hand of forbearance and conciliation, to forgive and to forget, and to join in making for the land they love a new era of peace, contentment, and goodwill."

Something had to give. American public opinion was firmly against the war. In addition, a new home-grown peace movement had sprung up in Britain, which included an eclectic mix of the Labour Party, *The Times*, members of the House of Lords, and celebrities like George Bernard Shaw.

Brigadier General Cockerill, a Tory party politician, sent an open letter to Lloyd George in the *Times* demanding that a peace conference should be organised. Even the Pope waded in with calls for a negotiated end to the violence.

On 6 June 1921, Lloyd George made his first conciliatory gesture. He called off the policy of burning civilian houses in revenge for attacks on the military. Then he invited the Irish to send representatives to London to see if a treaty could be negotiated.

During the uneasy truce that followed, Jack was sent on an IRA refresher course in the nineteenth century Duckett Grove mansion in Carlow. While he was honing his terrorist skills, Collins returned with the Treaty.

Apoplectic with rage De Valera told the Dáil they should not only reject it, but they had had no right to approve it in the first place.

If they did, he threatened,

> "the fight for freedom would still go on, and the Irish people, instead of fighting foreign soldiers, would have to fight the Irish soldiers of an Irish government set up by Irishmen."

Despite his objections, the treaty was ratified, and Collins took over as party leader. Almost immediately, De Valera began touring the country, calling for the vote to be overturned. On his graduation from Duckett's Grove, Jack offered his support. For a while, he acted as De Valera's driver and as he toured the country the Long Fella didn't mince his words. In a speech in Thurles, he warned that,

> "The IRA would have to wade through the blood of the soldiers of the Irish Government, and perhaps through that of some members of the Irish Government, to get their freedom."

This was incendiary stuff, and with what he thought was a majority behind him, he stood for re-election. To his frustration, he suffered a resounding defeat.

Most democratic politicians might have accepted the will of the people and retired to lick their wounds. Not De Valera. His retort to his opponents was to become one of the most famous quotes in Irish history: "The majority have no right to do wrong."

At that point, he stormed out of the Dail and effectively kick started the civil war.

In Borris, Jack was surprised at how many of his old friends backed Collins. Hynes stayed loyal to the cause. Dundon decided to sit on the fence, but the Hogans and practically everyone else in the Brigade sided with the Big Fella. Kennedy's assassination had taught Jack that patriotism could be a smoke screen for self-interest. Certainly, a lot of scores had been settled over the past couple of years, and on the whole the people who'd risen to the top of the new food chain were keen to stay there.

Self-interest had never been a motivator for Jack, and he wasn't content with a job half-done. Ireland was still a divided puppet state, and as far as he was concerned, the struggle had to continue until that changed.

Initially, things looked good for the anti-treaty men. The new Free State army had only eight thousand volunteers compared with De Valera's fifteen thousand. Not only that, but they included most of the heroes of the Anglo-Irish war, holed up in some of the best positions.

One of them was the public records office at the Four Courts in Dublin. Collins hesitated to attack his old comrades there but found himself in a tricky position. If he couldn't regain control of the country, Churchill threatened to send in British troops and do the job for him.

Reluctantly, he ordered his men to bombard it. Within days, they blasted their way in, but it was a pyrrhic victory. The attack only strengthened anti-treaty opinion that the new Free State was merely a continuation of British rule.

Taking the name "IRA" for their own, the anti-treaty men decided to fight on, but despite their superior numbers, they were soon on the back foot. The Free State army was well-paid and well-armed, and as time went on their numbers grew. In only a year, it expanded to over thirty-eight thousand men. A year later, it rose to fifty-eight thousand, many recruited from experienced war veterans. The IRA, on the other hand, had no source of income and hardly any weapons. To fund themselves, a directive was issued to resume robbing banks and post offices as they had during the War of Independence.

For the first year or so, the Civil War was fought along conventional lines — the sort of head-to-head conflict De Valera favoured. It didn't take long, however, before the IRA concluded that they could never win that way. Their only chance was to adopt the same guerrilla tactics Collins had used during the Anglo-Irish war.

Their problem was that Collins knew exactly how to counter them.

William Cosgrave

Within weeks, he ordered Republican sympathisers to be rounded up and imprisoned. The Kielys had never made a secret of where their loyalties lay and in early 1922, pro-treaty neighbours and some of Jack's ex-comrades drove into the yard at Kilcloney and broke down the kitchen door. Unlike raids they'd had from the British, this one was far more personal. Jas was arrested on the spot and severely beaten. He received nine months for sedition, but his injuries were so bad he had to spend most of the time in a military hospital. Jack managed to hide, and in a frantic search to find him, the Free State ransacked the mill, smashing up furniture and destroying the weaving and carding machinery.

For the first time in a hundred and fifty years, the mill had to close. The army had also taken their cattle and, now in his late seventies, all John had left was the old house and a few sheep.

Business had been bad before, but now Kilcloney was firmly between the crosshairs of the Free State. Neighbours who would have previously helped- turned away. Others went out of their way to snoop on the mill — especially if they thought Jack was around. Some shopkeepers refused to serve him. Even church was difficult. The clergy were firmly behind the Free State, and when he and Biddy filed up the aisle to receive communion, he could sense the animosity.

Without a source of income, John was forced to sell the houses in Dublin. The stress played havoc with his health. After a while, he stopped going out. Nell and Mary were left to take the ass and cart into town to collect the groceries while Biddy stayed at home to look after him. That August, as his health continued to deteriorate, Michael Collins decided to take a trip to his native Cork.

By 1922, the Free State controlled most of the country — bandit country, Cork was one of the exceptions. Collins was advised against going but seemed confident his old friends wouldn't attack him there.

His convoy stopped off at Long's Pub near Beal na Blath to inquire about directions. The man they asked was IRA and recognised him. He told his superiors and an ambush party was put in place in case the convoy returned. A few hours later it did, and after a short gunfight, Collins was killed with a bullet to the head.

It was the ultimate irony. The man who'd gained Ireland its independence, killed by his own men. A few months later, his Sin Féin party split. The anti-treaty element went its own way, while his successor, William Cosgrave, set up a new pro-treaty party called Cumann na nGaedheal.

Cosgrave was angry. He'd played an active role as captain of the South Dublin Union during the rising, and he was no stranger to war. Collins had been his friend, and his feelings towards the IRA were uncompromising. He told the Dáil,

> "I am not going to hesitate if the country is to live, and if we have to exterminate ten thousand Republicans, the three million of our people is greater than this ten thousand."

As he settled into his new portfolio, Jack met up with his old commanding officer, John Hynes. Hynes was now part of an anti-treaty flying column operating around Enniscorthy and Borris. In it were the big names of the Four Court escapees: Seán Lemass, Ernie O'Malley, and Paddy O'Brien. Jack was invited to join them, and the unit began carrying out raids across the region — including attacks on the barracks in Carlow and nearby Myshall. Then they moved to Blessington in Wicklow.

Because of its proximity to Dublin, Blessington was of enormous strategic importance to the IRA, and O'Malley set up a base there with the idea of attacking nearby Army posts and drawing troops out of the capital.

With other units to organise, he headed off towards Carlow with the 3rd Tipperary Brigade. Jack and Hynes were among the men left behind, and a few days later Oscar Traynor came down to take charge. He was appalled at what he found:

> "We had neither policy, nor military leadership, nor provisions, nor proper clothing and neither had the reinforcements which came to help us,

leaving the whole south-east exposed. We were easy prey to a sudden attack by Free State soldiers."

Ernie O'Malley

Realising he was on a hiding to nothing, he disbanded the garrison and instructed his men to use what resources they had to attack neighbouring barracks. They were partially successful, but soon the Free State decided enough was enough.

In a pincer movement, they attempted to surround the rebels. The Curragh and Dublin brigades moved in from the southeast while a unit commanded by Commandant McNulty bore down from the mountains.

They were more than ready to deploy their formidable — mainly British — weaponry, but the battle they hoped for never took place. Crucially, McNulty's unit was delayed, which allowed Traynor's men to slip through the net.

For the next few months, wet, dishevelled, and badly armed, the IRA continued to be a thorn in the side of the Free State. They shot Private Peter Kenny when he was out driving in an open-top car. Two days later, one of their own men was taken out by a Free State ambush at a disused lodge in Sally Gap. A month later, in the early hours of the morning, they attacked a makeshift garrison at the Glendalough Hotel until it was relieved by reinforcements.

By now Jas had joined Jack in Wicklow. While he elected to fight on there, Jack decided to head back to Carlow with Hynes. To avoid Free State roadblocks, they made their escape by wading across the Slaney. They intended to join up again with O'Malley, but unknown to them he was already in Dublin debating strategy with the IRA commander, Liam Lynch.

It turned into a heated argument. Lynch had originally agreed that Dublin should be their primary target. Now he'd changed his mind. His idea was to leave Dublin for the moment and set up an alternative capital in Cork. O'Malley was furious — the whole point of Blessington, he argued, had been to recapture Dublin.

While they slogged it out, a Crossley Tender packed with nine Free State soldiers ran out of petrol on the relatively quiet Athy road. It was 24th October 1922, and the commandant in charge sent a motorcycle messenger ahead to request more fuel. After they'd topped up, he decided to give the journey a miss and turn back.

Including a stop at the local post office to buy cigarettes, his men had spent over an hour hanging around. This wasn't lost on the anti-treaty locals, who quickly notified the IRA. When the Crossley finally began its journey back to barracks, more than twenty heavily armed men were waiting for them at Graney Cross.

One of them was Jack. Graney was on his way back to Kilcloney, about twenty-five miles from Blessington. He and Hynes had walked there a few days earlier, and as the Crossley appeared around the bend, they attacked. Most of the firing came from the Thorpe house at the side of the road. The Free State soldiers stood little chance. Outnumbered two to one, and with the exit roads blocked by felled trees, they were bombarded by grenades, rifles, and Lewis guns. The first volley achieved nothing. The second knocked out the driver. As he lost control, the Tender careened into a ditch. Three Free State men were killed outright. One of them a sixteen-year-old, Ed Byrne from Bagnalstown, had only joined up a few months earlier.

Graney Cross

His death had a profound effect on Jack. He would have been the same age as his youngest sister, Bridie, and as Free State weapons were being gathered up, he approached his body, hoping to see a sign of life. There wasn't.

For Cosgrave, the capture of the men involved became a priority. As the net widened, Kilcloney was raided again. Somehow, Jack kept out of sight, but another Bagnalstown man, James Lillis, wasn't so lucky. Roughly the same age as Byrne, he was tracked to Borris, where he was found with a rifle and some ammunition. A few months later he was executed. To make matters worse for his family, the Catholic church had recently decreed that anyone involved with the IRA should consider themselves excommunicated. A church burial for Lillis was therefore out of the question, which meant his soul wasn't going to heaven. In a country so overwhelmingly devout, it was yet another disincentive to oppose the Free State.

A month later, O'Malley was captured. After the meeting with Lynch, he'd been involved in a shoot-out with Free State soldiers in Dublin. Despite being severely wounded, he was transferred from Portobello military hospital to Mountjoy prison on 23rd December. He thought the authorities would wait for him to recover and give him a show trial. When he refused to recognise the court, they'd have the ideal excuse to execute him.

He was resigned to his fate, but he was lucky. The trial never happened. There seemed to have been reservations about having an Irish hero carried "Connolly-like" to his execution on a stretcher. His friend, the writer, Erskine Childers, was less fortunate. He'd been executed a month earlier for possessing a small Spanish-made "destroyer" pistol. As it happened, it had been a gift from Michael Collins — but that didn't seem to hold much weight with the judge. Childers was shot at Beggars Bush Barracks in Dublin after shaking hands with the firing squad.

Over the following months, the fighting became more intense, personal, and dirty. In March 1923, eight Free State soldiers were sent to investigate a tip-off about an IRA arms dump in Kerry. It was a trap and six of them were killed.

Two of the dead were close friends of the Kerry commandant, Paddy Daly. Enraged, he ordered that in future, if an IRA mine needed to be defused, it would be Republican prisoners who'd have to do it. A day later, he ordered nine of them to be brought from Ballymullen gaol in Tralee to a place called Ballyseedy.

Paddy Daly

His troops had been instructed to select men who were, "all fairly anonymous, no priests or nuns in the family, those that'll make the least noise."

When the prisoners arrived at the barracks, they were tied to a Free State landmine and blown to pieces.

Liam Lynch

As atrocities on both sides began to escalate, thousands more IRA men — including De Valera — were arrested. While Jack holed up at Kilcloney, Jas found himself interred in the severely overcrowded Wicklow jail.

Cosgrave's Minister of Justice was a man named Kevin O'Higgins. Jack vaguely knew him. After failing to become a priest, he'd joined the Carlow brigade in 1915, and his attitude to almost everything was evangelic and uncompromising. To up the ante, he introduced a Public Safety bill to expand the number of offences that merited the death penalty. They included "aiding or abetting attacks on state forces, possession of arms and ammunition or explosives without the proper authority" and "looting, destruction of public or private property or arson."

Eight thousand Republican prisoners went on hunger strikes in protest. Already weak with beatings or malnourished after being on the run, many collapsed or became so ill they never recovered. Jas was one of the lucky ones. Close to death, he was moved to the Curragh military hospital in Dublin. Eventually, he was released on compassionate grounds — essentially because the authorities were convinced he would die.

On 30 April Lynch accepted that he'd run out of options. He told the IRA to cease military activities. A month later, he proclaimed a ceasefire.

On hearing of the defeat, De Valera's instruction to his followers was characteristically opaque:

> "The Republic can no longer be defended successfully by your arms. Further sacrifice of life would now be in vain and the continuance of the struggle in arms unwise in the national interest and prejudicial to the future of our cause. Military victory must be allowed to rest for the moment with those who have destroyed the Republic."

Lynch was ambushed and shot a few months later — one of his assassins initially mistaking the body of the bespectacled IRA leader for De Valera. At the time of his death, 13,000 IRA prisoners were in jail. Conditions were appalling by any standards: dark, cold, wet, cramped, and rat-infested. At the end of July, the High Court ruled that as a state of war no longer existed, their incarceration was illegal. Cosgrave, concerned that fighting would break out again if they were released, instructed O'Higgins to introduce two more Public Safety Acts to make sure they stayed inside.

At the end of August, he called a general election. His Cumann na nGaedheal party took 40% of the vote, the Republicans, represented by Sinn Féin, just 27%. It seemed the country was very much on his side — although in fairness, most anti-treaty sympathisers were in prison and not allowed to vote.

The Civil War was a conflict the Irish could have done without. The damage to property alone came in at £50 million (£2.1 billion). The military cost, another £17 million (£718m). Friends, neighbours, and families were split along partisan lines and the historically "us versus them" glue that had held the island together during seven hundred years of British rule had gone. Roads and railways were decimated. Continual bank and post office robberies had drained the exchequer, and there was a mood of general distrust and ill-feeling throughout the country.

The new Free State ended 1923 with a budget deficit of £4 million (£168m). Over a thousand people had been killed, and Collins had been assassinated. As far as Jack, was concerned that last one wasn't a bad thing — although to him, his replacement was as bad, if not worse.

Certainly, Cosgrave found himself in an unenviable position. With no cash left in the bank, his government couldn't afford to repay the huge imperial debt it owed to Britain. To write it off, he agreed to accept that the border with Northern Ireland would remain unchanged in perpetuity. He was also forced to pay for damage inflicted on British property during the war.

A few weeks later, Jack's father died. As he was being interred in the family plot, Jas was released from prison. Kilcloney, for what it was worth, was now his. The beatings he'd suffered and his time living rough on the run had taken their toll. It took him months to recover — and even then, not fully. With the help of his mother and his sisters, he went back to work, trying to make a go of the farm and keep the family afloat.

The civil war was officially over, but as far as De Valera was concerned, the fat lady still hadn't sung. Behind the scenes, he was still secretly advocating economic disruption. Somehow the Free State had to be brought down, and Jack was still in total agreement.

While Jas tried to piece Kilcloney back together, Jack continued in the same vein as before — robbing banks and post offices. This time, however, things were different. Many of his old anti-treaty comrades were dead or had given up the fight. The civil war had been a huge strain on their finances, relationships, and health. They were tired of conflict, and despite the outcome not being what they'd hoped for, they'd come to accept the new status quo. By the end of 1924, the IRA men didn't have the community support or sympathy they'd enjoyed in the old days, and by 1926 Jack found himself reassessing his position.

He'd been trying to keep off the radar since Graney, and now he was a suspect in a litany of misdemeanours, including a bank robbery at Bunclody. If the Free State manage to pin any of it on him, he could be facing a long sentence or possibly worse. Concluding that discretion was the better part of valour, he decided it would be prudent to disappear for a while.

He asked Josie, his long-term girlfriend, to go with him. They'd met at Kilcloney years earlier, when her father used to bring wheat over to the mill. Even as a child, she was a great dancer, and John would often get them out together for a reel or a jig while he accompanied them on his concertina. Years later, they met again. Josie was an active member of the Cumann na mBan. She also worked at Floods in Borris, and occasionally their paths would cross when she carried messages for the Brigade or brought food when they were hiding out.

Gerrymandering

To his surprise, she agreed, and they caught the train out of Borris at the start of 1927. To cover his tracks, he adopted an alias: John Doyle. At first, they went to England and got married, and then a few months later caught the ferry to Belfast. With a small inheritance from his Aunt Kate, he rented a grocer's shop in the Protestant area, a few hundred yards from the Harland and Wolff shipyard.

He guessed it would be the last place the Free State would look for him. On the other hand, it was a risky choice. Northern Ireland had a system of apartheid as onerous as any in the southern states of America. Catholics were regarded as an underclass and the War of Independence hadn't helped. In 1921, Unionist mobs, upset at the British defeat, stormed the shipyard and forced thousands of

Catholics out of their jobs. Since then, four hundred people
— mainly Catholics — had been murdered in sectarian
pogroms. Mass burnings of Catholic property were
commonplace, and their homes, businesses, and churches
were systematically destroyed.

James Craig was the PM — a Protestant viscount and,
thanks to his father's whisky business, a millionaire. He was
the man who'd so vehemently opposed Gladstone's Home
Rule bill and created the UVF. He facilitated and encouraged
the ultra-right-wing Orangemen to march in full regalia
through Catholic areas and he'd overseen the creation of
the Ulster Special Constabulary, a police force comprised
of hard-line Protestants who spent most of their time
harassing Catholics.

By the time Jack reached Belfast, only 420,000 Catholics
were left in the country — about one third of the
population. Being outnumbered, they had little chance of
getting into government anyway, but where they had clear
majorities, like in Omagh and Derry, Craig had the electoral
boundaries re-drawn to stop it happening. The technique
was called gerrymandering, after Elbridge Gerry who, as
governor of Massachusetts in 1812, gave the Democrats
power in Boston by drawing up boundaries in such a
convoluted manner the resulting electoral map looked like
a salamander.

To belt and brace Union supremacy, Craig retained the
archaic property qualification for local elections.
Essentially, if you didn't own property, you didn't vote. As
most Catholics couldn't afford to buy a home, this
hammered home the final nail in their electoral coffin.

It was here, in a hostile Northern Ireland, that Jack decided
he and Josie should settle down. They married a few

months later, and as they moved into their shop, they told their Unionist neighbours and customers they were Protestant.

Kevin O'Higgins

On the 6th of August 1928, their daughter was born. She was christened in the Holy Cross Catholic Church on the Crumlin Road as "Bridget Doyle."

While they tried to make a go of the shop, De Valera decided to re-enter the political mainstream. This time he set up his own party, Fianna Fail, or "Soldiers of Destiny." Back in 1918, he'd wrapped Sinn Féin's Republican agenda inside a more populist anti-conscription message. This time he wrapped it inside a promise to address the concerns of the poor. By the time he finished writing his manifesto, it was so labour-like that Fianna Fail was perceived by many as more labour than the Labour Party.

The USP was perfect, but the Long Fella's underlying objective was still the same: to destroy the Free State so he could take power and correct the wrongs of the treaty. His subterfuge didn't fool Cosgrave, who accused Fianna Fail of being a party for communists and gunmen. De Valera parried the accusations and, true to form, refused to take the oath that had been a key part of Collin's treaty. The result was that whilst his party members were allowed to run for election, they couldn't take their seats in parliament.

This didn't seem to bother him. Refusing to take an oath to a foreign King merely reinforced his mystique as a man of integrity. He'd started the Civil War on that principle and nothing or no one was going to change his mind on the matter.

Then he did.

Just before twelve on Sunday 10 July 1927, O'Higgins was on his way to Mass. Halfway there, he ran out of cigarettes and sent his bodyguard back to fetch a pack. As he walked on alone, a man jumped out from a parked car and began firing. O'Higgins managed to stagger a few yards before collapsing. As he lay wounded, another man finished him off.

Both were soon captured and found to be members of the IRA. The assassination, they claimed, was in revenge for him ordering the execution of seventy-seven IRA prisoners during the civil war.

Cosgrave was enraged. He felt De Valera was behind it, and within days he introduced a new law making it compulsory for Dáil candidates to take the oath. If they didn't, not only would they not be allowed to sit in the Dáil, but they wouldn't be allowed to contest an election in the first place.

De Valera was faced with what seemed like an intractable problem. If he continued to refuse to take the oath, he couldn't get elected — and if he weren't elected, any chance of him gaining power would be out of the window.

The devil, as he once said himself, was in the detail. The wording of the oath, which had been incorporated as Article 17 into the Irish Free State's 1922 Constitution, read:

> "I (name) do solemnly swear true faith and allegiance to the Constitution of the Irish Free State as by law established, and that I will be faithful to H.M. King George V, his heirs, and successors by law in virtue of the common citizenship of Ireland with Great Britain and her adherence to and membership of the group of nations forming the British Commonwealth of Nations."

Ironically, the hated oath hadn't been written by the British government, but by Michael Collins — and his wording had been based on a draft suggested by De Valera himself. Collins had cleared it with the IRB long before he presented it to Lloyd George.

Some might say De Valera backed down, others that he was a canny operator. Either way, in the end he decided to take the oath. His justification was that it merely involved signing a worthless piece of paper. The oath, he argued, required him to swear allegiance to the constitution — not the King. It merely required him to be faithful to the King, which in essence meant nothing.

Many pro-treaty supporters wondered why he hadn't reached that conclusion back in 1921 and avoided the Civil War — but to his die-hard supporters like Jack, it was yet another sign of his studious ingenuity.

In the June election of 1927, Fianna Fail came in a close second to Cosgrave's Cumann na nGaedheal. The margin was so small that another vote had to be held in September. That time, with the support of the farmer's party, Cosgrave scraped a workable majority.

While De Valera licked his wounds yet again, Jack and Josie were returning from a day out at the seaside. As they reached the shop, they saw a bloody pig's head nailed to the door. Jack hadn't marched in the Orange Day parade the week before, and their Protestant neighbours had put two and two together. It was time to get out — and fast. Only a year after they'd tried to make a fresh start, they loaded their new baby into the family car and headed south to Wexford.

CHAPTER FOURTEEN
The Ballyanne bus

I got up early on Thursday morning, pulled the car as quietly as I could out of the drive, and headed towards Wexford. My wife insisted this had to be my last day at the Archives — we were sailing back to England on Monday, and I needed to keep the weekend free for the kids. Besides, I'd promised I'd call in to see Larry and Michael at Kilcloney. Nell having died a few years earlier.

In the meantime, I was anxious to pick up where I'd left off. On Tuesday, I'd read something about Jack and a bank robbery in Bunclody. That night, I borrowed my father's road atlas and a book on local history and did some background research.

Up until the end of the Civil War, the town had been known as Newtown Barry. The river there was the Slaney. I'd heard Jack complain he'd been injured crossing it in Wicklow. As to how or why, he didn't explain.

It seemed that over the years it had seen its fair share of bloodshed. Back in '98, a Catholic priest called Mogue Kearns led an attack on the English Barracks. The English beat a hasty retreat across the bridge to Carlow, and the rebels cracked open some porters of ale to celebrate. As they did, a few yeomen who were still in the town started to pick them off. Their retreating colleagues heard the gunfire and returned to help. In the rout that followed, Kearns lost four hundred of his men and had to flee back to Wexford.

There was another fatal clash just before the famine. The peasants — 100% Catholic – refused to pay for the upkeep of the local Protestant church —a church - almost exclusively used by a small but rich group of landowners. When the police arrived, they arrested the peasants and began seizing their land. In the ructions that followed, twelve people were killed outright and another twenty fatally wounded.

A hundred years later, in October 1922, "Nacey" Redmond, an officer in the pro-treaty Free State army was shot dead on the old Bunclody-Kiltealy road. Two months later, another officer suffered the same fate when he was ambushed at Ryland's Cross just outside the town.

Bunclody might have been picturesque, but it has seen plenty of action – and not all of it particularly pleasant.

The next morning, I hit the archives early and asked for the 1925-29 file. The same girl who'd helped me before brought it over and asked if I was looking for anything in particular. I smiled at her and shook my head. Not really, I said — just general research.

As soon as she'd gone, I opened the *New Ross Times* where I'd left off. Monday 1st February 1926. According to the editorial, a special court hearing had been held under the auspices of district judge J.V. Fahey — the man in the dock being Jack.

The robbery had taken place in December of the previous year. The article was long — at least one foolscap page of small typography. Fortunately, I'd brought my glasses, and I slipped them on and started reading.

The gist of it was that on that morning, seven men were seen marching toward Bunclody from the mountain road —

presumably the one I'd cycled on over Mount Leinster. Before they reached town, they spotted a car backing out from a garage called Colliers. After forcing the owner out at gunpoint, they pushed it to a nearby pump and topped it up with petrol. They then commandeered a second car and drove off in convoy.

When they reached the bank, the drivers remained in the cars. One of the men stood guard outside the bank while the others stormed in. According to an eyewitness, they were all wearing masks and heavily armed with shotguns and revolvers.

Hearing the commotion, the guards rushed out of their barracks with guns drawn. Before they could get far, they were stopped by three of the men. Two, they claimed, had revolvers, the third a Mauser rifle. The men locked them in Mulligan's Pub a few doors along. Three others, who for one reason or another failed to help their colleagues, were then dragged from the barracks and forced to join them.

William Beveridge was an accountant working in the cash office. He described to Fahey how around ten past two he saw a mob rushing in through the main doors waving guns and shouting for everyone to put their hands up. He said Paddy Byrne, the manager, refused. The bank had been robbed many times before, and it seemed he was sick and tired of it. When he tried to give them a piece of his mind, one of them cracked him across the head with the butt of a revolver.

According to Byrne, a small man then forced him at gunpoint into the cash office. He collected £147 (£11,000) in notes from the table and stuffed them into his pockets. He told Fahey the whole thing lasted only ten or fifteen minutes.

On their way out, the raiders were approached by the local priest, Father Butler. He begged them to give themselves up. Hardly surprisingly, they ignored him. Instead, they headed to the post office and destroyed the telecommunications equipment. Then they climbed back into their commandeered cars, and, like the British yeomanry a hundred and fifty years before, took off across the bridge to Carlow. As soon as the raiders had gone, the guards managed to free themselves. Along with four local men, they armed themselves to the teeth and set out in pursuit. Eight miles down the road in Myshall, they found the cars abandoned. As they began combing the vehicles for clues, someone spotted the bank robbers. They'd climbed up a steep ridge and were running across the upper slopes of Mount Leinster towards Borris.

The guards told Fahey they reckoned they were about a mile away. Despite the odds stacked against them, they gave chase. The men were fit, and after an hour or two they still hadn't closed the gap. Around four, as the sun sank beneath the horizon, they reluctantly gave up.

Over the next few days, the usual anti-treaty suspects were rounded up. At a police line-up on January 19th, several men were identified, including Luke Dwyer. This, I assumed, had to be the same Luke Dwyer Jack had introduced me to years ago.

It seems the guards found him and another man when they raided Dwyer's house the day after the robbery. He'd answered the door exhausted, and his boots were wet and covered in grass — proof, they suggested, that he'd recently been running across the mountains.

As Dwyer was taken into custody, the police hunt continued. Four days later, they raided Kilcloney, and Jack was pulled in for questioning. At another line-up, Paddy Byrne identified him as the small man who'd forced him into the cash room and taken the money.

Luck was a commodity Jack seemed to have had in spades. A few days later Byrne, changed his mind. There was no doubt, he said, that Jack was the same height as the man who stole the cash, but the robber had been wearing a flat cap, a trench coat, and a mask — so in hindsight, he couldn't be 100% sure.

It seemed odd to me that Byrne changed his mind. Perhaps it was the blow he'd received to the head, or maybe he honestly couldn't be sure — or perhaps he'd been subjected to some unsavoury persuasion. I didn't want to read too much into it, but I couldn't help wondering where Jas had been when all this was happening.

R.J. Brennan was Jack's defence lawyer. He submitted to Fahey that as Byrne couldn't be sure about the identification, his client should be freed at once — a submission with which Fahey had no choice but to comply. When the trial went before the circuit court a few months later, it turned out that many of Jack's old friends had been involved. When Luke Dwyer was sentenced, circuit judge Hannah said that as no one had been killed or seriously injured, he'd give him the shortest term he could — seven years penal servitude.

A James Keegan had been one of his accomplices, and his name triggered off a memory. Michael had told me years before that the house where he now lived — the one in Currane where we stayed while Jack built the bungalow — had been owned by a James Keegan. Always the storyteller, he said he'd mysteriously disappeared to America, but not before burying a hoard of stolen gold in the grounds.

Perhaps, I wondered, there was a twisted core of truth to the tale.

As the men were led away, Hannah took the opportunity to bemoan the vast number of similar crimes taking place across the country. In January 1925 alone, he said, there'd been two hundred and fifty-three armed robberies, sixty-six attempted armed robberies, eight armed raids on banks, and three incidents of bank officials being held up.

It seemed odd to me that two years after the civil war ended there was still so much social unrest. Initially, I wondered if it were just the usual ripples of a nation settling down. Like England with its highwaymen — mostly royalists who felt disenfranchised after Cromwell's victory — or the gunslinging, bank-robbing bandits of the wild west — mainly Southern soldiers unwilling to accept Yankee victory.

There was one major difference, however. From the snippets I'd picked up from Jack and John Nolan, the Irish civil war seemed to have had no real line drawn under it. The endpoint of Cromwell's war was the loss of the king's head. The American one ended in Liverpool when James Waddell, captain of the CSS Shenandoah, surrendered his ship to the British. In contrast, the Irish Civil War just seemed to have petered out with an unenthusiastic laying down of arms.

Maybe that's exactly what those raiders in Bunclody were doing. Continuing a below-the-radar war with the idea of just picking away at the Free State. Towards the end of the article, Dwyer told the judge he'd been operating under the orders of the IRA — which seemed to suggest the money was destined for their coffers. As to whether Jack was "the small man," it seemed likely to me. Although there had to be a plethora of "small men" around at the time, because so many of his friends were involved, because it happened so near to Kilcloney, and because he'd initially been identified as the man who'd taken the cash in the first place — I had to conclude that on the balance of probability, he was.

I continued leafing through the papers up until 1929, but there was no further mention of him. Hardly surprising, I supposed, as according to my mother that was when she was born in Belfast.

1930s bus

It was around eleven by the time I reached the end of the decade. I could have finished up then and driven back to the bungalow to make at least some amends for spending so much time away from the family. Still, I convinced myself, I could afford another just one more hour.

I decided I'd have a quick look at the 1930-35 file. My mindset as I opened it up was that I was wasting my time. The civil war would have been over six years, and surely by then Jack would have given up his Republican aspirations.

Yet the first article I hit told me otherwise. At 8.15 a.m. on the 3rd June 1930, two masked men —   one described as small, the other taller, were seen aiming their revolvers at the X876 bus as it rounded a sharp bend by the railway bridge at Ballyanne.

Ballyanne is about twelve miles from Kilcloney — and fifteen from Carrick on Bannow, where I'd been told Jack had moved to in 1929 after his sojourn in the North.

The driver was a man called Ben Boles, and according to his statement, the "small man" fired two shots that ripped into his cab and tore the skin off his forehead. The fact that he wasn't killed, he told the police, was a miracle.

There were quite a few witnesses, and the usual suspects were rounded up. Among them were Jack's brother Jas and another man called Danny McEvoy.

The local guards must have known that Jack was Jas' brother. That might have made them suspicious that maybe McEvoy wasn't necessarily the small man they were looking for. Still, as far as they knew Jack wasn't around. Word on the street was that he was away somewhere — probably England — and McEvoy would have to do. Besides, he was also a known Republican and reinforced his affiliation to the cause when he refused to recognise the court.

Jas was more circumspect. I imagine that by now he'd been around the legal block quite a few times and knew how to conduct himself in a courtroom. He made no mention of his political status, but employed the services of Mr. R. J. Brennan — the same solicitor who'd defended Jack at Bunclody. The district judge was again J.V. Fahey.

The charges were straightforward. McEvoy was indicted for attempted murder and Jas for the possession of an illegal weapon — in his case a Winchester rifle found in a house he was staying at in New Ross.

It appeared Brennan was a clever operator. He told the court that he was perfectly sure that he was voicing the feelings of everyone in the parish when he said that "such a murderous and blackguardly attack on the driver of the bus and its conductor was greatly to be deplored. It was an outrage of the worst kind, endangering the lives of the company's staff and passengers."

Turning to Superintendent Walsh, the man in charge of the case, he said he'd "never heard evidence for a prosecution presented in such a straightforward and fair manner." He added that he

> "didn't want to be seen even in the smallest way to be sympathising with the outrage. It was deplorable in a civilised community that people's lives should be endangered because of a strike between a company and their employees."

Then he went in for the kill. He slipped in the suggestion that despite what happened, there was no hard evidence "connecting his client with the major charges."

Fahey reminded Brennan that Jas had been convicted four years earlier for his involvement in an armed attack on Cork barracks. However, he concluded, "he did not want to be hard on him." He'd "adopted a reasonable attitude towards the court" and Fahey would take that into account.

Brennan thanked him, remarking that "rightly or wrongly, Jas was connected with the portion of people who did not see eye to eye with the Government. It was fair to say that he had suffered for his beliefs."

Beliefs? I assumed he was talking about political beliefs — but what, I wondered, had that to do with taking a potshot at a bus. Was Jas trying to rob it? The Archive girl who'd asked me if she could help earlier was still around and I decided to see if she could shed any light on it.

She could. Apparently in the 30s, the IOC — the Irish Omnibus Company — had bought out several bus garages. To rationalise the pay structure, they removed a weekly lodgings allowance and implemented a flat rate. The drivers weren't happy and went on a strike that affected the whole country. The IOC then began sacking them. As the economy was in meltdown, hundreds of men applied to take their place.

When I asked her what that had to do with the IRA, she showed me a copy of *An Phoblach* — a Republican newspaper at the time. It urged Republicans to stand up for the drivers and drive out the scabs.

From that, I assumed Ben Boles must have been a scab — or at least one of the unemployed who desperately needed a job.

Thanking the girl for her help, I returned to the papers. Further down the article, I read that Brennan told Fahey that Jas had ceased to have any connection with "that organisation and was prepared to give an undertaking that he would not be concerned with it." He added that he'd been working since last November with a Mr. Murphy, who would give him a glowing character reference and an undertaking that "he would not be again connected with that organisation and that he would mind his ordinary business."

The fact that Jas — and maybe Jack — had wanted to help the striking drivers told me something. I wasn't quite sure what. Maybe that they had a sense of fairness — a left-wing agenda — and a desire to stand up for the underdog.

Certainly, it suggested money wasn't their motivation. Holding up a bus was all risk and no gain. It also added weight to my growing conviction that the Bunclody raid was politically rather than criminally motivated.

The upshot of the trial was that Jas was sentenced to three months of hard labour and bound over to keep the peace for twelve months. Fahey concluded by saying he hoped he would, "keep clear of revolvers and ammunition in future. People could use propaganda as much as they liked," he added, "but they should not try to shove their opinions down people's throats with revolvers."

The paper didn't say where Jas did his time. I assumed it must have been Mountjoy. Certainly, his absence from Kilcloney couldn't have helped his mother. Two years later, I saw an advertisement.

> *KILCLONEY MILLS, BORRIS. MODERN WOOLLEN AND CORN MILLS, WITH VALUABLE FARM. TO BE SOLD BY PUBLIC AUCTION, ON THE LANDS, On Monday, the 7th day of July 1932, By directions of The representatives of John Kiely, containing 17 acres 3 roods 27 perches or thereabouts, in the Barony of St. Mullins Lower, and County of Carlow, held in fee simple subject to a terminable annuity of £4 4s.2d. payable to the Irish Land Commission, with a mix of Corn Mill and Woollen Mill thereon. The Woollen Mill consists of Water Wheal 14 feet high, a Greenhill No. 3 Improved Grinding Mill, a pair of Shelling Stones, Kiln, etc all in first-class repair. The Woollen Mill consisting of 14 ft Water Wheel, two Carding MacHynes, Condenser, Spinning Mille; also, carding shed attached, all in first-class condition. There is an abundant and never-*

failing supply of water for the mills. The lands, well known for high-class grazing and tillage properties, are laid out three acres (1 barley and the remainder in rich pasture. There is a substantial, 3-storey, three bed dwelling house consisting of drawing, dining room, kitchen and five bedrooms, all in good repair. The out offices consist of cowhouse (8 cows). stable, calf house, cattle house, fowl house, etc., all in 'good repair. There are also two good workman houses on the lands. After the sale of the above Holding, the following Stock, Chattels, Crops and Grazing will be sold by Auction: Two Working horses, 7 cows in full milk. 2 Springer, 7 Yearlings, 9 Calves, 4 Sheep, Poultry, Horse's Cart, Donkey cart. Tackling, Wheel Plough, Drill plough, Spring Tooth and Iron. Harrow, Mowing Machine, Turnip Slicer, etc; a quantity of Potatoes and Oats, and The (following Crops at Ballynasilloge 5 acres Lea Oats (white), 4 acres Matured Oats (white), 2 acres Potatoes, 1-acre Marigolds, 3 acres Turnips. For further particulars and condition of Sale, apply to THOMAS J. KELLY. LL.B.; Solicitor, New Roes; or to JOHN JOYCE, Es., Auctioneer and Valuer.

Business must have hit rock bottom. Jas was trying to sell up, and it looked like the end of the line for the Kielys. I was about to head home, but something told me I should carry on reading, at least to the end of the file.

It's just as well I did. While I had no concrete evidence Jack had been involved in the Bunclody raid or the holdup at Ballyanne, the next item left me in no doubt.

Another bank robbery had taken place on 2 February 1934. This time the bank in question was the National Bank of Taghmon and around £800 (£67,000) had been stolen.

Taghmon had been the name John gave me, and with renewed curiosity, I began leafing through the month. Then I caught a headline: *Planned by a genius*. Three men had been arrested. Jim Treacy, who I'd never heard of, Jas Kiely, and Jack. If I had any doubt whether this was what I'd been looking for, Jas' address was given as Kilcloney Mills.

CHAPTER FIFTEEN
The beginning of the end

Conditions in Ballymartin were among the worst in Europe. The Great War, the War of Independence, and the Civil War hadn't helped — and then on top of that had come the 1929 Wall Street crash. It started in America, but like a ripple on the transatlantic pond, it was now making its effects felt in Ireland.

For Jas, the crash initially looked like a godsend. Dozens of British farmers had sold up or become bankrupt and demand for beef and dairy products from Ireland soared. For the first time in years, he thought he saw a glimmer of light at the end of an exceptionally long tunnel.

Three years later, De Valera's Fianna Fail party won the general election. To the anti-treaty men, this was everything they'd fought for. The Long Fella was now in the driving seat, and he seemed to get off to a great start.

After removing the oath from the constitution, he released Cosgrave's anti-treaty prisoners. Then, on a victory tour of Skibbereen, he made a point of saluting a line-up of IRA men rather than the Free State police officers who were waiting to greet him just a few yards further up the road.

Like Jas, De Valera believed Cosgrave's Free State had betrayed Ireland. Now the IRA had emerged like a phoenix from the flames, and they wanted revenge.

A Fianna Fail TD summed up his party's anger at the old government: "as long as we have fists and boots, there will be no free speech for traitors."

Sean Lemass, a future PM of Ireland and someone who'd fought alongside Jack in O'Malley's flying column, added that Fianna Fail was only a "slightly" constitutional party. "If we can achieve our goals by the present peaceful methods, we will be very pleased...but we will not be held back if not."

With such inflammatory rhetoric, it wasn't surprising that Cumann na nGaedheal meetings started to be attacked. The police weren't sure how to react. Their new President not only condoned the IRA, but seemed to have granted them quasi-legal status.

To protect Cumann na nGaedheal events, a former commandant in the Free State army set up an organisation called the Army Comrades Association. It started as a reasonable attempt to discourage IRA attacks, but when Eoin O'Duffy took over, it moved in a more sinister direction.

A fan of Mussolini, he re-modelled the organisation along the lines of his "Blackshirts." Unimaginatively, he called his men "Blueshirts" and encouraged straight-arm Nazi salutes.

The optics weren't good, even before Hitler began goosestepping across Europe. Jack and Jas had seen them in Carlow, marching up and down with their right-wing agenda and getting into pitched battles with anti-treaty supporters.

It was an echo of the Civil War, but less violent. Fist fights often broke out, but guns were rarely used. As annoying as it was, it was a small price to pay for what now looked like the real likelihood of a Republic.

Up until then, De Valera had done no wrong. Then, in October 1932, things changed. He told the British PM Ramsay MacDonald that Ireland would no longer be repaying its land annuities.

Land annuities were loans the British government had made to tenant farmers to buy their land. Their repayment had been agreed in the treaty, but that didn't concern De Valera. He argued that as Britain had stolen the land from Ireland in the first place, they had no right to sell it back to them. He then demanded £30 million (£2.7bn) to cover rents illegally collected, plus £400 million (£36bn) as a tax rebate for the years 1801 to 1922.

For Jack and Jas, this was the fighting talk they'd wanted to hear. The Long Fella was squaring up to the old enemy, and he wasn't afraid to tighten the screws.

It was good populist stuff, but it was a fatal miscalculation.

MacDonald responded by levying a 20% duty on agricultural products coming in from the Free State. As Ireland exported virtually all of its agricultural goods to Britain, the effect on its already crippled economy was devastating.

Prices soared, the value of cattle halved, and unemployment — which was already historically high — rose higher. Coal and fuel prices went through the roof, and even though the land annuities weren't being paid over to the British, De Valera collected them anyway.

Some people refused to pay. De Valera responded by having their livestock impounded and auctioned off. Thousands who'd managed to hang on to what little they had through famine, wars, and the Depression now lost everything.

He told his supporters that this hardship was the price they had to pay for true Irish freedom. The island had to stand on its own feet without being beholden to Britain — and his economic war was just another growing pain to be endured.

As a result of the economic war, Ireland continued to sink to the lowest depths of the world economic quagmire. Rents were going up and it was impossible to sell livestock. There was also no escape route. Even during the famine, it had been possible to emigrate to a better life. Now England was going through its own economic crisis and America an even worse one, with no jobs and millions out of work.

While most new homes in England were routinely being fitted with electricity, Kilcloney wouldn't have mains power until the mid-sixties. As for communication, the only information coming in from the outside world was via De Valera's highly censored newspapers or what was preached from the pulpit. TV wouldn't appear for decades and there was just one radio station: 2RN, a division of the Post Office. It reached just 5% of the population — the few who could afford a licence.

It was in that climate of austerity that at 7.30 pm on Friday 2nd February 1934, nineteen-year-old Jim Treacy climbed up on his old Raleigh bike and cycled home from work.

Jim was Jas' neighbour and that night it was cold — particularly cold for him, as he didn't own an overcoat. It was also bright. There'd been a full moon the night before, and although it was now on the wane, its pale glow lit his way home along the narrow lanes.

Whilst many of his friends were out of a job, he was lucky to have secured himself a position at Jack Cummins' farm. The work was hard, monotonous, and poorly paid. His main tasks were spreading slurry, mucking out the livestock, and making sure they had enough feed and hay. On top of that, he was expected to handle the repairs, painting, cleaning, and pretty much anything else that needed doing.

The hours were long. Six in the morning until seven at night — longer in the summer season — but there was one perk. After he hung up his spade and fork, Mrs Cummings would invariably invite him to share supper with the family.

Jim lived in a small two-up, two-down terrace near the Fenagh Road crossroads in Ballymartin. His parents, James and Anastacia, shared one bedroom and he and his seven younger brothers and sisters the other.

There was nowhere to hang clothes, there were no washing facilities except the well outside, and no chance of privacy. The slope on the bedroom ceiling was so steep that the only place possible to stand up and get dressed was the centre of the room.

The kitchen was downstairs — the only room with a fire — and it was Anastacia's responsibility to have it lit and ready in the winter months for when her men came home.

Ballymartin is a stone's throw from Currane and is particularly exposed to the cold winds blowing down from Mount Leinster. In the thirties, glass was expensive and where the panes were cracked or broken, Anastacia had stuffed the gaps with newspaper to try and keep out the draughts. Apart from the fire, the only way of lighting the house was with a paraffin lamp.

That night Anastasia re-heated the week's stew — a few carrots, onions, and potatoes. Jim, his father, and elder brothers, all back from work now, drew their chairs up to the fire and warmed their hands.

While James started reading the *Leinster Leader*, the girls laid the table with a few plates and mugs. The youngest was sent out to fetch water from the pump, and Jim took his usual chair near the fire.

The house next door to Jim Treacy's

Most winters the yard was a quagmire of mud and dung. That year, with the drought, the ground was unusually hard and the heavy stench of pigs from the lean-to outside was stronger than usual.

As he settled back, he reflected that his future looked bleak. Ireland had the highest rate of single people in western Europe and living in his father's house with nine others, little money, and no prospects, his chances of getting married or making something of himself were slim. It was a depressing thought and after dinner, he concluded he needed cheering up. He was still tired after the day's work, but he had to do something. It was a Friday night after all. His siblings were bickering, as always, and he needed to get out.

To relieve the boredom, he decided to ride down to see Jas. At thirty-six, Jas was the same age as his father — but a lot more entertaining. He always had a story to tell: if not about the unfairness of British tariffs and Blueshirt violence, then his time fighting the British, and then the Free State.

When he told his mother where he was going, she wasn't keen. In her day, the Kielys had been a respectable family. Her father had even worked at the mill. They were still friends as well as neighbours, but she worried about their politics. The last thing she wanted was for Jim to become radicalised. His father's views were Republican enough, but the Kielys — particularly Jas — took it to a whole different level. Still, she concluded, she couldn't stop him.

She kissed him goodbye as he let himself out. Collecting his bike from where he'd left it beside the wall, he pushed it onto the lane and climbed on board. It was less than a mile and a half to Kilcloney — about a five-minute ride, most of it downhill.

As he began freewheeling towards the Wexford Road, he could see the Big Dipper directly ahead. According to his father, it was part of the Big Bear constellation, a sequence of stars he'd never been able to recognise. As the cold wind bit into his face, he pulled his pullover tight to his neck. James Keegan had sold his farm at Currane ten years earlier, after he got out of prison for robbing the bank at Bunclody. When he emigrated to America, new tenants had moved in with fierce dogs. As Jim cycled past, he pedalled furiously, hoping they wouldn't run out growling and snapping at his ankles. Another reason not to hang around was what he'd been told years ago: the road to Kilcloney was haunted. He was sure he'd seen a ghost there himself one night after a dance at Ned Breen's house, when he was riding home worse for wear.

He'd told Jas about it. An old man carrying a lamp — at least that's what it had looked like. Maybe the priest his grandfather said continually walked the road. It wouldn't have been surprising. If the stories he'd heard were true, there had to be hundreds of lost souls trying to make their way up the old road back to Wexford.

At the crossroads, he turned right and cycled on until he reached the bridge. Pulling up at the mill, he swung a leg off the bike and freewheeled into the yard.

As always, it was a mess. An old plough and a tractor lay abandoned in the mud. Bales of mouldy hay that should have been stored in the barn months ago were randomly piled against the walls.

The sheds were just as bad. He'd seen inside them once. Most were filled with broken machinery: wooden looms, belts, and pulleys that hung haphazardly from the ceiling. Remnants of the mill's better days.

Jas told him the damage was caused by Free State soldiers looking for Jack. When they couldn't find him, they broke the place up. He told Jim that whenever he came around, he should leave his bike in the stable in case it rained. It was usually empty, but that night Jim noticed a car parked inside. This was unusual. As far as he knew, Jas didn't own a car. Perhaps he'd bought one; more likely he had a visitor.

Deciding to leave the bike propped against the shed instead, he wiped his boots on the mat by the kitchen door and let himself in.

The fire was blazing as usual. Biddy was huddled on the little wooden bench beside it, rubbing her hands in the flames. Jas was at the table reading a newspaper by the sickly glow of a paraffin lamp. To his surprise, Jack was next to him.

As he walked in, so did a gust of cold air. Biddy stood up and invited him up to the fire. As she went to fetch a saucepan of water for the tea, he warmed his hands and then joined Jas and Jack at the table.

He'd expected to see Jas, and maybe one of his sisters, but certainly not Jack. As he sat down, the old IRA man glanced up from a copy of *Ireland's Own* and asked how he was doing.

The last time they'd met was when he was twelve and he felt as he had done then, nervous, yet excited to be in the presence of a man regarded as a local hero.

He told him he was middling and after a while summoned up the courage to ask him where he'd been for the last few years.

Jack smiled. Since he'd left Borris, there'd been all sorts of rumours circulating. Some said he was dead, others that he was in prison. There was even a theory he'd faked his death to escape the Guards. Even Jas didn't know where Jack was — or at least that's what he said.

As Biddy handed out the tea, Jack folded up his *Ireland's Own* and placed it neatly on the table. Jim noticed that he looked different. His nails were bitten to the quick and his hair, once a thick mop of black, was peppered grey. It was unlike him not to be bubbling with enthusiasm. In the old days, nothing affected him. Now he looked down, almost defeated.

Jas explained that Jack would be staying with him for a while. Then he looked across at his brother, as if to ask whether he should say anything else.

Jack shrugged his characteristic shrug. It was pointless trying to keep a secret in rural Ireland. He also knew the

Treacys were people he could trust, and he assumed the same was true for Jim. He gave a deep sigh, took a sip of tea, and leaned dangerously back on his chair. Then he told his story.

After the robbery at Bunclody, Josie thought they should move away and make a fresh start. Although he was an innocent man, there were too many people who thought he wasn't. The police wanted to put the finger on him for a variety of crimes, and he concluded that she was probably right, and it was the best thing to do.

They caught the train to Dublin and then the boat to England where they got married. They toured around for a while, taking up digs in places like Liverpool and Manchester. Then they headed back across the Channel to Ulster, and tried to settle down. He rented a shop in the North and had a baby girl called Birdie – who he'd named after his mother.

Jim hadn't thought of Jack as the settling down sort, let alone the having children sort. He told him what he thought, and Jack grinned. He told him that Birdie was six now, and that he had another who was still a toddler. Josie had taken them up to her mother's place in Clomoney while he was laying low in Kilcloney.

He took another sup of tea and told him things hadn't gone well in Ulster. They had to get out, and he moved the family to Wexford, to a place called Carrick on Bannow. To be on the safe side, he kept the alias he'd used in the North and rented another shop. He managed to scrape by for a few years, but then, just two months ago when some of his big credit customers couldn't pay up, the business went bankrupt.

Jim shook his head. After all the sacrifices he'd made, Jack was no closer to seeing a united Ireland now than he had been in 1916. What's more, the well was dry — he'd lost everything, and it looked like he had nothing else to give. Jas' position was as bad, if not worse. Once the mill had been one of the most thriving in the County. Now it was worth nothing. His father had shown him the auction ads in the paper where they'd tried to sell it. Twice now — once in 1930, and then just last year.

He was sorry to see that the Kielys had hit such tough times. They'd always been good to his family, but now they were on the breadline — just like they were.

It was in an atmosphere of collective hopelessness that the three men talked into the night. The future seemed bleak until Jack suggested the robbery.

Every bank, post office, and mail train hold up the Kielys had carried out over the years had been for the cause. Without the money men like them raised for arms and ammunition, the IRA could never have continued its fight against the Free State. Now that they had been reduced to penury, surely it was only fair that DeValera new Ireland repaid at least a little of its debt.

Jim had hero-worshipped the Kielys for years. Jas had told him most of what they'd done and got away with. The ambush of Kennedy, the Graney attack, Jack's stint with O'Malley in the flying column — not to mention what happened to Fin the spy. Both had spent time years on the run. They'd been sent to prison and roughed up to such an extent that both had wound up in military hospitals.

If Jack believed they could make money, it was good enough for Jim. Besides, it was a chance to share some of his glory.

220

He suggested that they rob his local bank, the one at Taghmon. It was isolated and easy to break into. He'd been contemplating it for weeks and he'd already done a full risk assessment.

The consensus around the table was that it was a good idea. No one would get hurt and, with luck, they should come out with at least £500 (£40,000) each. More than enough for Jas to pay off the arrears on his land annuities, Jack to buy another business, and Jim to find himself a wife.

By 11 pm, it was settled. They'd head off in the early hours. While they were waiting, Jack finished off his "Kitty the Hare" story in *Ireland's Own* while Jas prepared a last supper of bread and butter. Jim went out to the yard to have a quiet smoke and relieve himself behind the sheds. By the time he returned, there was a rifle on the table.

He'd never seen one up close — and he certainly hadn't handled one. Jack saw the bewilderment on his face and asked if he was sure he wanted to come. When he confirmed he did, Jack gave him a handful of ammunition and helped him load up.

With him sorted, Jack pushed a long-nosed parabellum into his coat pocket. Jas followed suit with a shorter one. Jas handed him a spare coat, then led the way into the yard. A frost was settling on the ground as he dragged open the wooden doors to the stable.

Inside was the car Jim had seen earlier, a large four-seater banger. Jack explained that it was a Clyno Saloon he'd bought years ago and that the headlights were on the blink. As he tied two carbide lamps to the mudguard, Jas started the engine with a crank and told Jim to get in the back.

Clyno saloon, 1927 model

He did as he was told and laid the rifle on his lap. Once the lamps were lit, Jack and Jas climbed into the front. Jack took the driver's seat and waited a minute or so for the engine to warm up. When it reached temperature, he pushed the choke back in and slowly edged out into the yard.

There were two routes to Wexford. Either via Borris or left along the haunted lane to Scullough Gap. Jack took the latter.

CHAPTER SIXTEEN

Mrs. Love and the fair

The previous day — the 1st of February — had been the big fair in Taghmon. As usual, farmers and jobbers had come from across the County to buy and sell livestock. Most had arrived the night before to mark out their spots, often ones their families had claimed for generations.

Along Main Street, three-sided pens packed with sheep, pigs, and cattle had been tied outside the houses. Times were hard, and so many farmers were desperate to make a sale that they ran half a mile out of town — on both sides.

For most of the day, Elsie Love had her hands full looking after the children. Just five and ten, they'd usually be at school, but on fair days the schools were closed. She didn't mind. It was a good excuse to share quality time. Besides, they loved the theatre of it all, watching the deals being done, the slapping of hands, and course the animals — especially the horses that were traded in a little paddock just down the road from her husband's bank.

That February was particularly cold. Clouds of steam rose from the backs of the cattle, and now and again there was a flurry of snow. As she knelt to make sure the children's coats were buttoned, her nostrils filled with the earthy stench of dung that would need to be cleared away the next day. Above her head smoke from turf fires spiralled up from almost every chimney in long streams of blue smoke.

The sights and sounds of a fair day were vibrant and exciting, and she loved them. She also loved being the bank manager's wife. It wasn't just the financial package — although George told her it was very good — it was the fact that they got to live above the bank itself — effectively the best house in town — and of course there was the prestige that went with it.

Blueshirt salute

Elsie was in her mid-thirties, a good ten years younger than her husband, and she accepted that part of her wifely duties was to present herself in a way that reflected well on him.

These days it was difficult. She needed to look fashionable and well-dressed, but not too well-off. George had recently foreclosed on half a dozen local farms, and she didn't want to send out the wrong message.

That day, she'd chosen a modest — albeit deceptively expensive — three-piece skirt, blouse, and jacket. To top it all, a white cloche hat, and a suede coat — certainly not the beaver George bought her before the Depression. She'd leave that until times improved.

Many of the traders weren't so self-deprecating. It paid to look like you had money when you were striking a deal, and she noticed that one of the more ostentatious was sporting a broad-brimmed hat, velvet-collared Crombie, and bright ox-blood slip-on boots.

The farmers were less well-heeled. On the breadline, most were still wearing dusty old suits they'd put on for Mass that morning, along with flat caps and overcoats. The only wardrobe addition for the fair was a pair of old boots or wellingtons.

Most recognised her, addressing her as "Mrs. Love" and doffing their caps as she walked by. She nodded back in a modest but confident style, in keeping with her standing in the community.

Around midday, she made her way past the cock fighting booths and three card tricksters to her friend's house near the pub. While their children played together, they discussed the news of the day. The big item of course was the continuing violence between the IRA and the Blueshirts. George was appalled. As a staunch Free State man, he believed Cosgrave had been the voice of reason. When he'd been in power, the IRA had been kept under control. Now, the country was a mess. Hundreds of IRA men had been let out of prison, and they seemed to have carte blanche to do what they wanted.

To add insult to injury, De Valera had been elected on the promise of making life better for the poor — especially the farmers. That, in George's opinion, was hogwash. His real agenda was the usual Republican claptrap. A united Ireland that any reasonable person knew could never happen. Not because of the British, but because the Unionists in the north would never let it. To cap it all, his pig-headed economic war was making it impossible for his customers to make ends meet.

Elsie knew little about politics; she left that to George. Besides, there were many more interesting things to talk about. The Irish sweepstake for one — and what would you do with all that money if you won? Then there was the question of who murdered Lindbergh's baby. Would he ever be found? There was also that strange little man in Germany who'd just been elected chancellor. George thought he'd be good for the country — give it the shake-up it needed.

After lunch, she took the children back to the fair. Her daughter wanted to see the pony sale — and like most little girls she begged her mother to buy her one.

It was difficult to pull her away, but the promise of seeing her father did the trick. Fair days were always busy for George, and as they entered the bank, she could see he had a queue stretching out of the door.

He saw them from behind the iron bars of the counter and waved. She and the children waved back, but she knew he was too busy to talk. That was the funny thing about fair days. George was always rushed off his feet, but by the time he closed, his safe would be practically empty.

Farmers who wanted to buy stock took their savings out. Ones who'd sold stock bought more or gave the proceeds to their wives to pay their bills. If they had any money left, they'd stock up on provisions like biscuits, sausages, or maybe a side of bacon. If they'd done particularly well, their wives might give them pocket money for the pub and go to the drapers to buy a new dress or some balls of wool.

As usual, the bank closed at six. When the cashier, Ed Conry, finally shut the doors, George slumped down on his stool and breathed a sigh of relief. Elsie was already in the kitchen making dinner, and while Conry and the rest of the staff headed home, George locked up and joined her and the children.

His bank was part of the National Bank of Ireland. When he became the manager, the group was already a hundred years old — set up by, amongst others, Daniel O'Connell — the man who'd spent most of his political life trying to get rid of the Act of Union.

It was located on the outskirts of the town, on the old road to New Ross, and it was one of the grandest buildings in the village. Slightly set back from the road in its own landscaped grounds with neat wrought iron railings, it was the envy of most of their friends.

Old bank of Taghmon

Later that evening, George let himself out through the gate and walked the two hundred yards or so into town. At 8 pm, it was already dark but there was still a lot going on. Groups of men were chatting on the corners, and families were laughing and making their way back home by paraffin lamp. In the streets, farmers were packing up their pens and getting ready to drive their livestock to new homes or the slaughterhouse.

As he walked into the pub, he could see it was packed. Someone was playing an accordion. Another had joined in on the fiddle, and one of the girls who used to work for him stood up, worse for wear, and to great applause began singing Skibbereen.

Oh father dear, and I often hear you speak of Erin's isle
Her lofty scenes, her valleys green, her mountains rude and
wild
They say it is a lovely land wherein a prince might dwell
Then why did you abandon it? The reasons to tell

My son, I loved my native land with energy and pride
Till a blight came o'er all my crops, and my sheep and
cattle died
The rent and taxes were to pay, and I could not them
redeem
And that's the cruel reason I left old Skibbereen

This well I do remember the bleak November day
When the bailiff and the landlord came to drive us all away
They set their roof on fire with their cursed English spleen
And that's another reason I left old Skibbereen...

He stayed until around ten, then walked home on his own. After Elsie put the children to bed, they shared a pot of tea until around eleven. Then he re-checked the hall and kitchen doors to make sure they were locked and climbed into bed around ten past.

He was a light sleeper, and just after four in the morning, he heard footsteps. A few seconds later, he noticed a bright light under the door.

His ten-year-old son had a habit of sleepwalking, and as he opened the door to the landing, he expected to see him there.

Instead, he saw three masked men, one with a shotgun and the other two with pistols. As they pushed him back into the bedroom, the smallest of them told him not to be nervous. Then he said he wanted the keys to the safe — adding that he planned to take all the cash in the bank.

CHAPTER SEVENTEEN

Is this the new hall porter?

A "small man."

According to the papers, it was a small man who'd jumped over the cashier's table in Bunclody. Another small man had helped Jas ambush the bus at Ballyanne. Now George Love described a small man breaking into his bank.

It was becoming a pattern, and after a cup of tea, I continued leafing through the report in the Times.

According to George's statement, Elsie woke as he raised his hands. He tried to reassure her, but it appeared she didn't need reassurance. Instead, she sat up clutching the eiderdown to her nightgown and demanded the robbers keep the noise down, as her children were crying in the next room.

It was one of those observations that gave the report a realism that spanned a gap of sixty years. I can't imagine how scary it must have been for her to find three strange men in her bedroom, yet she felt confident enough to stand her ground and tell them off.

I'm not sure how most armed bank robbers would have acted, but the small man — who I assumed had to be Jack — did what she asked, lowering his voice to a whisper and giving her permission to go to check they were okay.

Once she'd left the bedroom, he asked George if there was anyone else in the house. George assured him there wasn't.

To make sure George wasn't lying, he poked the parabellum hard into his chest and repeated the question. George gave the same answer, which was backed up by Elsie when she returned.

George's age wasn't stated in the paper, but I guessed he must have been in his forties, well old enough to have fought in the War of Independence and the ensuing Civil War. On the other hand, he might not have fought in either, preferring to keep his head down and work his way through the banking hierarchy from cashier to manager.

Either way, according to his evidence, he acted bravely. Initially, he refused to hand over the keys. When he was told he'd be shot if he didn't, he changed his mind.

There were three bedrooms in the house. One for him and Elsie, one for the children, and the other for their maid — a young girl who was fortunate enough to be staying with her parents that night. The bedrooms sat above their living quarters: a kitchen and a drawing room. The bank itself was tagged on the side and comprised the public foyer, the cashier's office, and the strongroom.

Keeping the gun in George's back, the small man followed him closely down the stairs. Elsie followed on behind carrying an oil lamp with the two other raiders on her heels. I imagine his idea was to get George - to open the safe, take the money and make a getaway ASAP.

As they entered the downstairs hall, he asked how much cash he reckoned was in the safe. When George told him there was only around £300 (£27,000), he accused him of lying. George assured him he wasn't. The day before had been a fair day, when bank deposits were typically at an all-time low.

That must have been the first blow. The second was when George explained that there needed to be two sets of keys to open the safe — his and one belonging to his cashier, Ed Conry. Conry, he explained, lived in the town above a shop called Sweeney's.

Jack must have been devastated. He'd picked the wrong day and now he needed two keys from two people who lived in two different places.

In court, George told the judge that he then had to wait while the raiders had an emergency confab. The small man, he guessed, must have been in his thirties and about 5' 5". He was the one who did most of the talking and was most likely the ringleader. When asked to describe him, George said that he was wearing "a tweed overcoat, darkish flannel trousers and a flat cap. Not the sort of clothes a farmer would wear." On his feet were "dark canvas rubber shoes" — an odd choice for a cold February morning.

The second man was taller, about the same age as the first, and also wearing a flat cap and dark overcoat. Their voices sounded similar, and George suspected they might be related.

The third man — the tallest — seemed the youngest, or at least the most inexperienced. He was wearing a similar coat and brown boots. He said very little, and when he did, he seemed nervous. All of them were wearing white linen hoods with crude holes cut out for the eyes.

When they'd finished their discussion, the small man took George into the cashier's office and insisted he try to open the safe with just his one key.

In the dim glow of the small raider's electric torch, George gave it a go, but it soon became apparent that it couldn't be done. He was telling the truth. One key wasn't enough.

According to George, the small man became agitated and began raiding the petty cash tin. Then an interesting observation. Taking out a ten-shilling note (£50), he offered it to Elsie and suggested she buy something for her children.

George of course was proud to tell the court that she refused, adding emphatically that she "would never touch stolen money."

Jack's offer somehow touched me. It demonstrated something. Maybe his humanity? Maybe he was thinking of his children? Maybe it was some sort of apology for being there in the first place?

If anyone cared about his motivation, it wasn't reported in the newspapers. George went on to tell the court that the small man then ordered him to take him to Conry's lodgings.

If I'd been Jack, I'm not sure I would have been so tenacious. Most probably, I would have given up and gone home. Obviously, he was made of stronger stuff. Besides, he was in for a penny and probably concluded he might as well be in for a pound.

George complained that it was too cold to go out in just a nightshirt. He asked if he could slip on a hat and coat. Jack agreed and when George was dressed, Jack took the safe key off him and led him out through the front door.

It seemed Jim must have gone with them. According to the article, only one raider was left to keep guard over Elsie, and it seemed unlikely Jack would have given that task to the man George described as being the most inexperienced.

As soon as they left, Elsie said she'd complained about a draft from the lounge window, presumably a result of it being forced open. It seemed like Jas did his best to make a quick repair, but being no DIY expert, failed abysmally.

In the meantime, Jack was marching George along the Ross Road. Jim was close behind, and as they approached the village, George said the small man asked if Sweeney's was far. He told him it wasn't, and as they turned the corner, he pointed out the shop ahead of them.

As soon as they arrived, Jack began knocking on the door. When no one answered, he knocked again. George told him he shouldn't be impatient, as Conry needed time to get up. He said the small man just shrugged, complained that time wasn't on his side, and began rapping again.

It seemed Conry was a heavy sleeper. Besides, it was still only five a.m., and I'm not sure I would have woken up too easily at that time either. The court heard that in the end, Mr. Sweeney himself had to get him out of bed. Bleary-eyed Conry staggered across to his window to see what all the fuss was about.

George told the court that by then the two raiders were hiding to the left of the front door. Conry had no idea why his boss had called around in the middle of the night. Before he could ask why, George shouted up that he should come down — that they needed to talk. Conry gave a grunt and shouted back that he'd be there in a minute.

Conry then slipped on a dressing down and made his way to the foot of the stairs. According to his evidence, as he opened the door, a small man shoved his foot into the jamb, pointed a gun at him, and told him to put his hands up.

It seems likely Conry was a war veteran. He told the court that as the small man tried to push open the door he pushed back. For a few seconds they tussled, until the small man said that if he didn't pull away, he'd "plug him through the door" and "smash it down anyway."

Conry decided to do what he was told. As he retreated into the hall, the small man told him he needed his keys to the strongroom. He added that there was no need for him to be nervous. Conry told the court that he might have been angry and frustrated, but he wasn't "bloody well nervous." He said that he told the small man just that and added that he was going up to his room to get dressed.

While Jim kept George covered, Jack followed him up the stairs. As they entered his bedroom, he told him that he only had enough time to put on an overcoat. An angry Conry slipped on a coat and a pair of shoes. Then he reluctantly retrieved the key from his bedside drawer and handed it over. The small man, he said, led him down the stairs at gunpoint. At the bottom, he claimed to have turned to him and said that he was a "fool if he thought he'd get away with it." The small man's answer was quietly confident. "We aren't fools...we'll get away alright."

Once they were back on the street, Jack marched both men back to the bank with Jim following on behind. As they walked into the hall, Conry saw Jas, parabellum in hand, keeping guard over Elsie and the children. "Is this the new hall porter?" he asked sardonically.

If Jack appreciated the wit, he didn't say so. Instead, he told him that there were men keeping guard in the garden and that he shouldn't try anything. Then he gave both bankers their keys and told them to unlock the strongroom.

As soon as it was open, he and Jim followed them in. Conry reluctantly pulled the cash box from the safe and, on Jack's orders, emptied it onto the floor. Immediately, Jack began picking up notes and coins, stuffing them into a bag. Jim was more reticent. George noticed how the small man seemed exasperated by the tall man's unwillingness to help himself. "Don't you want any of this money?" he heard him say. "Come on, hurry up."

Once the cash was collected, the bag was handed to Jas, who was still in the hall with Elsie. Before he left the strongroom, Jack double-checked the safe to make sure it didn't have a secret compartment. When he was satisfied, he allowed Conry and Love to lock up again.

By now, it seemed Conry had had enough. According to his evidence, he told the raiders that now they had the cash, they'd better clear off. Not only that, but he was cold and wanted to get back to bed. The small man told him that couldn't happen. He had to remain on the premises with George and Elsie until at least daybreak. If he tried to leave or warn anybody before then, the men outside would know, and there'd be trouble.

Before Jack left, there was something else, he wanted to say. George was able to repeat it to the court almost verbatim. "I'm sorry," he said, "for all the trouble I've given you at this hour of the morning. Believe me, it's the result of dire necessity."

It's not usual to feel sympathy for an armed bank robber, but as armed bank robbers go, Jack wasn't what I imagined to be the norm. There was no need for him to apologise. There was no need to offer Elsie ten shillings for her children. Knowing the circumstances that led him there, I couldn't help feeling sorry for him. He'd lost everything, and he had two young children to feed. As he told George, what he was doing was an act of "dire necessity."

George, however, made it clear to the court that the small man's apology didn't wash. Stony-faced, he said that he pointed to the open window in the dining room and asked if that's where they got in.

The small man said it was, adding apologetically that they'd "made as little mess as they possibly could" and "that he was very sorry for any damage caused."

It was time to go. With Conry and George gaining confidence, Jack needed to find somewhere to lock them in while they made their getaway. After testing a few doors, he realised there were no good options and, reminding them of the guards in the garden, he led his fellow raiders out through the front door.

George made a note of the time. It was 5.20 and by his reckoning, they'd been there just over an hour.

CHAPTER EIGHTEEN
An Englebert tyre

George wasn't sure whether to believe the small man's story about guards in the garden. Conry was certain he was lying. The bank didn't have a phone, but there was a police barracks in New Ross, and he was all for cycling there and raising the alarm. George decided it was best if they all stayed put, and Conry reluctantly bowed to his boss's decision.

Three hours later, he headed home in the freezing cold, dressed in just a nightshirt and overcoat. In the meantime, George contacted the police and by 10.30, Sgt McNamee and Guard Stack from the Wexford barracks were sitting in his kitchen drinking tea and taking statements.

While Elsie played with the children, George took the police on a quick tour of the house, explaining as far as he could remember what happened. After showing them the strong room and giving them a rough idea of the amount stolen, he took them out to the garden.

The bank faced directly onto the road. To the side was a six-foot-high wooden gate. McNamee tried it and found it unlocked. George was sure this had to be where they'd gotten in. Being a creature of habit, he'd not only checked the doors to the house that night, but also the gate.

McNamee took a closer look and found a footprint halfway up — the print of what he suspected was a rubber canvas shoe. One of the raiders had obviously climbed up, reached over the top, and undone the latch.

He then turned his attention to the house. According to George, the small man said they'd got in through the dining room window. It was still open and a Sgt Rabbit and Sgt Pat Summeries, who'd just arrived, noticed the catch had been levered up.

Outside on the grass, they found a piece of wood with an iron hook — presumably, a tool for prising open the window. While McNamee and George returned to the house, Summeries took the hook and broken sash back to the police car. Rabbit used a small saw to cut away the part of the gate with the print of the rubber-soled shoe.

A few hours later, Sergeant Tom Keating and District Officer Compton began to examine the road. They found nothing heading into the village itself, but out of town about four hundred yards up the road to New Ross there was a lane to the left. There they noticed what looked like fresh car tracks. There weren't many cars around, and immediately they suspected this was what they were looking for.

They followed them three hundred yards to a place known locally as "the buildings." From there, it looked like the car had turned full circle and headed back. A hundred yards on they found deeper tyre impressions which suggested the car had been parked there. Two patches of oil on the ground confirmed their suspicions.

There was a house at the point the car turned, and they decided to knock at the door and ask the occupants if they'd heard anything. It was leased to the Kavanagh family, and a man called John Kavanagh answered. He told them he was a labourer who worked nearby and that he had heard a car earlier that morning — quite a rare event he added.

After having breakfast and a shave, he'd walked down to where he thought it turned, about twelve yards from the house. He noticed a mask on the verge. He described it as white and flimsy and concluded it was best to leave it where it was.

Englebert tyre

The officers then interviewed John's son, Phillip. As it happened, Phillip was a motor mechanic. He told them he'd gone to bed around 11:30 and was woken around 1.30 by the sound of a car and the dogs barking.

Like his father, he walked down the lane to see where the car had turned. Then he continued another hundred yards until he saw where it had been parked up. From the oil and the depths of the tracks, he reckoned it must have been there a considerable time. He'd had the foresight to measure the tracks, which he recorded as four foot one between the rear wheels, four foot two between the front, and nine feet from front to back. The tyres themselves were quite unusual. Three were Pirelli or Goodrich but the fourth — the right rear wheel — was an Englebert. As a car mechanic, he found this particularly interesting. Oscar Englebert, he said, had been making tyres since 1898 and they were the first choice in most big races. An Englebert, he added, had been the first tyre to complete the 24-hour Le Mans without change.

From his observations, it seemed the robbers had sat in the car for around four hours before plucking up the courage to raid the bank.

While Sargent Rabbit and Summeries took plaster casts of the tyre prints, Keating and Compton returned to examining the road. Initially, the tracks were easy to follow. They managed to follow them six miles to a place called Scullabogue — infamous as the town where two hundred Protestant Loyalists were burnt to death by Catholic rebels in '98. Then they disappeared.

In the meantime, Conry was helping the police with their enquiries. Being the meticulous cashier he was, he was soon able to provide them with the exact amount stolen: £796.6.8 (£67000).

Intriguingly, he remembered two distinctive coins taken in the haul. A half-sovereign — an oddity that he'd stuck to a postcard with red sealing wax — and an old British half-crown. George also remembered the half-crown. He'd pointed it out to Conry the day before and they'd put it to one side, concerned that it might not be legal currency because a strange "snip" had been taken off the edge.

Having taken their evidence, the police headed back to their barracks and contemplated their next move. From the direction the car had taken, it looked like the robbers had been heading out of Wexford and probably into Carlow, but they couldn't be sure. To be on the safe side, they decided to cast the net wide and take a close look at the usual suspects: the anti-treaty men.

One of the first to be arrested was Bob Lambert. He'd recently returned to his mother's house in Kyle after being in Australia since the end of the Civil War. One of the reasons he'd made his antipodean move was because of his anti-treaty activities — most memorably when he ambushed a mail train packed with Free State troops in an attempt to release their IRA prisoners.

His mother had organised a dance held to celebrate his homecoming and many of his old comrades had been invited. As it began, a contingent of Guards appeared, threw him in the back of their police van, and in a scene reminiscent of Coppola's *Godfather* wedding scene began questioning the guests and giving their cars the once over.

A few days later, the same thing happened to Peter Daly, another prominent Republican. He'd also left Ireland after the Civil War — in his case to join the British Army. This, however, wasn't because he'd had a change of heart. As was subsequently discovered, he was using his position to channel guns and ammunition to the IRA.

Daly was arrested and brought before District Judge Fahey. At a preliminary hearing, he told him that on the night of the robbery, he'd been on armed duty with the IRA miles away.

Eleven days later, the inevitable happened. On 13th February, Superintendent O'Brien, Sargent O'Neil, Superintendent Desmond, Sargent Keating, and District Officer Compton turned up mob-handed at Kilcloney. There was no sign of Jas or Jack — just their mother, Josie, and her two children. As Biddy offered them tea, the officers showed themselves around. It didn't take long to find a car in the stables. It was an old Clyno, and O'Brien noted the registration as YO5165.

As they pushed it out to take a closer look, Keating noticed two patches of oil on the stable floor. He also found an impression of a rubber-soled shoe on the mudguard.

The Clyno seemed to be the car they were looking for. To make sure, Compton measured the distance between the tyres. Four-foot one at the back. Four foot two at the front. The distance from front to back came in at nine feet.

The measurements were identical to the ones Phillip Kavanagh took. The icing on the cake, however, was what O'Brien found on the rear right wheel: an Englebert tyre.

They left around five o'clock. The next day, they were back early and found the key to the Clyno hanging behind the kitchen door. To make sure the car could make it to Taghmon and back, Keating and guard Kearney drove it to the barracks in Wexford. Kearney noted that it was a good runner and that it took an hour and twenty-five minutes. He found two pennies on the back seat and noticed the headlights weren't working. There were also some odd scratches on the mudguard.

While Kearney wrote up his report, other police officers began searching the house.

Upstairs in Jas' bedroom, he found a half-sovereign wrapped in what looked like wallpaper. The bed wasn't made up, and even though there was no sign of Jas, it looked like it had recently been slept in. Compton also noticed some sort of red material on the coin — possibly sealing wax.

The case against Jas seemed pretty strong. The question was, who else was involved? The bank manager had said there'd been three raiders and he'd described the ringleader as a small man. O'Brien had known the Kielys for years and he'd often heard that description when witnesses were describing Jack. The strange thing was, he hadn't seen him for years. Yet there was a smoking gun. Josie and his children were staying at the house. She'd told him Jack was working in England — but suppose he wasn't?

The only thing to do was put out the feelers. See if anyone had seen him around recently. As for Jas, he needed to track him down and bring him in for questioning.

Back in Bagnalstown barracks, O'Brien was about to draft a letter requesting Jas come to see him ASAP when his sergeant rushed in to tell him that they'd picked him up at the station and he was waiting outside.

It was an unexpected surprise. He fetched Jas in from reception and sat him down in the interview room. After offering him a cup of tea, he told him that he was a suspect in the Taghmon bank robbery and that he'd asking him some questions that he was under no obligation to answer.

Jas nodded and took the tea. Over the years, O'Brien had always found him gentlemanly and reasonable. Besides, Jas knew the ropes. He told him he understood the caution and said to fire away. Taking him at his word, O'Brien's first question was straight to the point. Was there a half-sovereign in the house? Jas replied that there was. It was his, and it had been around since 1914. O'Brien made a note and asked where he kept it. Jas replied that he kept it in his bed — in a bit of paper tucked under his pillow.

There was no doubt he was going to be a slippery customer. O'Brien decided to change tack and asked him where he'd been for the last few days. Jas replied that he'd been over the water. On the 12th, he'd taken the cattle boat to England in an attempt to persuade his brother to come home. Jack had been working there for about a month and wasn't aware that the guards wanted to question him about the robbery.

He said Jack wasn't keen. He felt the Guards in Borris blamed him for everything and if they wanted to question him, they'd have to come and get him. He added that before that he hadn't seen him in years. He confided they hadn't been friendly for quite a while.

O'Brien offered him another cup of tea and asked for Jack's address. Jas seemed hesitant. He explained that he didn't want to betray any confidence and that it was better if he asked Jack's wife, Josie.

O'Brien sighed and scribbled down his answer. Then he asked about the Clyno. Jas confirmed it was his, but said that he'd only bought it a few weeks before, from a man in Bannow. As far as he could remember, his name was Doyle. He had no idea of his Christian name.

When asked about the registration number, he said he'd had the car such a short time he couldn't remember what it was. He also said that he'd bought it to do up, that it was partly dismantled, and not in a fit state to be driven anywhere.

Throwing him a curve ball, O'Brien asked how often Jack used the car. Jas smiled and replied he never did as he was never around. Then why was Josie living at Kilcloney — wasn't it odd she and the children were there without him?

Jas explained that she'd had a falling out with a brother she'd been staying with and had nowhere else to go. He was just taking care of her while Jack was away — it was as simple as that.

He went on to describe how, on the night of the robbery, he'd gone to bed around eleven and got up at eight. When he lit the fire in the morning, he distinctly remembered looking over at the stables and seeing the car still in there.

O'Brien asked again if he'd give him Jack's address. This time he seemed more conciliatory. He asked for a piece of paper and wrote down: *Lodge Terrace, Bellefield, Rochdale.*

O'Brien thanked him for his help and told him he was free to leave. Jas shook his hand, slipped on his heavy coat, and let himself out.

O'Brien poured himself another cup of tea and sat back down at his desk. He might be able to prove that the Clyno was the car used in the robbery, but if he couldn't prove Jas had been in it, he wasn't in the frame. As for the half sovereign — he doubted that on its own it was enough to bring about a conviction.

He needed to keep following up his leads. The latest being that address in Rochdale. Jas told him it was a bedsit rented by James Coburn from Bagnalstown. Unfortunately, Coburn was also an anti-treaty man and it didn't seem likely he would rat on his old comrades.

His best bet, he concluded, was to keep an eye on Kilcloney. If Josie was there, there was a good chance Jack was close by. As for him working in Rochdale at the time of the robbery, O'Brien didn't buy it.

He instructed his men to stake out the bridge beside the mill. The box hedge outside the kitchen window had been cut short, so from there they'd have a good vantage point of the yard and the house.

A few days later, the watchers reported back. One officer noted that when Josie hung out the washing, she always closed the kitchen door firmly behind her. He also noticed that the low wooden seat to the left of the kitchen fire was always occupied by either a sleeping child or the boy's mother.

Something wasn't right. On Sunday 18th, he convinced the magistrates that there was a good chance weapons were hidden inside. He was given a warrant that gave him a right of entry under the firearms act. The next morning, he gathered up his officers and went back to the house.

As he began knocking on the kitchen door, he heard scuffling. He tried the handle, but the door was locked. There was more scuffling, but still no one answered. Suspecting something was going on, he tried to force it open. The first time it didn't give way. The second time it did.

As he burst in, he saw that the room was in a state of confusion. Josie was rushing towards him with a baby in her arms. Another child was holding onto her skirt, crying. Over by the fire, he could see old Biddy Kiely settling herself down on that low wooden seat.

He asked her to stand up and made a long search around the fireplace. There was nothing there. Confused, he checked out the seat itself. As he tried to move it, he saw that it was attached to the wall. He tried again and this time it came away, ripping away a piece of timber covering a hole.

It was an extraordinary discovery. He guessed this must be where the guns in the raid were hidden. As he peered in, he expected to see them in there. Instead, he saw a man's arm.

CHAPTER NINETEEN
The informer

A quick glance at the clock told me it was only coming up on one. It seemed I'd discovered more about Jack in the last few hours than I had in the last thirty years.

There were a few other things I needed to know, though. First, what exactly was a Clyno? Second, what was a long-nosed parabellum? And third, what was a carbide lamp?

I'd never heard of any of them and asked the girl at the Archives how I could find out more.

She directed me to the general library on Mallin Street. I reckoned I had plenty of time, so I bought a sandwich on the way and eventually entered what looked like an opera house.

The library was big and impressive, and the reference section was excellent. I quickly found "automobiles" and a small red book on vintage cars.

It told me that back in 1909, two cousins — Frank and Alwyn Smith — designed a pulley with a variable drive ratio. They called it the "inclined pulley," which soon became abbreviated to the "clined" or Clyno.

By 1918, they were supplying motorbikes with machine gun attachments to the British. Ironic, really, given that Jack was to wind up with one of their cars.

Their first car trundled off the production line as the Civil War started, and their low prices made their sales start to rocket. By 1925, their turnover had quadrupled, and by the time Jack got married, they were producing three hundred and fifty cars a week.

At a guess, I'd say that's when Jack's Clyno rolled off the assembly line, making it around eight to ten years old at the time of the robbery.

Long nosed parabellum

Satisfied about the car, I turned my attention to the long nose parabellum. After further research, I discovered it was another name for a German Luger. The reference book gave a lot of detail about calibres and magazines, but the bottom line was that it had been introduced in 1900, and one of its variants was a long, eight-inch barrel model — presumably the one Jack had.

Where he got it from, I didn't know, but I had a vague recollection that he'd once told me he'd bought a gun from an ex-British soldier coming home from the war.

Certainly, he used to tease my father about it. When we'd go to Ireland in the seventies, he often told him he'd owned a parabellum, and that he'd hidden it somewhere in Kilcloney. He said it was greased up, wrapped carefully in oilskins, and ready to go. Every year, my father would ask where it was, but Jack would just grin and shrug. I guess by then he'd kept the secret forty years, and he wasn't going to give it up lightly.

As for carbide lamps, another book told me they'd been used as lighthouse beacons and car headlights. They were bright, and they worked by putting calcium carbide in the lower part of the lamp, water in the top, and hey presto — you got acetylene gas, which you could light up.

Carbide lamp

When I got back to the archives, I bought myself another coffee and sat back down with the 1930-35 newspaper file.

I'd left off where O'Brien had found someone hiding in a hole. I was pretty sure I knew where it had been. Even in my day, there'd been a low wooden stool next to the fire. It had been Michael's favourite spot. Whether there was any sort of passage behind it then seemed unlikely. Certainly, he'd never mentioned one, and I suspect it must have been filled up long before his time.

As for O'Brien, he told the court that as soon as he saw the arm behind the wall, he suspected it was Jack. According to the *New Ross Times*, he shouted that he should come out and put his hands up.

The man refused and disappeared back into the hole. Josie asked if she could talk to him for a few minutes. O'Brien agreed, and after a while, the man appeared again. This time, O'Brien grabbed his wrist and, with the help of Kinsella, managed to pull him out.

As he thought, it was Jack, and his first words to O'Brien were remarkably blasé.

"Now Super, I was just going to come up to you tomorrow and make a statement."

I strongly doubt O'Brien believed him. Instead, he merely noted that Jack had no shoes on, and that he was wearing a pair of blue engineer's dungarees.

He told his officers to hold him while he explored the hole. As he crawled in, he saw a compartment just big enough for "two men to stand together upright and a roof that couldn't be reached with outstretched hands." Beyond that was a hole in the wall leading to a similar compartment. There was no other exit and no window, and after asking for a torch, he found an old straw quilt on the floor — presumably a makeshift bed where Jack had been sleeping.

More damningly, he also found a "Lee Enfield service rifle complete with magazine and strap, a double-barrelled hammerless shotgun, a .22 rifle, a .32 revolver (bulldog pattern), two military holsters, a leather belt and a sword."

The sword was a surprise. I can imagine O'Brien wondering if he were a forerunner of "mad Jack" Churchill, the man who'd fought in the Second World War with a sword and bagpipes. Fortunately, I knew that wasn't the case. Jack told me years ago that a sword had hung over the fireplace in the parlour for as long as he could remember, apparently given to one of his ancestors for saving a drowning woman.

Next to the weapons, O'Brien found a "bag of silver coins and some coppers." As he crawled out of the hole, bag in hand, Jack asked him to "make a note that there were no notes in it." O'Brien said he would, and as he lay it on the table, he read him the usual caution: "I suspect that you were implicated in the bank robbery at Taghmon County Wexford on 2nd February. You need not make any statement unless you wish to do so. Any statement you do make may be used in evidence afterwards."

Jack's reply was like something out of a 1930s "B" movie. "I was going to come up to make a statement, but every time I tried to make a move-out, the place was surrounded by tecs."

He always had a dry sense of humour, and I imagine his reply was as much tongue-in-cheek as anything else. O'Brien, not to be outdone, said that if that were the case, then perhaps he'd like to take the opportunity to make one now.

Jack apparently mumbled something to the effect that it wouldn't be a good idea.

Both men then sat at the table while Jack pulled on his shoes. The kitchen was probably full of police, and I can imagine Biddy offering to make them tea. The newspaper reported that Jack lifted my mother onto his lap and pointed to the bag.

"That silver," he said, "is my life's savings. I am a fellow who moves around from place to place, and I carry my money with me — and I never carry notes. You must know I got a share in this place left to me and there was a good sum in it."

O'Brien spilt the contents onto the table and made a quick count. He told the court that it came to around £109 (£8000), but in that moment he kept that to himself. Then he spotted a half crown. It was nicked just to the left of the date, exactly like the one Conry said had been stolen from the bank. Again he kept quiet about that.

Jack, on the other hand, kept talking. He told him the money in the bag comprised what he'd got when he'd left home, plus what he'd saved in Carrick. "The only thing in the dugout that was mine was that bag," he insisted.

It seems O'Brien wasn't convinced. Presumably, to catch him out, he asked if he'd like to confirm how much was in it.

I can imagine Jack grinning as he answered, "Haven't you just counted it? I trust you to do so, and I'll tell the amount to the District justice."

As he put my mother down and got to his feet, O'Brien told him Josie had been to see him on the ninth and said he'd wanted to make a statement. Jack said that was true but repeated that he, "couldn't come because the place was surrounded by tecs."

O'Brien then asked him where he was on the night of the robbery. "I know about the raid," Jack replied "but I wasn't there — and I have witnesses to prove it."

He then pulled on a coat and asked if Jas had given a statement. O'Brien said he had.

Jack must have wondered what was in it. Apologising to O'Brien for his impertinence, he asked if his brother had been "pinched."

O'Brien merely replied that Jas had been taken to Wexford for further questioning. With that, he had Jack loaded into a Paddy wagon and driven under escort to Bagnalstown.

I can imagine there must have been a lot of weeping and wailing in the house that day. As the Guards filed out, the children would have been crying. Biddy would have sat back on the remains of her wooden stool and wondered how things could get any worse. Josie would have been putting on the children's coats so she could get them over to her parents in Clomoney and join Jack in Bagnalstown

I've seen the barracks in Bagnalstown many times. Fortunately, not from the inside. They're in Kilree Street, near the centre, and after Jack arrived, he was taken in, offered a cup of tea, and put in a holding cell. An hour or so later, O'Brien returned with pad and paper. According to his report, he repeated his caution and asked where he'd been for the past few years.

On the face of it, Jack seemed remarkably cooperative. He replied that he'd been living in Carrick on Bannow under the alias "John Doyle" and he'd been renting a shop there.

Then he gave O'Brien the full story — or at least his version of it.

Before leaving Borris in 1927, he'd been a member of the IRA. Since then, he'd lived in England and Belfast. When he left home, he received £156 (£12,000) from his father's estate and £50 (£4000) each from his sisters — presumably, Mary and Nell. As he had explained back at Kilcloney, the silver in the dugout partly came from that. The rest was from what he'd saved in Carrick.

When O'Brien asked him why he'd moved back to Kilcloney, he said it was because he'd been made bankrupt. He and Josie had been evicted from their shop in November 1933, and while she went to stay with her parents in Clomoney, he moved in with his sister at New Ross. On the 26th of January, he returned to England to get a job. He'd stayed at his friend James Coburn's house in Rochdale and the first he'd heard of the robbery was a week or so ago, when Josie sent him a letter telling him about it. He then returned to Ireland with his brother and had remained at Kilcloney ever since.

As to why he was living under an alias, he said, "Now Super, I've had a rough time of it for the past two years. Everything that happened around this place was pinned on me."

When O'Brien asked him the exact date he'd come back to Kilcloney, his reply was more evasive: "Sure, you know that yourself."

Asked how he travelled the thirty miles or so from Carrick to Kilcloney, he looked down at his feet and replied cryptically, "Look at them old shoes."

O'Brien's last question related to the car. He asked if he had one. Jack said he did but when pushed to disclose what make it was, he told him, "That would be a washout – I won't tell you that."

I assume O'Brien must have found Jack's answers exasperating. On the other hand, maybe as a seasoned interrogator, he expected nothing less. Finishing the interview, he told him that he'd be taken to Wexford to join his brother.

In his usual laid-back style, Jack asked if he could have a shave with Denny Rowe before he went.

I don't know how police interrogations are carried out. I imagine a modern-day suspected armed bank robber wouldn't be allowed to pop into his local barbers before being shipped off to prison for a severe grilling. Those days, things seemed far more civilised. O'Brien said that he could and "he'd arrange it once he'd had a cup of tea."

According to the *Times*, Jack was then taken to Wexford barracks. Around midnight he appeared at a special hearing before Justice Forde, who remanded him in custody at Waterford jail.

Things weren't looking good. Even so, it struck me that if he kept to his story, he might get away with it. What I read next wasn't so encouraging.

A day or so after his arrest, O'Brien was woken at his home in Bagnalstown and told he had an urgent message. It was from James Treacy senior — a labourer In Ballymartin — and it was about the robbery.

O'Brien called in three of his officers and headed over to the house. James answered the door and led him upstairs to where his son was asleep. According to the report, O'Brien put a hand on the young man's shoulder and said, "You're Jim Treacy, and as a result of the information I have received, I arrest you."

He then added the usual caution that he need not say anything unless he wished to, but anything he did say would be noted and might be used against him.

Jim must have been taken totally by surprise, although it didn't say so in the paper. I imagine his father, knowing he'd been out all night with the Kielys, had put two and two together.

It couldn't have been easy to shop his son to the police. On the other hand, from what he must have read in the papers, it would have seemed likely that it was only a matter of time before the truth came out. Certainly, it would look a lot better to a court if he fessed up rather than getting tripped up in the interrogation process.

Jim was allowed to get dressed and was then driven to Bagnalstown barracks. Sargent Kinsella sat him down in the interview room and asked where he'd been on the night of the robbery.

Jim, presumably still bleary-eyed, told him he was at home. When asked to expand, he said that as usual, he'd been working at Cummins's farm. When his parents went to bed around ten, he followed them up, leaving his brother Bill asleep in the kitchen. He distinctly remembered locking the back door behind him and according to Kinsella's report added, "I am satisfied that I didn't leave the house until 7.30 the next morning."

Asked why he was late for work the next day, he said he had to walk as his father had been up early and taken his bike.

It seemed he was anxious to prove he'd been to work. According to the paper, he told Kinsella that his boss, Cummins, would never let him get away with missing a day. After all, when he didn't turn up for work after a dance at Jack Fenlon's house, hadn't Cummins come over and physically dragged him out of bed?

To add what he thought was a further credible detail, he explained that usually when he was out late, his mother would wait up for him, but on the morning of the 2nd

February, she hadn't — because he hadn't been out. Quod erat demonstrandum.

Whatever Kinsella believed, he kept it to himself. According to his report, he scribbled down Jim's answers and offered him another cup of tea. As someone went to brew up, Kinsella asked if he knew Jas Kealy. Jim said he did. Jas, he said, had inherited his father's corn and woollen mill in Kilcloney.

I assume that wasn't a surprise to Kinsella. They were bound to know each other. It would have been more surprising if they hadn't. After all, both families had lived in the area for well over a hundred years.

When he asked if he'd spoken to him recently, Jim said he had, on Sunday 4th, on his way home from Mass in the Sacred Heart Church in Borris. He explained they'd made light conversation and that he'd asked him if he'd heard what happened in Wexford. Jas said he had, but only after reading about it in the papers.

Kinsella must have known he was lying. The plethora of evidence coming out of Kilcloney compounded with his father's statement made it a sure-fire certainty Jim was involved — more than likely as the third man.

For the next few hours, he kept the questioning going. Eventually, Jim's resolve began to waver. He asked if he was sure they had the right two men in Jack and Jas. Kinsella assured him they did.

Jim must have been torn between loyalty to the Kielys and wanting to please his father. It was a difficult position for a naïve young man, and I couldn't help feeling sorry for him.

In the end, the inevitable happened. He wasn't a veteran of interrogation, and when Kinsella assured him that his best bet was to make a full confession, he did just that.

Less than an hour later he dictated a new statement: "Well, I was in it alright...and this is how it happened..."

CHAPTER TWENTY
The verdict

Pro-treaty Free Staters like George Love were horrified when De Valera got into power. They were even more appalled when he started releasing IRA men from prison.

Not surprisingly, they were firm supporters of the Blueshirts. Although they increased street violence by clashing "Mods and Rockers" style with the anti-treaty men, the Free Staters felt that at least they kept their excesses under some sort of control.

Then, just three months before the trial, De Valera banned them.

It was something the Long Fella had been contemplating for a while, and his chance came when the National Guard decided to hold a parade in Dublin. It was to commemorate iconic pro-treaty Irish leaders like Arthur Griffith, Michael Collins, and Kevin O'Higgins, and it spooked him. Just six months earlier, Mussolini had led his fascist followers to Rome and carried out a coup d'état. It wasn't beyond the bounds of possibility that O'Duffey had something similar in mind.

Immediately, he invoked Article 2A of the constitution to ban the parade. Years later, he confided that he hadn't been sure if the Free State Army would obey his orders.

In the end, they stayed loyal. O'Duffy graciously accepted the ban, insisting he was committed to upholding the law. However, a few provincial parades still went ahead, which gave De Valera - the opportunity to ban the organisation altogether.

Eoin O'Duffy

A situation that already looked good for the IRA now looked even better. Jack and Jas hoped this pro-IRA zeitgeist might help their position in court — but they weren't banking on Jim Treacy's new confession.

In the interview room at Bagnalstown barracks, Kinsella sharpened his pencil, opened his notebook, and cautioned Jim for the third time. Jim confirmed he understood, and without further prompting began to spill the beans.

Kinsella wrote down his statement verbatim:

> *I came home from work about 7.30 and went over on my bike to Kilcloney and it was all arranged in a few minutes. I had bread and butter. Jack gave me a rifle. He gave me nine*

rounds, one in the breech and put on the safety catch. Jas had a short para the stock like a scow — Jack had a long one — it had a piece for the pillbox for the magazine and a long thin barrel. We got things ready and drove off. Jas lent me his coat. I don't know what time we got to Taghmon, and I don't know what road we took but we had a bit of a delay. We stole up the stairs and the manager opened his bedroom door. When he saw Jack, he tried closing it, but Jack said "There's no use shutting it" — so he opened it again.

After the manager put on a top coat and cap Jack and I escorted him to Sweeneys. Jack beside him, me behind. Jas was at the hall door when we got back. The manager opened the safe, Jack had a torch and the manager's wife an oil lamp. Jack Kiely took the money and gave some to Jas and me. Then we cleared off to the car up a laneway about a quarter of a mile from the bank. I handed the money to Jas, and I never saw it again. We came home St. Mullins way. We came into Borris and turned under the viaduct. We had no lights on the car except two bike lamps tied onto the mudguards. It was daylight when we got back. We pushed the Clyno in. Jas said it's better for you to go now. Jack said have you any money to get dumped — I said whatever I had I gave to Jas. I left the rifle and all in the car and cycled home. When I got home my mother and brother Matthew were in the kitchen. I don't know what happened to the money and I never saw it since. I didn't know a ha'porth about the raid until the very night I went over and went off in the car. There was no one else in the raid.

Kinsella couldn't have asked for a better result. Once Jim had signed his confession, he was locked in a holding cell for the rest of the night. Early next morning, as he was being taken to the barracks at Wexford, Superintendent O'Brien ordered another in-depth search of Kilcloney.

Mary and Nell, having heard about the arrests, had come over to look after their mother. O'Brien ordered them to remain in the kitchen, along with Josie and her children, while his men began to systematically take the place apart.

He'd already made a full exploration of the dugout, and - had a fair idea how it worked. When the stool was pulled away from the wall, a piece of timber came with it. The timber was a door to a passage that led to a space under the stairs — the ones that ran from the kitchen up to the main hall. Beyond that, the passage opened out into another space, this time under the outside steps, the ones that ran from the drive up to the official front door.

He didn't anticipate any more surprises, so when one of his officers called him over to look at the dairy, he wasn't sure what to expect.

It was another hole. Smaller than the one where he'd found Jack, but still big enough to house a child of six or seven. According to his officer, it had been disguised beneath a neatly whitewashed wooden board in the same manner as the dugout. When he peered in, he could see it had only recently been excavated — but whatever might have been inside had gone.

He felt like Howard Carter. The house seemed a myriad of secret holes and chambers, and he was beginning to wonder what else was in it.

Spurred on by the discovery in the dairy, he ordered his men to beef up the search. Over the next few hours, they found other oddities. A gable window, visible from the outside but boarded over and wallpapered on the inside. Yet another secret compartment.

In one of the bedrooms, guard Dalton of Gorsebridge was searching a wardrobe. As he checked it over, he discovered a false top. Inside he found a five-chamber Smith and Wesson revolver, a cartridge for a shotgun, a bullet for a machine gun, and an oil bottle.

The wardrobe in the next bedroom had already been checked, but he ordered it to be checked again. This time another false top was found containing a hand grenade and a detonator.

Kilcloney was beginning to look like an arsenal. O'Brien had fought in the Civil War himself — in his case on the side of the Free State. He knew the anti-treaty men were short of guns and ammunition and it looked like Jack might have been in charge of one of their weapons dumps.

As the search continued, Sargent O'Leary noticed that the top step of the stairs leading to the attic was loose. On further examination, he found it was also a secret compartment. Inside was a copy of *Ireland's Own* and two cocoa tins. One contained nine .303 rifle bullets and eighteen rounds of automatic revolver ammunition. The other a dozen or so .22 bullets. He also found a pair of rubber-soled shoes.

Sargent Kearney had been left in the kitchen to keep an eye on the Kiely family. While he was there, he spotted two carbide lamps. They looked like they'd had wire or string tied around them. They also still contained carbide water, suggesting they'd been recently lit.

While O'Brien continued his search, Jim Treacy arrived at the barracks in Wexford. As Kinsella led him through the courtyard, Jim saw a car parked outside one of the garages. It was Jack's Clyno.

"That's the old bus," he said. "I'd recognise it anywhere."

He also noticed a coat lying across a chair in the interview room. "That's the coat I wore in the raid," he said. "Jas Kiely gave it to me."

With the evidence gathered, a preliminary hearing was held before District Judge Fahey on March 3rd.

As usual, Brennan was defending the Kielys. He told the court that he strongly objected to Jim's statement being heard as evidence. His reasoning was straight out of a legal textbook. The three defendants were co-conspirators. Anything said or done by a conspirator was a case of "common conspiracy in furtherance of a common design." Jim's statement was unlikely to have been in the common design and was therefore not submissible.

Such semantics weren't swaying Fahey. He suggested it was better to let matters of law go before the trial judge.

Brennan graciously agreed, taking the opportunity to heap praise on the police and Fahey, as was his custom. "In the course of my long career," he said, "it has been my fortune to appear in a great many enquiries, and I have never seen such efficiency with which the depositions were taken — and with such expedition and fairness." He added that "his brethren at the bar would agree with him when he said they owed a great deal of gratitude to the Justice for the exceedingly thorough way the work had been done."

He then went on to apply for bail — the low-hanging fruit being Jas, for whom, he argued, there was little incriminating evidence. He added that he was a man of substance who could well afford to pay.

Foley, who was Jim's solicitor, said he too wished to associate himself with Brennan's tribute to Fahey. He also had a great deal of experience and had never seen depositions taken in such an organised and concerted way. He said his client was also prepared to give substantial bail, and he couldn't see why the prosecution would have a problem with him being released.

Fahey was buying none of it. He said he was sorry, but he couldn't take the responsibility. Having given regard to the nature of the charge and the evidence, he had no choice but to return the accused to the circuit court in Wexford. He fixed the date as June 24th.

He went on to thank them for their comments and in turn praised the guards. "If anyone needs a mention," he said, "I would single out Inspector O'Neill, Sergeant Sommerville, Sergeant Rabbit, Detective Sergeant Keating, Officer Compton, Detective Sergeant O'Leary, and Guard Dalton." He then gave Superintendent Desmond and O'Brien an additional metaphorical pat on the back.

Three months later, the circuit court in Wexford was packed. The charges were defined as:

> *While armed with firearms the accused stole from George Stephenson Love £796.6.8 (£67000) and before and after such robbery did*

> *use personal violence to the said George Stephenson Love and to Edward Conry-*

and

> *That the defendants on the second day of February and dates immediately prior did conspire together to rob the National Bank Ltd in Taghmon and in furtherance and in pursuance of said conspiracy did on the second day of February rob from the said bank £796.6.8 (£67000).*

For the next three days, Josie, Nell, Mary, and Biddy were there to watch every moment — as were the Treacys. It was particularly hard on Biddy. At sixty-nine, she wasn't in the best of health and coming to terms with losing her livelihood and her husband had taken its toll. Since her nephews had been murdered by the Tans, she'd also been of two minds about her politics. Previously she'd been against fighting, per se. Now she accepted that the War of Independence had had to be fought. She also agreed with the boys that the Free State were no better. The fact that it was close neighbours and friends in Free State uniform who'd smashed up the mill was proof of that. On the other hand, she didn't want to see her boys perpetually in trouble or on the run.

Since John's death, she'd struggled to keep the wolf from the door. For the last few years, she'd been particularly dependent on Jas. When Jack left for the North, she'd tried to make a go of the farm, but with De Valera's trade war, and with livestock impossible to sell, it was an uphill battle that seemed impossible to win. As for the girls, Mary was still grieving the death of her second husband, and Nell seemed to be having some sort of trouble with her marriage. She said it had to do with the robbery. Her husband, Michael, had been a manager at the prestigious drapers, Power, and Co. in New Ross, when the boys were arrested. She said he couldn't cope with the shame. In fact, she confided, he'd tried to commit suicide.

One of Biddy's biggest regrets was falling out with the Treacys. It was sad but not surprising. The prosecution depended on young Jim's statement — which circuit Judge Davitt had now ruled fully admissible.

Certainly, prosecutor Joe McCarthy was confident that Jim's evidence would be his coup de gras — the biggest nail he could hammer into the defence. There were other nails, however, ones he'd diligently gathered to ensure his case was insurmountable.

One such nail came from Frank Doyle.

He owned a car repair garage in New Ross, and he told the court that sometime in December 1933, a man had dropped a 1927 Clyno off at his place in Priory Street. He said he'd given his name as John Doyle — no relation — and that the Clyno's registration number was JO 1565.

Over time, he'd gotten to know John Doyle. He'd done work on the Clyno's Magneto and sent the bill to him in Carrick on Bannow. As far as he remembered, the car had been stored there until 10th January, and during that time it had been taken out about thirty times. Mostly at night — but it was always there in the morning when he came into work.

One Sunday night, Doyle paid him to tow it back from the quayside at Ross Bridge. The tyres were old, maybe as old as the car itself, and one had a puncture. He said he couldn't remember what make they were, but the new one he fitted was an Englebert.

Sometime after the 10th, he bumped into Doyle again. He asked him if the car was all right. Doyle told him it was, but that he was going to put it up for sale in Stafford's garage in New Ross. When Frank was asked if he recognised John Doyle in the courtroom, he said he did and pointed to Jack.

McCarthy then presented the fingerprint evidence. Chief Warden Tim Sullivan had taken Jack's prints at Waterford prison. Expert Henry McNamara then compared them with those found on the rod and the window sash. He said he was able to get a match with Jack's middle finger.

Apart from Jim, the most damning witness was Dick Coburn. He should have been Jack's alibi, but elected to appear for the prosecution instead. He told the court that on 13th February Jas paid him a visit in Rochdale. He told him he and Jack were suspected of raiding a bank in Wexford but that they were innocent.

He asked if he'd tell the guards that Jack had been staying with him from before the 6th. Coburn said he'd refused ten pounds Jas offered — presumably as a sweetener — but agreed to give the alibi. When he discovered the raid wasn't political, he changed his mind.

By three o'clock on the third day, all the evidence had been presented. The Jury had completed their deliberations, and as they filed back into court, Judge Davitt resumed his seat at the bench.

June 1934 was the hottest and driest month since 1743. As a special dispensation, he'd given the court officials leave to loosen their ties and take off their jackets. Windows had been opened as far as security would allow, but even so, the courthouse was still sweltering.

Once the jury had taken their seats, Judge Davitt wiped his brow and asked the Foreman for their verdict.

The word was spoken quietly, but its impact echoed around the hushed courtroom. "Guilty."

People started shouting — some in support of the defendants, others against them.

Jim broke into tears. Jack and Jas stared impassively ahead. James Treacy put a comforting arm around his wife and waved to his son, a wave that tried to say everything would be all right.

George Love got to his feet and clenched his fist in victory. A smiling Conry waved back and gave him a thumbs up. McCarthy grinned. It was a good result — dangerous bank robbers would be put away for a long time, and it was another feather in his KC cap. Brennan slumped back in his chair and loosened his wig. Most of his previous attempts to get the Kielys off the hook had been successful, but not this time. Foley twirled his pencil around in his fingers. He had known his client would be found guilty — now he just hoped he wouldn't receive a custodial sentence.

Josie sat, bemused, not yet taking it in. Nell was on her feet, shouting her defiance. Davitt brought down the gavel to demand silence. When the court quieted, he leaned over the bench and addressed his first comments to Jack.

"You have been found guilty of a very dastardly crime," he began. "It is clear you are the ringleader. To hold up a man in his own house in front of his wife makes you a man not fit to live in a civilized society."

He spoke to Jas with less vitriol, but added, "I cannot overlook the fact that you had a repository of arms in your house — and tried to cloak that in an air of false patriotism."

He was more conciliatory with Jim. "There's some excuse for you," he began. "You at least tried to minimise the enormous trouble caused to the guards." He went on to expound that Jim had been caught at the threshold of life. He was only nineteen, the eldest of ten, and he'd received none of the money. He'd assisted the state, and he would take that into account when passing sentence.

Banging down the gavel again, he leaned forward. Jack was to receive the harshest punishment: seven years hard labour for robbing a bank while armed, seven years for having a revolver with intent to endanger life, two years for conspiring, and twelve months for having a gun without a licence — all to run concurrently.

Jas got five. Two years for conspiring, five for having a revolver with the intent to endanger life, and twelve months for having a gun without a licence — all again to be served concurrently.

Jim was sentenced to twelve months hard labour on all accounts.

Davitt went on to say that it would be in Jack's best interests to tell him where the guns and money were hidden.

Jack, defiant to the last, shouted back that he didn't have the money, he hadn't stolen it, and he wasn't guilty.

CHAPTER TWENTY-ONE
A dangerous lunatic

was surprised to read what Jack yelled out when Davitt sent him down. I would have thought that, faced with the overwhelming weight of evidence against him, he would have shrugged his usual *c'est la vie* shrug and taken it on the chin.

Perhaps he hoped that if he maintained his innocence, he had an outside chance of getting off on appeal. Certainly, I couldn't take issue with the sentence. To paraphrase Davitt, robbing someone at gunpoint in their own home wasn't exactly a nice thing to do.

Having said that, I knew Jack. He was stubborn and determined, all right, but his default factory settings weren't those of a callous bank robber.

I remember Michael telling me years ago that someone in Graney had asked to see him. It was to chat about old times — in particular, an ambush that had taken place there during the Civil War. He agreed to go, but Josie put a stop to it. She said he'd seen a young lad shot, and it still upset him. Michael didn't tell me who he was or how Jack was involved. Perhaps it was the sixteen-year-old James Lillis John Nolan told me about. The anti-treaty lad from Bagnalstown who was hunted down and executed after the ambush Perhaps it was someone on the other side. -

I'd also seen him cry over Kennedy, the chemist in Borris who was shot from behind the wall of the Kavanagh estate. There was no doubt he had a conscience. He'd wanted the

British out, and he would have done anything to facilitate that, but he wasn't cruel. According to Josie, they'd gone bankrupt in Bannow because of his misplaced generosity. She said he'd always been a mug for a hard luck story, and in the end, he gave too many people too much credit for far too long.

Jack's compassion even shone out from between the lines of the newspaper reports. Apologising to George Love for the inconvenience. Explaining he was only there because of "dire necessity." Offering Elsie 10 shillings for their children.

It was a stretch, but maybe not too much of a stretch, to compare him with the likes of Dennis Whelan. John Nolan had told me about him in one of his history lessons. He'd stolen a couple of sheep in Tipperary during the famine, His family were starving, and he told the court that he'd taken them out of "dire necessity." The same words Jack used.

Whelan was transported to Bermuda, locked up in a rat-infested prison hulk, and forced to work with African slaves. In comparison, Jack's sentence was a walk in the park, but there was a similarity. Both men had been desperate — and their desperation came from the same source: centuries of brutality, indifference, and oppression.

What would I have done if I'd have been Jack? I don't know. The shop was gone, the mill broken up, and he had no profession, property, or money. With De Valera's economic war, there were no jobs, and even if he could have found one, the wages would have been so low he wouldn't have been able to find a place to live. To cap it all, he had a wife and two young children to look after. The only thing he could fall back on was his IRA experience and the arsenal at Kilcloney.

As I headed off to get another coffee, I tried to imagine what it must have been like for him in prison. It couldn't have been easy. Having said that, it couldn't have been easy for Josie either. She would have had to fend for herself as a single mother. Poor law relief was a pittance, and to get it she would have had to face a panel of local do-gooders who'd decide whether she was worthy enough to receive it. It must have been soul-destroying and embarrassing. Especially in such a small community, where everyone knew your business.

Despite that, my mother said Josie always held her head high. She made their clothes, bred and sold pigs in the back yard, and kept the family from going under. She cycled everywhere and was sometimes gone for hours. I imagine some of those rides took her into Kilkenny to buy groceries and bits and pieces for the house. I guess others would have taken her the fifty miles or so to Portlaois.

As for Jack — it seemed that when he told me he'd been quartermaster for the brigade, he'd been telling the truth. In his statement to O'Brien, he said he'd had those weapons since 1919 — the start of the Anglo-Irish war. It must have been dangerous. If James Lillis had been executed for possessing a single rifle, I dread what would have happened if the Free State had found his store. It also begged the question, did his parents know? With so many secret nooks and crannies built into the house, I would have thought it impossible they didn't. He told me his father built the extension to the old house when he was a teenager. Maybe Jack excavated the dugout then. If that was the case, not only did his father know about it — he probably condoned it.

This must have been where he'd made the nitro-glycerine he told me about. Maybe he'd hidden there after the

Graney ambush. Perhaps he was hiding there when the Free State soldiers broke up the mill. As for the smaller compartment O'Brien found in the dairy, my best guess was that it served the same purpose as that hole beneath his shed in Sparkhill. To hide the still he used to make poteen, the offence he was arrested for back in 1925.

Jack's story was coming together, albeit in bits and drabs. It seems he'd told me a little of what he'd got up to in the Anglo-Irish war and hardly anything about what he did in the Civil one — and he certainly hadn't spoken about the bank robbery. I suppose the war with the British was generally accepted as a battle that had to be fought and one he was proud to have been part of. The Civil War was far less civil. It was brother against brother, friend against friend, and I can imagine it got very dirty and hurtful. As for the robbery, I can totally understand why he never spoke about it. For him, it was an embarrassment. Something out of character he bitterly regretted.

When I returned to my desk, I re-opened the A1 folder. I wasn't expecting to find anything else, but this time I had more of an open mind. It was just as well. Three months after the robbery at Taghmon, I found another item. This time it was about Nell. She'd been arrested by Sargent Cody, one of the men Fahey singled out for praise after Jack's arrest. It read that between the 3rd and 18th of February, she "unlawfully and feloniously received one national bank consolidated note for £10 and one for £5 — knowing both to be stolen from the national bank of Taghmon."

It seemed that Conry had recorded the serial numbers of the stolen notes and circulated them amongst the banks. When she tried to pass them off in New Ross, they were spotted and the manager called the police.

When Cody read her the usual caution, she politely answered, "Thank you." Then he took her to Bagnalstown barracks. A quick rummage through her handbag revealed she was carrying "two, ten-pound notes, (£900 each) a pound note, (£90) two half-crowns, (£45) three florins, one shilling, two six pennies, eight pennies and three half pennies." She also had "5 national health insurance cheques worth around five pounds" (£450).

Cody predictably asked if they were hers. She predictably answered that they were. A quick check through the serial numbers confirmed she was lying. A few weeks later, she was brought up before the omnipresent district judge Fahey.

By now, Fahey must have known the Kielys well. One or other of them had been up before him for a plethora of offences, including Bunclody, Ballyanne, Taghmon — maybe others I wasn't aware of. As for Nell's defence lawyer, I wasn't surprised to see she'd chosen R.J. Brennan.

As usual, he began by praising Fahey, then slipped in a request for bail. When he refused, Nell burst into tears and begged to see her children. Her reaction took me by surprise. The Nell I'd known in the seventies had been wiry and strong, with that same devil-may-care attitude Jack had. I would have thought she would have kept her emotions to herself and stonewalled it out. Still, having to leave children so young must have been heartbreaking. Nancy, the eldest, would only have been four, Larry three. At her brother's trial, she'd been pregnant with Michael, so he couldn't have been older than three months or so.

Fahey obviously took pity on her and agreed. After she'd kissed them goodbye, she was taken under police escort to the station. Half an hour later, she was put on the 4 pm train to Dublin. From there, by armoured car to Mountjoy.

At the subsequent hearing in Wexford, Davitt again was the circuit judge. After a short trial, he sentenced her to fifteen months hard labour. The caveat was that if she persuaded her brothers to reveal where the guns and money were hidden, he'd ask the Minister of Justice to be lenient.

Predictably, she refused.

Fifteen months was a long time, and I wondered who looked after her children when she was away. Maybe her husband, Michael — although I doubt it. The newspaper report said she and the children moved out of the family home in New Ross during the Taghmon trial and had lived at Kilcloney ever since. Why she left him, I have no idea. Perhaps he threw her out when her brothers were arrested. He had a good job, and it couldn't have looked good when his in-laws were arrested for armed robbery. On the other hand, it might have had something to do with baby Michael. The family rumour was she used to dye his hair red — the same colour as her husband's. Perhaps Mike Sr. had doubts about his son's paternity.

I took another sip of coffee and glanced up at the clock. Four forty-five. The Archive would be closing in just less than an hour. Still amazed by the torrent of information I'd discovered in just one morning, I decided to leaf through to the end of 1935 and leave it at that. Nell's sentence for trying to pass off the stolen money surely had to be it, but there was one last surprise. An article in the *New Ross Times* dated 3rd November 1935. It was a few weeks after she'd been released from Mountjoy, and it was headed up: "Dangerous lunatic arrested."

The "dangerous lunatic" was Nell and this time it was her sister Mary who'd shopped her to the police.

Mary told the court that when her husband died in 1931, she'd moved back to the family home. She paid the rent and rates and around the time of the robbery, Nell moved in. When Nell went to prison, Mary looked after her children. A few days earlier, she'd left Kilcloney to visit her Uncle Mike at Coolnabrone in Kilkenny. "I left at around 9.30 and returned at 5 or 8 in the evening. When I got home, my mother, the accused, Ellen Doyle, and her three children were there."

It seems Uncle Mike had some sort of accident, and she was looking after him. She told Nell she'd have to stay the night as "it wasn't fair to leave him by himself."

Mike was another of Biddy's brothers, and I'd heard Jack say he'd died in 1935 in Coolnabrone — so it all neatly fitted the narrative.

Nell asked if she was coming back the next day. Mary said it depended on how he was. She then went to fetch her hat and coat. When she returned, Nell told her she had to sign over control of Kilcloney when she got back. That's when it all seems to have kicked off. Mary told her that wasn't going to happen until she received her inheritance and Nell repaid some other monies she owed her.

This was interesting stuff. Another part of the family history I never knew — yet one that fitted in so well with the few fragments I'd been told. There were two big questions here: Why did Nell want control of Kilcloney, and why did she think she was entitled to it? I suppose there was also a third. What did she mean by control? Even though Jas was in prison, he still owned the place, so control must have meant something different.

Either way, according to the papers, Nell then got feisty. "We'll see," she said. "Remember I have a revolver." According to Mary, she started "jumping up and down" threatening to "blow her brains out." Then she leapt on a chair, reached up to the top of a partition near the fireplace, and asked again if she was coming back. Mary must have thought she had a gun- hidden up there somewhere, as she told the court she was frightened out of her wits and promised she would.

That night she stayed at her Uncle Mike's. The next day, instead of returning home, she headed to the barracks in Borris. According to her statement, she told Sergeant Evers what happened, and he immediately drove over to Kilcloney.

I assume the Guards were still anxious to find the weapons used in the bank raid, and Evers must have thought this was his chance to shine. When he arrived, he arrested Nell as a "dangerous lunatic" and took her to the barracks. Leaving her locked in a cell, he then drove back to Kilcloney with Mary.

From what I'd read about O'Brien's exhaustive search of the place, I would have thought he would have found every weapon that could conceivably have been hidden there. It appeared he hadn't. Mary pointed out the spot Nell reached up to in the kitchen and Evers climbed up to take a closer look.

He found a piece of wallpaper that had been whitewashed over. When he ripped it away, he saw a board covering yet another secret compartment. Inside was a long-nosed parabellum, a short-nosed one, a Colt revolver, and six rounds of ammunition.

I couldn't help smiling to myself. So that explained where Jack had hidden the guns. All those times he'd told my father they were still at Kilcloney were just a wind-up. On the other hand, perhaps no one told him they'd been found. After all, he was in Portlaoise at the time — and maybe after he got out, he never had the chance to go back and check.

When Evers returned to the station, he read Nell a caution, to which she responded with what seemed to be her characteristic reply: "Thank you." Then he had her examined by a Dr. Pat Reid, hoping to have her certified insane. Reid refused.

Mr O'Hare, who was her defence lawyer, said that "her brothers, as everyone knew, were in prison." They as well as his client had certain political "interests and sympathies" and it was clear that "what happened on that night had come about because of those."

It seemed like an odd thing to say. I wasn't sure what part of Nell trying to shoot Mary was down to politics — apart from the fact that she had access to IRA revolvers hidden in the wall.

Foley was the prosecution's lawyer and argued that Nell should be sent up to the circuit court for trial. Judge Tommy O'Shea wasn't keen. He said that if Foley didn't object and Nell pleaded guilty, he could deal with the matter himself. He added that "no order could be made that could increase the torture already endured by the two women."

"Torture." That was a harsh word. Reading between the lines, I was becoming more convinced this wasn't just your usual run-of-the-mill disagreement. Maybe politics did have bigger part to play in all this than I'd thought. I'd read about families being pulled apart by civil war before, and maybe this was an example in my own. Certainly, If Mary had been pro-treaty, it offered a better explanation as to why Jack had sent me off to enquire after her but wouldn't follow up with a visit of his own.

Back in court, Foley agreed with the judge. Despite being the prosecutor, I'm pretty sure he would have known the Kielys personally. Even I knew Foley. Not that Foley, of course, but his grandson, who still has a practice in Bagnalstown. Ireland is a small place, and back then it would have been even smaller. Reading between the lines, he and O'Shea seemed to have an empathy for Nell you wouldn't find in the Old Bailey.

Despite the severity of the threat, and the fact she'd been found in control of yet another arsenal of unlicensed weapons, O'Shea merely bound her over to keep the peace. He also ordered that she shouldn't enter Kilcloney without being accompanied by a guard.

It seemed a shame politics had caused so much animosity between the sisters. Mary looked after Nell's children when she was in Mountjoy. She'd taken care of their mother, she'd paid the rent and rates — she was even looking after their Uncle Mike. It seemed to me she was only doing her best to help out. Certainly, the guns in the wall story explained that tale Michael told me back in the seventies. The one where he pointed out the dent in the wall and told me it was where his mother took a potshot at her. Someone probably told him the real story when he was young, and over the years it grew and twisted in his mind to a fully-fledged gun battle.

I left the Archives around five and was home by six thirty. The next day was Friday, and I woke early and made up for lost time by taking the kids go-carting. That evening we had dinner in a new restaurant near New Ross, and on Saturday we dropped into Kilcloney to say our goodbyes.

Like the "Johns" and "Jameses" before him, Nell's eldest son, Larry, had inherited the mill and married a woman named Mary. As their children were roughly the same age as mine, they occasionally played together, and that Sunday they did just that in the yard outside.

I hadn't been inside Kilcloney since Larry got married, and while I was there — and in the light of what I'd discovered in the Archives — I took the opportunity of taking a more well-informed look around. The dent in the wall that Michael pointed out was no longer there. Nor was the wooden stool in the corner. The open fire had been replaced by a shiny new range.

From my conversation with Larry, it seemed Mary as the new woman of the house had insisted on making a few changes — not dissimilar, I suppose, to the Biddy and Mary that went before her. She'd had the place gutted and a new modern kitchen installed. I daresay if her workmen had found any more weapons, I would have heard about it. As for stolen cash, I'm pretty sure that would have been spent long ago.

Having said that, its disappearance was still a mystery. Jack had been caught with some silver in a bag and Nell with a few pounds — but there was no real account of the bulk of it. I'm pretty sure Jack hadn't had it. When he got out of prison, he moved into the old house in Ballinagree and lived a far from ostentatious life. As for Nell — if the state of Kilcloney in the sixties was anything to go by, I doubt she'd had it either.

After tea, Mary, Larry, and the kids waved us off from the yard. As we turned onto the Dublin Road to head up to the ferry, I suspected the old mill still held more secrets. What they were, I didn't know, and I didn't have the time to find out. I'd gone as far as I could in my quest for Jack's truth, and it had thrown up a whole can of worms I hadn't been expecting.

Perhaps it was finally time to let sleeping dogs lie.

CHAPTER TWENTY-TWO

A new chapter

After the sentence was read out, all three men were led down to the holding cells of the Wexford court. A day later, they were taken under armed escort by train to Mountjoy gaol in Dublin.

As they sat together with their guards, Jim Treacy was worried. He'd turned King's evidence on his neighbours. They'd seen him relish the attention he received when he turned them in. Now it was reckoning time. He knew what the Kielys were capable of. He knew they were well connected with the anti-treaty prisoners inside. Whichever way he looked at it, his twelve-month sentence wasn't going to be easy.

As for Jack and Jas, they felt betrayed. The majority of evidence given during the trial had either been circumstantial or could have been batted away by Brennan. Jim's statement put them firmly in the frame, and once he'd opened his mouth, there was no going back.

The "Joy" predominantly housed "local" prisoners or "in-outers" — career criminals who spent most of their lives in and out of the system. It also acted as a temporary clearing house for convicts waiting to be allocated elsewhere.

While Jas was there, Nell wrote to him saying that it would be better if she had control of Kilcloney rather than Mary. As the eldest sister, the courts had granted control of the place to her until he got out of prison. Nell wasn't happy about it. Mary had never supported their struggle, and it didn't seem fair that she was now able to pull the strings. Besides, she couldn't be trusted. She might do something underhand like sell up and take the money.

Jas had no reason to believe that might happen. Having said that, he was in no position to argue and wrote back to say that if Mary agreed, he had no objection. Every letter sent from the prison had to be read and censored by the Governor. Before he went out, it was stamped in red ink: *Mountjoy prison*.

Discipline in the Joy was lax. Portlaoise wasn't like that and six months into their sentences, they were taken from their cells and loaded into an open-backed transport wagon to be taken there. As the wagon left Dublin, Jas — still handcuffed — jumped out. The wagon had slowed down at a corner, but it was still doing twenty when he hit the ground.

The guards, annoyed at his attempted escape, gave him a beating. When they returned him to Mountjoy, they dragged him to the hospital to be examined. Years on the run and ill-treatment in Wicklow had taken his toll. With a low muscle mass and a weak core, it turned out that his injuries were life-changing. The prison doctor concluded that either from the fall or the way he'd been treated by the warders, his back had been broken.

The governor signed his release papers a few months later on compassionate grounds. Until his death twelve years later, he was confined to his room in Kilcloney, bedridden and in constant pain.

Jack and Jim's transfer continued a month later. As they were driven into Portlaoise town, the prison loomed up like a mediaeval castle. Its walls were grey foreboding granite, and it looked as stark as they'd been told. Once through the gates, however, they found themselves in a well-tended flower garden. Above the entrance to the Governor's office was a colourful canopy of roses.

Still in handcuffs, they were escorted into the reception area and placed in a waiting room. A few minutes later, they were taken to the office to be weighed, photographed, and fingerprinted.

The prison uniform was a heavy, coarse wool suit printed with the iconic thick black stripe of a convict. As Jim was a first — or what the prison termed "Star select" — offender, he was given an additional outfit for Sundays, made from lighter wool with a more subtle stripe. To complete the transformation, they were both given matching caps and neckcloths.

Treadmill

Jack couldn't get Jas out of his head. He hadn't been allowed to send or receive a letter from his brother since the accident. Jim was more concerned about himself. Not only did he need to worry about Jack, but he'd also seen Jas being beaten up and heard that prisoners could be flogged. As he was escorted to his cell, a million questions flooded his mind. Not least was to what his "hard labour" sentence meant. He'd heard it defined somewhere as that "which kept a man always breathing hard and perspiring." An old lag at the "Joy" had also mentioned the treadmill.

A Mr. Cubbitt of Ipswich had invented it back in 1817. Its purpose was to pump water up a gradient using manpower. When it was adopted by the prison system, it morphed into something more insidious. Prisoners were forced to face a wall and climb an equivalent of 14,000 feet in a gruelling ten-hour day. No water was being pumped and human interaction was strictly verboten. Cubbitt's friend, the prison reformer Rev Sidney Smith, was a great fan.

"I advocate the treadmill," he wrote, "on some such species of labour where the prisoner cannot see the results of his toil and pushing." He went on to say that "a prisoner should not profit from his prison labour, not a single shilling. There should be no tea or sugar [for them] — nothing but beating hemp, pulling oakum, and powdering bricks. No work but what is tedious. The treadmill should prove a perpetual example before the eyes of all those who want it, affecting the imagination only with horror and disgust and affording great ease to the government."

Fortunately for Jim, neither flogging nor the treadmill had been used at Portlaoise for thirty years. Nor had "picking oakum," where hard labour prisoners had been forced to unravel ropes as tough as iron to make hemp for caulking ships. These days they were merely expected to manage the gardens on the thirty-acre farm or work in the on-site factories dedicated to shoemaking and laundry work.

Jack plumbed for shoemaking. He was good with his hands, and he had an eye for detail. Jim took work anywhere he could to keep out of Jack's way.

Their new home was the three-storey E block. Homosexuality wouldn't be legalised in Ireland until 1977, and the ground floor housed sex offenders — mainly gay men. Jack and Jim were housed in E2, the floor above. Even numbered cells on one side held "Star select" prisoners like Jim. Odd numbers on the other were for old offenders like Jack. Floors E3 and E4 took the temporary overflow from gaols like Limerick and Mountjoy.

Over the first few days, Jack paced out his cell. It was twelve feet by seven. The door was solid metal with a spy hole the size of a 10p piece. Opposite was a small, curve-paned window set high in the wall. Thick bars lay behind it. To the left were two shelves. The one on the top was for books. The one at the bottom for toiletries. In the centre was a table. On it were two enamel mugs and a plate. The authorities also provided a salt cellar, a tin knife, and a spoon — but oddly enough, no fork. Beneath the window was an enamel hand basin and a chamber pot. An iron bedstead with a hard mattress coconut mattress was to the right of the door. There was also an electric light, a few thin blankets, and a bell that could be rung in case of an emergency.

Discipline was tough. Jack was expected to keep his cell pristine by getting down on his hands and knees each morning to scrub the floor an almost iridescent white. Breakfast at 08.30 was a pint of thick oatmeal porridge, a few slices of bread, and a hot mug of sickly-sweet tea. Dinner on Tuesdays and Thursdays was a pint of soup with meat and vegetables. On Mondays and Wednesdays, Irish stew and more soup. Sundays offered the best fare, with a generous helping of corn beef, cabbage, and fresh potatoes from the garden.

Every Sunday, holy day, and bank holiday, the warders took the day off, and Jack and the other prisoners were kept locked up in solitary. There was time for exercise, but little chance to fraternise. Six paved circuits separated by thin strips of grass ran like racetracks around the yard. When allowed out to walk, each prisoner had to keep four yards from the man in front, and talking wasn't allowed.

With such a regime, it was easy for Jim to stay out of Jack's way. Within a year, he was home in Ballymartin. He was lucky. If Nell hadn't been in prison herself, she would likely have made his life as much a misery there as it had been in Portlaoise.

Jack still had six years to go, and it wasn't until two years into his sentence that he was officially allowed to read a newspaper. The big headlines of the day were George V dying at Sandringham, Charlie Chaplin releasing *Modern Times*, and Adolf Hitler winning the German parliament with a record 92.1% of the vote. There was also great optimism that the economy might lift. The British had agreed to ease their economic embargo and had signed an agreement to increase the import of coal and cattle.

As far as Jack was concerned, De Valera was handling things well. He'd released Cosgrave's IRA prisoners, banned the Blueshirts, and now he'd forced the British to back down on their embargo. If he continued in a similar vein, perhaps semi-political prisoners like him might be released early.

What Jack didn't know was that De Valera was having second thoughts. The IRA were champing at the bit for him to lead a military action against the British, and in their enthusiasm, they were getting out of hand. Using the 1931

Public Safety Act first introduced by the Free State, he decided to ban them.

The move came as a total surprise. Within a few hours, Moss Twoomey, the IRA leader, was arrested and sentenced to three years for membership of an illegal organisation. De Valera faced a possible mutiny from his supporters, but gambled that his next move would recover his hard-line support.

While Edward VIII complained he couldn't rule "without the woman he loved," the Long Fella took advantage of the chaos and rewrote the Irish constitution. In it, he defined Ireland as the whole island of Ireland, along with its islands and seas. Its name would be Éire and its first language, Irish. It was to have its own flag, and he as President would replace the King as head of state.

Jack was delighted but confused. It was all well and good unilaterally declaring a one-island Ireland, but the British wouldn't just hand over the North. There was no way De Valera could realise his vision without an armed insurrection — and without the IRA, how could that be done? Certainly, his chance of being let out anytime soon seemed highly unlikely. By 1936, the status of Republican prisoners — a status Jack felt he deserved — had once more moved from freedom fighter to enemy of the state. That summer, a number of plays and cinema performances in Dublin were interrupted in protest. The statements read out by young Republican women during the intervals said, "We don't intend to interfere in any way with the performance, but we want to tell you some facts which the daily papers are prevented from publishing."

They went on the complain about the conditions for Republicans in various prisons — including Arbour Hill, where *An Phlobacht* publisher Donal O'Donahue and Tomas MacCurtain, son of the murdered Lord mayor of Cork, were at least twenty days into a hunger strike.

In support, Jack decided to follow suit. Over the following couple of weeks, he was subject to a regime of force feeding. In a procedure likened to rape, he was strapped to a chair while a thick rubber tube was forced into his stomach to deliver a concoction of milk and egg.

The lack of food and the brutality of the process left him weak and susceptible to disease. One morning, the wardens found him coughing sputum. His tongue and throat were covered with a thick white mucus, and they suspected diphtheria. They'd had outbreaks before, and in the days before antibiotics — particularly in a weakened state — it was often fatal. Immediately, they called an ambulance to take him the short distance to Abbeyleix Hospital.

Abbeyleix was run by the Sisters of the Little Company of Mary, known as the "Blue sisters." They were disease specialists, and they sent a telegram to Josie telling her to come immediately, as there was every chance Jack might die.

As the sisters encouraged him to eat and pumped him full of anti-toxins, Josie cycled into Borris and hired a cab. Stopping off to leave Maureen with her mother, she took six-year-old Birdie with her in case it might be her last chance to see her father.

Two hours later, a nun met them at the hospital entrance. She led them up a flight of metal steps to the isolation ward. Jack was in a room on his own. Josie, in tears, asked how he was. When the nun shook her head, she took a bottle of holy water from her handbag. It had been sold to her by one of the priests at the Sacred Heart, and she sprinkled a few drops across him. The sister who'd led them in held her hand as she knelt by his bedside and began a round of Hail Marys. Birdie, overwhelmed, looked on, transfixed by the grey-white fur that covered her father's tongue, a memory that would remain with her for the rest of her life.

Josie managed to persuade him to give up his hunger strike. Even so, Jack remained at Abbeyleix for nearly three months. As he slowly recovered, many IRA hard-liners saw the writing on the wall. De Valera had unilaterally declared an independent united Ireland, which was what they'd always wanted. There didn't seem to be any point in continuing the struggle in the South, and many started to drift off. Over the next few years, their numbers dwindled to just a handful of extremists.

One of those was Sean Russell. A veteran of the Easter Rising, he'd recently taken over the IRA leadership — and he was as much anti-British as pro-Republican. As Jack was escorted back to Portlaoise to complete his sentence, Neville Chamberlain signed the Munich agreement. At the same time, Russell proposed his "S" or sabotage plan. His idea, as always, was to attack Britain when it was at its weakest and, like Roger Casement thirty years earlier, he had no problem asking the Germans for support.

On 12th January 1939, just nine months before war broke out, his army council sent the following letter to the British foreign secretary, Lord Halifax:

> *I have the honour to inform you that the Government of the Irish Republic, having as its first duty towards its people the establishment and maintenance of peace and order here, demand the withdrawal of all British armed forces stationed in Ireland. The occupation of*

our territory by troops of another nation and the persistent subvention here of activities directly against the expressed national will and in the interests of a foreign power, prevent the expansion and development of our institution in consonance with our social needs and purposes and must cease.

The Government of the Irish Republic believe that a period of four days is sufficient notice for your Government to signify its intentions in the matter of the military evacuation and for the issue of your Declaration of Abdication in respect of our country. Our Government reserves the right of appropriate action without further notice if, upon the expiration of this period of grace, these conditions remain unfulfilled.

A week or so later, the first IRA bombs went off in Manchester and London.

At the time, most people thought De Valera was behind it. He'd refused to join Britain in the war, and now it looked like he was trying to exert military pressure to realise his vision for constitutional change. That wasn't the case. Beneath the gruff Republican exterior, his relationship with the British was good. A year earlier, Chamberlain had agreed to lift the trade tariffs if he settled the land annuities disagreement. De Valera offered a one-off payment of £10mn (£915mn) — a drop in the ocean compared with the actual amount owed. To his surprise, the ever-genial Chamberlain agreed and, as a bonus, he handed back the treaty ports.

De Valera had established a good working relationship with Chamberlain, and he didn't want Russell messing it up. On the other hand, he couldn't openly condemn him, as that would alienate his grassroots support. It might also start another civil war. Pragmatic as always, he concluded that his best course of action was to help the British stop Russell while appearing to his public to be, at best, neutral.

In 1939, he secretly wrote to Churchill, asking him to provide intelligence that could smear the IRA leader as a communist agent.

> It is believed that some 10 or 12 years ago, he [Russell] was in Soviet pay as an agitator; If there is any information which could be made available to show that this was the case, or that at present he is in receipt of pay from foreign sources, it would be of the greatest possible assistance to the Dublin authorities in dealing with him since it would practically eliminate the risk of him being treated as a patriotic martyr....

Not content with subterfuge, he then introduced the "Emergency Powers Act." It included the death penalty for subversion and was every bit as draconian as legislation introduced by Cosgrave's cabinet during the Civil War.

Paddy McGrath, Russell's right-hand man in Britain, was one of the first to fall foul of it. He was arrested when he returned to Ireland and faced the death penalty. He immediately went on hunger strike, and the Labour Party pushed for his release. Some TDs cited his record as a hero of 1916, and Liam Tobin, a leading political figure in Fianna Fail, said that it "...would be a tragedy if he lost his life, no matter what we may think of the aims and methods pursued by himself and those associated with him."

Under intense political and moral pressure, De Valera released him.

It turned out to be a mistake. On Christmas day, the IRA broke into the Magazine Fort in Phoenix Park. The culprits got away, but six months later, following a tip-off, the Guards raided a house in Dublin. There they found McGrath and a man called Harte, who'd also been involved in the S-Plan campaign. As they tried to escape, they shot and killed two police officers.

Eventually, both men were captured and sentenced to death. Again, hard-liners — including Kathleen Clarke, the widow of the famous 1916 leader, Tom Clarke — called for their executions to be halted. Despite this intervention, De Valera was determined not to make the same mistake again. He ordered that they should both hang.

Throughout the war, he hung more IRA men than the British ever did. He even borrowed their executioner, Albert Pierrepoint, to do it. He also interred over 1,500 suspects, and for anyone insisting on political status, he made sure conditions were harsh. Refusal to wear prison uniform resulted in solitary confinement, twenty-four hours a day, with just a blanket to keep out the cold.

There were hunger strikes, of course, and one of the most memorable was in Portlaoise. – In the same year Jack was released Seán McCaughey, an IRA officer who'd been carrying on the fight in the North, started a life sentence. He complained that he should be held as a political, rather than a criminal, prisoner and refused to wear prison clothes. Three years later he went on hunger strike and after ten days without food or water, he died. At the inquest, the prison doctor said that during his time in Portlaois, he hadn't been allowed to "exercise or get fresh air or sunlight," adding that, "he would not treat his dog the way Seán McCaughey had been treated..."

On his release, Jack went home to live with Josie and his children in their new home in Ballinagree. While she continued to breed and sell pigs, he tried to bring money into the household by mending shoes — a skill he'd learned in the prison workshop.

His mother died the same year, tended to the last by Mary. She didn't want him coming to the funeral. He'd brought disgrace to the family and heartache to their mother. In the end, she changed her mind, but not before insisting Bridie be buried in Ballinkillen — twelve long miles from her husband's grave in St. Mullins. After all, it was John who encouraged the boys to take up arms in the first place and it was she who'd been left to pick up the pieces.

Bridie had drawn the short straw of having to care for a much older man and a dysfunctional family. She'd suffered years of misery and heartache as her livelihood crumbled around her As far as Mary was concerned she deserved to rest in peace as far from the troublesome Kielys as possible.

Over the next couple of years, Jack commuted to England to find work. Eventually, he secured a permanent position at the United Wireworks in Birmingham. As the war in Europe was coming to an end, he locked up the house in Ballinagree, said goodbye to his old life in Borris, and headed off to start a new chapter with his young family in England.

CHAPTER TWENTY-THREE

The last word

Last year, I made my annual pilgrimage to Ireland. It had been twenty years since I'd found those newspaper reports in Wexford and a lot of water had gushed under the bridge since then. I was divorced, my children had grown up, and my father had died.

My mother was still living at the bungalow, and I'd stayed with her while I was there. Before heading home, I decided to make St. Mullins my last port of call.

I left the car in the small car park by the river and walked up the steep hill to the cemetery. It was wet and windy, but as usual the views across to Mount Brandon were Scandinavian and spectacular.

As I reached the top, I looked across to the Norman Motte. As a child, I would run up and down it like a lunatic, and remembering those times plunged me into a mire of nostalgia. A lot had changed in Ireland since I'd first come over. Back in the sixties, men wore flat caps and dusty old suits, smoked pipes, and drove a pony and trap. Since the Celtic Tiger, they sport Raybans, suck on vapes, and drive Mercedes. It was tempting to hark back and bemoan the loss of a more simple and innocent life. But if I did that, I told myself, I'd be accused of being a tourist. And as Jarvis Cocker said, "Everyone hates a tourist."

Times back then were hard, and whilst dusty flat caps looked quaint, I know they hid a lot of despair. Maybe it was good they'd been consigned to the dustbin of history, but one thing that had changed for the worst was community spirit. Neighbours rarely dropped in to see my mom. The Sacred Heart was practically empty on Sundays, and the glue that held Borris together didn't seem quite as sticky as it had been — or at least, that's the way it looked to me.

I opened the little gate into the graveyard and walked a few yards down the path. There, on the right, was the Kiely headstone. It was remarkably well maintained, and it struck me this was one of the many contrasts with England. Over there, headstones were invariably choked with weeds, covered in lichen, or sunk into oblivion. In contrast, the Irish seemed to have a neolithic veneration of the dead. The fact that there wasn't a weed in sight was down to an interesting piece of theology. Each year, a festival called a "Pattern" was held, usually to coincide with "cemetery Sunday." People came from miles around. Prayers were said and devotions were held. Relatives of the dead would spend the day cleaning their graves and decorating them with fresh flowers. It was a clever way for the church to save money — and how some people went about it, you'd think it was a competition.

I wasn't sure who cleaned the Kiely grave that year. I suspect it was Nell's grandson, Laurence.

When Jas died in 1947, Mary was living in New Ross with her third husband. Jack had moved to Birmingham. Young Bridie was studying nursing in England, and Nell found herself the unlikely inheritor of the old mill.

She died in 1978, leaving it to her son, Larry. Larry died in 2018 and left it to his son Laurence. Just a year or so later, Laurence built himself a fine new house opposite the old mill, roughly where a Mr. Fox — a dyeing expert and one of Jack's father's old hands — lived in the nineteenth century.

Michael died a few months before his brother, and both their names had been added to the headstone. I wasn't religious, so I didn't offer up a prayer, but I sat on a nearby bench and conjured up memories of them helping Jack to build his bungalow back in the 70s. They were great dancers, often touring around to different feis, doing their jigs and reels and so on. It was sad to see them gone. Larry the perfect gentleman. Michael the joker, good friend to my father and teller of ghost stories.

Holy Cross Church

St. Mullins had a comforting air of permanence about it. Nothing had changed much since I was a child — and I suspected it still looked frightening similar to how it did in Johannes's day.

The same wasn't true of Taghmon. I'd driven there that morning, and as odd as it was to say, I'd never been there before.

It was nothing like I imagined: essentially two roads bustling with shops and businesses overlooked by an old Norman tower. After a coffee, I found the road to New Ross and a hundred yards or so out of town I found George Love's old bank. Of course, it wasn't a bank anymore, but the building was still there. A large, picturesque private house with roses in the front garden and a neat metal rail running around the front wall. I tried looking for the gate Jack had climbed over. There was one, but I couldn't swear it was the same. I also took the liberty of walking down a side entrance and peering over the fence. From there, I could see a low window looking out onto the garden. Again, I wondered if this was the one he'd climbed through — but again I couldn't be sure.

A few hundred yards on, I found a narrow lane off the main road. It fitted the description of where Jack had parked the Clyno, and I reckoned it didn't look much different than it had in the thirties. There was still an outhouse with a muddy layby outside — possibly the one where Phillip Kavanagh found the mask and the tyre tracks. I also timed how long it took for me to drive there from Borris. About forty-five minutes, which beat Kearney's drive by a good half an hour — although in fairness, I probably used different roads.

A couple of days earlier, I'd driven up to Belfast. Like Taghmon, it was my first time there and I wondered what sort of reception I'd get. My knowledge of the place was based on 1970s TV reports of armoured vehicles and loud, rough people shouting and throwing petrol bombs. As it happened, it was nothing like that. My reason for going was to see the Holy Cross Church. It was slap in the middle of the Crumlin Road, and I had an odd feeling when I walked in. I assumed nothing much had changed, and there at the end of the aisle was a font, presumably the one my mother had been baptised in ninety years before. The priest was around, and I decided to tell him my story — or at least part of it. He disappeared into the vestry and returned with a large red book. He flicked through a few pages and showed me an entry in large, black, flowery writing: "Bridget Doyle. The 6th of August 1928." The book also noted that there were some witnesses. They were the Byrnes, and my first guess was that they were probably the Byrnes of Glynn — relatives of Jack through his Aunt Kate. The priest, however, said they might be related to a family that lived opposite the church, and he gave me their address and told me to pop in.

Initially, I wasn't sure I should disturb them — then I decided that since I'd come so far, I might as well. I left my car with its English registration plate in the church carpark and walked down to their house. When I knocked on the door, they invited me in without a question. Bearing in mind the history of the province, I thought it decidedly odd. I was a total stranger, and for all they knew I might have had an Armalite tucked under my coat. The lady of the house asked me if I wanted a cup of tea and invited me to sit by the fire. It was scorching hot outside, but it would have been rude to refuse. It was only then her husband asked what I was after and how he could help.

I gave them the potted history, but as it turned out, they weren't related to the Byrnes at that christening. Still, they were helpful. I told them Jack had lived in Foyle St. They told me it had gone years ago, bombed out of existance during the war. In its place was Foyle court, and it was down near the Harland and Wolff shipyard in the Protestant area.

I finished off my tea and bade them farewell. When I picked up the car, I thought it would be just a quick two-minute drive to what was only a couple of roads along. As it happened, huge concrete bollards forced me to drive around the estate for another ten minutes before I got there. This was obviously a way of keeping the two communities apart, and it brought home to me that normality for the people up there was still a long way off.

On my detour, I got to see some of the murals I'd seen on TV — and I had to admit that although tasteless, they were quite well done. On the Catholic side was a landscape of the Irish Tricolour surrounded by the hunger strikers who'd died in the Maize. On the Unionist side, a painting of the Queen and a soldier in Oliver Crowell's new model army, running some unlucky peasant through with a pike.

Jack's mugshot

Foyle Court was effectively a new housing estate. I parked the car and approached a man cleaning out a rabbit hutch. I told him the same story — omitting that Jack was a Catholic. The man, presumably Protestant and equally as friendly as the Byrnes, put his rabbits back in the hutch and did his best to fill me in with the local history.

It seemed such a pity – such kind people divided by so much hatred. As Frankie once said "War, what is it good for?"

Jas' mugshot

I was quite sad to leave the North. I would have liked to have got to know the people better — but then again, it probably would have ended in tears, most of them mine. As Dublin was on the way back, I'd made plans to visit the records office in Bishop Street. Parking wasn't easy, but once I was there, I settled in and, as usual, elicited the help of the librarians. Within a few minutes, there was a folder on my desk with Jack's court records. As I opened it up, I saw his photograph in crystal clear black and white. It was the first one I'd seen of him under the age of sixty. He was thirty-four, and I knew that because it was his mugshot for the Taghmon robbery. He was wearing a flat cap and a thick coat — which I found odd because even to have a passport photograph accepted these days you need to at least take your hat off.

It seemed odd I'd never seen a photograph of his young self before that — but with the benefit of hindsight, I suppose it made sense. If he'd spent most of his life on the run or trying to evade the police, he would have gone out of his way to make sure there was no record of what he looked like.

As for his mugshot, I noticed that his jaw was slightly swollen on one side. In later years when he felt anxious or under the weather, that would often happen to him. Perhaps he was feeling poorly when the picture was taken — more likely it had been brought on by stress.

There was also a photograph of Jas. It was the first time I'd seen him "in the flesh." He was leaner than Jack, with finer features and a slightly bent nose. He looked very much like Nell's son, Larry. He also resembled an old photograph I'd seen in Kilcloney of his father. Like Jack, he was also wearing a cap and a coat.

As I turned over his photograph, I had another surprise. A mugshot of Nell with horned-rimmed specs, a fur coat, and a cloche cap. She was staring down at the camera and looked as defiant as I might have imagined.

Nell's mugshot

That week was a week of looking around. The day before, I'd driven to Bunclody, which was pretty much as I remembered. Then I headed south to Carrick on Bannow. I'd never been there before, either, and I was surprised that even as one-horse towns in Ireland went, this one took the biscuit. There were two pubs, a village store, and of course, a church. My mother told me that when she was little, she caught pneumonia, and her parents brought her there. It was the church of Mary Immaculate and St. Joseph and she remembered being placed on a table in a room full of candles. A lot of prayers were said, and the priest gave Jack and Josie a small leather pouch filled with something holy they were to keep in her cot. My mother still has it, and it did the trick.

Looking around, I struggled to see where Jack might have had his grocers. I made some enquiries in the newsagents and was surprised that the woman behind the counter still remembered him. "John Doyle, the man who robbed the bank at Taghmon." She brought me out and showed me an empty field where his shop used to be. Apparently, it had been knocked down a few years earlier, the land presumably earmarked for future development.

She spoke about the robbery as if it had happened yesterday. She told me that when the Guards found the dugout at Kilcloney, they removed the outside wall under the front stairwell to get in. Literally hundreds of people from over the County flocked to see where he'd been hiding, and the incident seemed firmly etched in local memory.

A year later, a quick Google search told me that since 1934 there'd been quite a few bank robberies in Taghmon — in fact, the village seemed to be a magnet for them. The one that stuck in my mind was the 2004 raid on the Credit Union, where the raiders creatively used a JCB to rip the cash machine out of the wall. They managed to get away with around £140K. Adjusting for currency value, about twice as much as Jack.

Even so, despite its sheer audacity, it hadn't quite captured the public imagination in the same way as the 1934 raid. I suspect the reason was what followed on afterwards: the discovery of the secret room and the vast haul of military-grade weapons. There was also the Robin Hood factor. Back then, there was still a large minority of hard-liners determined to disrupt the system. Compounding that with the slump in the economy and crippling poverty, people were looking for anti-heroes. Mavericks they'd read about in De Valera's highly censored newspapers, like John Dillinger, Bonnie and Clyde, or "Machine Gun" Kelly. For anyone lacking the courage to pick up a gun and improve their lot, those who did earned their grudging respect. Certainly, from how I saw Jack treated by his peers in the sixties, he'd earned more than his fair share.

By the time I returned to the car, it was beginning to drizzle. I turned on the lights and drove out of St. Mullins towards Borris. My plane was leaving Dublin at three and I had plenty of time to get to the airport. The new motorway had made it so much easier to get there — although the toll charge was a pain. It was so easy to miss or forget that I usually wound up with a fine in the post when I got home. I'd already said my goodbyes to my mother. Now it was time to bid adieu to my father.

I arrived at the New Cemetery just before lunch. It was built on a sports field overlooking Borris, a few hundred yards from Art Kavanagh's viaduct. As a boy, I remember being taken there by Michael to watch the hurling. When they started using it as a burial ground, my father used to joke about how fast it was filling up. Now he was in it, his headstone lonely and cold at the far end.

I stood beside him for a few minutes. He'd been funny, but like his headstone, he'd also been lonely — at least until he met Michael. He might have been English, but he loved Ireland — perhaps as much as Jack — and I missed him dearly.

A few yards nearer the gate was Josie's headstone. Under her name, another had been etched into the marble. It was Jack's. He'd died in 1997, just a year before my father and a few months before the Good Friday agreement had been signed.

I always wondered what he would have made of "Chuckle Brothers," Martin McGuiness and Ian Paisley sharing a joke. I also wondered what he would have made of the Agreement itself. Essentially, that the Irish government would scrap De Valera's 1936 constitutional claim that Northern Ireland belonged to the South in return for the Unionists agreeing to a united Ireland — if a majority in both the North and South voted for it.

To me, it seemed a pragmatic solution. Like it or not, both communities had to live with each other and neither wanted perpetual mayhem. Jack may have felt differently. Peering through the Blairite smoke and mirrors, it might have crossed his mind that, not for the first time, the promise of a United Ireland had been kicked down the road into an uncertain future.

He died when he stood up to use the bathroom.

A nurse had injected a saline drip in his arm and in the dark, he tripped over a tube and smashed his head on the floor. I suppose he had to die sometime, but I wouldn't have been surprised to see him around today if that hadn't happened. I have fond memories of him sitting there in his vest, clenching his fists or giving that characteristic shrug of his depending, on his mood. He'd been in his right mind until the end, and he rarely complained — even though I know he would have preferred to be living in his Bungalow at Ballinagree.

Like Josie, he was waked at Joyce's. The mortician did her best to hide the bruising on his face, and he looked in fine health as he lay, arms folded across his chest in his best suit and tie. His coffin was draped in the Irish tricolour, and as we lowered him into the grave, a unit of hooded men appeared from literally nowhere, rattled some machine gun fire into the air, and disappeared as quickly as they'd arrived.

As we headed back to Shea's for sandwiches, I wondered what his epithet should be. Was he good or bad? Was he right or wrong? Should he have joined the IRA in 1918? Should he have supported De Valera? Should he have robbed the bank?

I'd been raised in a post-war Goldilocks zone. I'd lived through Korea, the Cuban missile crisis, Vietnam, Pol Pot, and Saddam — but to paraphrase Chamberlain, this was stuff that had happened far, far away in countries of which I knew very little.

Jack, on the other hand, understood what it was like to be oppressed. He'd heard about Asgill's atrocities. His father and grandfather had witnessed the horrors of the famine. His aunts, cousins, and uncles had to flee to America to avoid starvation — and he saw how his father had been totally at the mercy of aristocratic English Landlords.

Britain had been promising some sort of self-autonomy to the Irish for hundreds of years, and although Jack wouldn't have put it as elegantly as Newton, he felt British oppression would carry on in perpetuity unless booted out by an outside force.

I think if I'd been around then, I'd be of the same opinion. I'm pretty sure I would have supported an armed insurrection — although whether I'd have been brave enough to participate in it is another matter. Whether Jack should then have gone on to support De Valera in the Civil War is more contentious. Hundreds of books have been written about the Big Fella and the Long Fella. Who did what and why, and who was right and who was wrong?

Having given it some thought, I've concluded that it doesn't matter — at least not to me. Jack decided to support De Valera, and that's that. Whether he was right or wrong depends on your point of view. I suspect his point of view was that a treaty where only half of Ireland was on the cards to be handed back was fundamentally flawed. He believed Collins should have swung the treaty past De Valera before he signed it — regardless of Lloyd George's threats — and that as an ex-London post office oik, he'd been too susceptible to flattery from the likes of aristocrats like Churchill.

Jack was also of the opinion that, as the IRA controlled most of the country by 1921, the British were in a weak position. What Collins knew, and he didn't, was that they'd run dangerously short of guns and ammunition. As Collins confided — possibly foolishly — to Hamar Greenwood, the chief secretary and one of the men who'd introduced the Black and Tans into Ireland: "You had us deadbeat. We couldn't have lasted another three weeks. When we were told of the offer of a truce, we were astonished. We thought you must have gone mad."

When De Valera lost the treaty vote and walked out, Jack was 100% behind him. My own stance might not have been so black and white. Once my patch of Ireland was free, I'd most probably have wanted to get back to a normal life, hope the economy would pick up, and expand the business at Kilcloney. Like De Valera, however, Jack was not a man for compromise. He saw Collins' Free State as a continuation of British oppression, and he was determined to keep the fight going until Ireland was a united Republic.

Again, whether he was right or wrong is a matter of opinion. What is a fact is that he was prepared to sacrifice everything to achieve that end — and ultimately, that's what happened.

Perhaps the real tragedy of Jack's story is something more personal. Despite all his bravery, the skirmishes, the ambushes, and his time with the flying squads, one event came to define him: Taghmon. As to whether he should have robbed the bank, the answer must be no. Then again, he was faced with a dilemma. To see his wife and children homeless, or use the experience he'd gained over the years to do something about it. Having never been in that situation myself, I have no idea if I'd have done the same — but I'd like to think I might have.

The summer before he died, I was in Ireland as usual. I picked him up at the nursing home and took him up to St. Mullins, then Ballymurphy, eventually stopping off for a sherry at Shea's. While we were out, we called into the New Cemetery so he could pay his respects to Josie. Once we were back at the home, I helped him into his room and sat with him for a while.

It was then I decided to broach the subject. Plucking up courage from somewhere, I asked him outright if he'd ever robbed a bank. He often seemed a bit hard of hearing, but this time he heard me clearly. A steel glint came into his eye as he gave me a one-word answer: "Yes."

I was quite surprised at his honesty. I asked him if he'd robbed more than one. He answered yes again. Then I asked him why. He rolled his eyes as if he couldn't believe I'd asked such a stupid question. "The money," he replied.

There were many other things I should have asked, but for some reason, I couldn't.

The only other ridiculously bland thing I enquired was what it had been like to be in prison. Again, I got a one-word answer: "Cold."

And that's all I got from the horse's mouth. As I headed back to the car, it struck me that perhaps the most important question I hadn't asked was what became of the money. It was fanciful to imagine, but maybe it was still at Kilcloney hidden in yet another undiscovered secret compartment.

There was another possibility however, that intrigued me. A few years after Jack died, Bridie's daughter, Maisie — the one who'd called my mother and told her she had something to tell her — rang me direct. We spoke about the robbery, and I asked her then if she knew what happened to the money. She said the bulk of it had been given to a fourth man, a collector on behalf of the IRA. Her mother told her about it, and she seemed adamant it was true.

Was that possible? The idea of a fourth man never came up in the trial or anytime afterwards — at least as far as I knew. Most likely, Maisie had been spun a yarn to excuse what her uncle did — but I had to admit, it wasn't totally beyond the bounds of possibility.

I suppose like those Channel 5 documentaries about aliens building the pyramids, we'll never really know.

A few years before Jack died, my mother told me something he'd said. Something that seemed to be his perfect epithet.

It was just after Josie's funeral, and she'd gone to make him a meal at his house in Sparkhill. As she sat down beside him, she decided to tell him how much she loved him and what a great man she thought he was. She said he just smiled, took her hand, and whispered, "Sure, I did what I had to do in the times that were in it."

End

EPILOGUE

My mother remembers Jack and John Hynes writing letters to each other in the sixties, discussing various applicants for IRA pensions and medals. I decided not to publish them because in many cases they reveal the claims to be either spurious or exaggerated, and I don't want to embarrass anyone.

The paradox was that while Jack received his medal in 1943, he never got the pension.

It seems the reason for this was because he was late in applying — and he was late because at the time he was in Portlaoise prison.

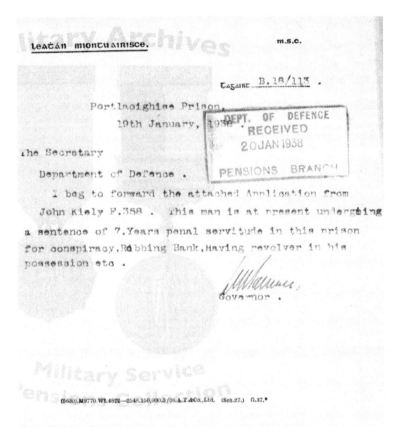

The first letter I found on the subject was one where the prison governor, William Borrows, writes to the Department of Defence on his behalf. The letter is dated 19.01.1938 and it states that Jack is applying for the pension and his application is enclosed.

On the 28th, he gets a reply telling him that the last date for application was the 1st — Jack is three weeks too late, and the Minister had no discretion to change it.

Fait a complis.

From then on, it seems Jack's chance of getting a pension is effectively nil. It's interesting, nonetheless, to see the progression of his attempts. I imagine one of his concerns was how much to reveal about his civil war activity.

28th January, 1938.

A Chara,

I am directed by the Minister for Defence to refer to your letter of the 19th instant, (Ref: B.18/113), enclosing a form of application for a Service Certificate under the Military Service Pensions Act, 1934, submitted by John Kiely (F.358), at present undergoing sentence in your Prison, and to state that in the Regulations made in accordance with the terms of the Act, it is laid down that all applications should have been made before the 1st January,1938.

The Minister has no discretionary power to accept an application made on or after that date. Consequently, the application cannot now be considered.

Mise, le meas,

Sgd.

Rúnaidhe.

William Borrows, Esq.,
Governor,
Portlaoighise Prison,
Laoighis.
MD.

In his original application, he only mentions what he got up to in the War of Independence.

APPLICATION FOR MEDAL.

- Give full particulars and nature of service rendered up to and
  including the 11th July, 1921: -

Period 1918 to 1919.

Removing of R.I.C. from within hearing of our Speakers night of anti conscription meeting at Borris. Organising the company and it outposts

Period 1919 to 1920.

Raiding for Arms. Destroying of Glynn and Killedmond R.I.C. barracks

Period 1920 to 1921.

Attack on Bagalnstown R.I.C. Barracks. Hunting down of Finn the Spy destroying of Bridges. Attack on important military post at Borris destroying of Searchlight. Enemy returned the fire with machine gun.
Holding and cutting of road night of attack on Gowran R.I.C. Barrack. Waiting in ambush of R.I.C. for 3 weeks. Taking of Revolver from Black & Tan at Borris

Full Christian Name
and Surname: - JOHN KIELY

Present Address: - Ballinagree
Borris
Co Carlow

When his application was dismissed, he appealed, revealing more of his post-truce service record, including the attack on Free State troops at Graney.

It still wasn't enough. The Ministry of Defence had drawn a line in the sand and that was that.

Hynes then sends a letter supporting Jack and, as his commanding officer, verifies his claim.

> G Coy = 4 ᵗʰ Batt
> Carlow Brigade)
>
> Owlbeg Borris
> Co Carlow
> 21ˢᵗ July 1943
>
> A Chara,
>   I have read the letter of appeal of John Kiely Ballinagh Borris. and found it corect in all details, he has always being a willing and active volinteer. I have sat on his assesment in Dublin after the time he was called before the Board, and I thought by the praise giveing him by the Chairman that he had passed out for a Pension
> this man held the Rank of Lieutenant in his own company and was responsable for the organizing of the outposts of the Coy; he was the only man of G Coy. who remained loyal when the Split came in 1922: at that period his Parents were wealthy but their Corn and Wollen milles was destroyed by Military while he was on the A S U he is now a very Poor man
>   Mise le meas
>   John Hynes,
>   4 ᵗʰ Batt Comandant
>   Carlow Brigade

He's refused yet again, for the same reason. Outgunned, but not outmanoeuvred, he then makes an application for a toe injury he suffered while retreating across the Slaney. To be honest, I never saw him with a bad toe, but the application itself is interesting, as it backs up his service in Tullow under Ernie O'Malley.

It's hard to take a bad toe injury seriously — unless you've had one yourself — and again his claim was dismissed.

STATEMENT OF JOHN KIELY.
_____

I claim for injury to left great toe which occurred about September, 1922, and heart trouble caused by strain of service and possibly by the toe injury.

We were wading across the Slaney near Tullow, coming from Myshall, Co. Carlow. Our object was to occupy Tullow. E. O'Malley was in charge. In crossing the river I stepped on a stone. The stone was slippery. I turned on my left foot and my great toe got jammed between that stone and another one. I had great pain at once. The toe was bruised. I got first aid treatment from John Hynes, Column leader. He put a bandage on it. The next treatment I got was from the column doctor whose name I cannot recall at present. He saw me at Tullow within three or four hours after the accident. He bathed the toe and dressed it. I resumed duty although the toe was still painful. About a month or so afterwards when still on the run the toe became septic. I returned home then to visit my people, after my brother's arrest and I showed the toe to Dr. Reid in my own house. He re-dressed the toe. He examined me for my heart and seemed concerned about it and my nervous condition. I returned to the column early next morning and carried on till cease fire. The toe was septic and painful at the cease fire. I could not get any treatment until my return home off the run about the end of 1923. From this time on to the present I have had treatment for my toe on four or five occasions. The septic condition cleared up when I was at home for some time and under Dr. Reid's treatment. The toe is inclined to swell and become inflamed and painful if I walk any great distance. Dr. Reid has treated me since my return home for heart trouble. I suffer from palpitation. Dr. Reid injected my arm on a number of occasions for the heart trouble.

Before my service I worked for my father at the Woollen Mills, Borris. He was the owner. I looked after the machines and generally supervised. During the civil war the machinery of my father's business was destroyed by F.S. Forces. No compensation was paid.

Since my return home off the run I have done no work as I am not fit. I am living on home assistance.

I never received compensation for my injured toe from any source.

I was never insured under the National Health Insurance.

I was perfectly healthy before my service.

SIGNATURE : John Kiely

WITNESS : Sir B Mungovan

DATE : 2nd April 1943

Tenacious as ever, I saw him apply for the pension again in the sixties. To his disappointment, his new application was refused, this time because he was earning too much money.

I'm not sure what the moral of Jack's story is. What I do know is that if it wasn't for people like him, or Nelson Mandela, or the man who stood in front of the tank in Tiananmen Square, the world would be ruled by bullies and dictators. Maybe it still is — but hopefully decreasingly so.

At least they had integrity. Others like William Stanley on Bosworth Field were more inclined to sit back and see which side their bread was buttered. Some, although not many big extant ancient Irish families did the same. What sacrifice did they make to improve the lot of the Irishman on the Dublin Luas?

One last thing I need to say — and it's essentially an apology to my English friends. When I speak about British oppression, it's shorthand for the oppression of the poor by the rich. Essentially, the big landowners. I'm British, but you can't blame me for Brexit. I didn't vote for it. I'm not a great fan of Cromwell, either, and the last place my English grandfather wanted to go was the Somme. During the famine, the poor Englishman had his own problems. Because of the Corn Laws, thousands starved because they couldn't afford bread. A few years earlier, eighteen English men, women, and children were trampled to death, with another seven hundred injured, when Wellington's cavalry charged into a crowd in Manchester. Their crime? Demanding the vote. Only 11% of the population had that right at the time — and they, of course, were the rich.

As Timothy said in the New Testament, "Money is the root of all evil."

Overall, I'm proud of what Jack did. Whether you agree with his politics or not, you have to admit he had the integrity to stick with his beliefs — and he was prepared to fight for what he hoped would be a better future. He was a good man, and as Edmund Burke allegedly said, "the only thing necessary for the triumph of evil is for good men to do nothing."

The Cross Examination

The New Ross Times of the 15th June 1934 reports some of the exchanges between McCarthy KC and the Kielys. They highlight the hopelessness of the defence and despite the levity of the charges, show amusing Irish wit from both sides.

Jas was the first of the brothers questioned. He told the court he'd lived with his mother at Kilcloney since his sister (Nell) moved out on 4th April 1931. His brother Jack had left in 1927. Their father didn't make a Will and Jack received £150 from "family arrangements" along with further money from his two elder sisters. He believed the bulk of the money had been paid to Jack in £10 and £5 notes.

Defence: Do you know anything about the bank robbery that took place?

Jas: No sir.

Jas explains that he had not seen his brother for 5-6 weeks before the 2nd February and that Josie and her children had moved into Kilcloney on 6th after a feud with her family. He then took the boat to Liverpool on 12th February to meet Jack.

Davitt: Jack was surprised to see you?

Jas: No, I understand he was informed I was coming to England.

He tells the court he met Jack off the boat in Liverpool. He then went on alone to Rochdale where Jack had been working with an old friend, Dick Coburn. He explained that the guards in Ireland were implicating Jack as a suspect in the Taghmon robbery and he wanted Coburn to confirm

Jack's whereabouts on 2nd February. He also wanted Jack to return to Ireland and give his alibi to the guards. In case Coburn was also required to return to Ireland he gave him £2 (£100) for the fare back. He and Jack then returned to Dublin by boat. Jack remained in Dublin whilst he returned by train to Bagnalstown.

He is then questioned by MacCarthy. First MacCarthy asks him about the guns discovered in the dug-out.

Jas: I was farming during the 3 years I was at Kilcloney. I have 11 cattle in 23 acres and two horses. The guns and revolvers were not used for working the farm – they were the property of the IRA.

MacCarthy: Don't be dragging the IRA into this Do you want to tell the courts you were custodians of the property for anyone?

Jas: Yes.

MacCarthy: Will you write down the names of these persons?

Jas: I won't give you them.

MacCarthy: Were the guns there before Jack came back?

Jas: Yes.

MacCarthy: The dug out was already there and ready?

Jas: There was nothing ready about it. It was there.

MacCarthy: And when jack came back there was ample room for him to sleep in a bedroom?

Jas: Yes.

MacCarthy: He need not have lived in the dugout?

Jas: No.

MacCarthy: Jack was a perfectly innocent man?

Jas: I believe so.

MacCarthy: Don't you know it? Haven't you already sworn he was in Liverpool or Rochdale when the raid took place?

Jas: I believe he was in England.

MacCarthy: You did not know it?

Jas: I was not there myself to see him.

MacCarthy: You believe him innocent?

Jas: Yes.

MacCarthy: Did anyone suggest he had something to do with the raid? The guards called on the house on 5th February enquiring about Jack?

Jas: Yes.

MacCarthy: Where was he then?

Jas: I don't know.

MacCarthy: Then you suddenly learned he was in Liverpool. When did you learn it?

Jas: During that week.

MacCarthy: You didn't know at that time whether he was guilty or innocent? You did not know anything about his movements on Feb 2nd?

Jas: No.

MacCarthy: Why did you come to Liverpool?

Jas: To tell him to come back.

MacCarthy: He didn't come?

Jas: He came to Dublin.

MacCarthy: Why didn't he come as far as Bagnalstown?

Jas: Let him tell that himself.

MacCarthy: You didn't know whether he was guilty or innocent except for what he told you?

Jas: No.

MacCarthy: Why did you go to Rochdale to discuss with Coburn?

Jas: I did it at Jack's request.

MacCarthy: He couldn't go himself?

Jas: He did not go.

MacCarthy: When you returned to Bagnalstown you met Superintendent O' Brien. Why didn't you tell him Jack was in Dublin?

Jas: John is finished with me, and I didn't want to get into any more trouble with his wife.

MacCarthy: Is there anything more favourable you could have said for him that he was on his way home?

Jas: I don't know.

MacCarthy: You gave Coburn's address to the guards as being Jack's address.

Jas: I gave it them as his address as on the night of the raid.

MacCarthy: Why didn't you give them Jack's address in Dublin?

Jas: Because he would not be satisfied. It was understood that if Jack made a statement he would not be arrested.

MacCarthy: Would it not be a simple thing to say Jack was in Dublin instead of misleading the guards by saying he was with Coburn?

Jas: I did not say he was at Coburn's at the time I returned.

Printer's Arms, Rochdale

Jas's evidence is in stark contrast to that given by Coburn and his employer. Coburn said he and Jack had served in the same flying column in 1922. He'd been living on Rochdale since 1928 and on 13th February around 6.30pm, Jas knocked on his door. He told him Jack was implicated in a robbery and asked if he could give him an alibi any time before 6th. Jas offered him £10 and told him that the raid was political. Coburn agreed and as a down payment, Jas gave him £2.

Coburn's employer, Albert Kershaw also appeared in the dock. He said he owned a demolition business where Coburn occasionally worked. That night around 9.15 pm he, Coburn and Jas went to the Printers arms. Jas said he wanted to catch the train back to Liverpool but when they went to the station they found the last one had left at

6.15pm. They went on to the Wine lodge for a couple more drinks. Jas told him he was a gentleman farmer (laughter in the courtroom), and that times in Ireland were bad. It was impossible to sell stock and he needed to get home as soon as possible as his sister was looking after the cattle. Jas then stayed with Coburn overnight and caught the train the next day to Liverpool.

MacCarthy then turns his attention to the car.

MacCarthy: Why did you tell the guards you bought the car from a man called Doyle who was a stranger to you in New Ross five weeks before February 12th?

Jas: Because I bought it.

MacCarthy: Maybe Jack Kiely was the Doyle you bought it off?

Jas: Certainly, he was (*laughter in the court*).

MacCarthy: Why didn't you tell me that before?

Jas: Because the car was registered in the name of Doyle.

MacCarthy: But you told the police Doyle was a stranger to you and you didn't know his Christian name?

Jas: I did not know what Christian name he was using.

MacCarthy: You were asked if your brother Jack ever used the car and you said he was never there to use it?

Jas: That was after the car came to Kilcloney.

MacCarthy turns to the cash found in the dugout.

MacCarthy: Where did you get ½ sovereign? (*gold bullion with a face value of ten shillings [50p]*)

Jas: 1914 I sold a heifer to a butcher who paid the money in gold, and it remained in the house.

MacCarthy: Did you see the wax? (*the ½ sovereign stolen from the bank had been stuck to a postcard with red wax*)

Jas: No, It wasn't on the 1/2 sovereign I had – besides I didn't see it being found.

MacCarthy: You don't accept it was found in a bed wrapped in wallpaper? Have you doubts about it being found?

Jas: I don't know.

MacCarthy: A number of people have sworn to finding it. Don't you think that's strange?

Jas: What's strange about it?

MacCarthy: Isn't it strange to have 2 stone (12.7Kg) of silver in your house?

Jas: That silvers not mine

MacCarthy: I agree it's not yours (*laughter in the courtroom*) Isn't it strange?

Jas: No

MacCarthy: If you had that much silver you would you carry it in your pockets?

Jas: No

MacCarthy: what would you do with it?

Jas: I'd put it in a bank (*more laughter*)

MacCarthy: Do you think it would be safe in a bank? (*more laughter*)

Jas: Certainly.

MacCarthy: How did the silver get in the dugout?

Jas: I don't know.

MacCarthy: You didn't bring it in there?

Jas: No, I believe it was my brothers property.

MacCarthy: You and he didn't bring it in there?

Jas: No, He didn't bring it in there until 12th Feb.

MacCarthy: But you left him in Dublin on Feb 15th?

Jas: Yes.

MacCarthy: So, he must have brought it in there after February 15th?

Jas: Yes.

MacCarthy: And the innocent man went into the dump with an arsenal to guard the silver?

Jas: I don't know. I was in custody at the time.

MacCarthy: You have been in jail with Jack ever since Did you ever dream of asking him where the silver came from?

Jas: No.

MacCarthy: You didn't care?

Jas: No.

MacCarthy: It was in your house?

Jas: Yes.

MacCarthy: Are you trying to put this over on your brother and keep out of it yourself?

Jas: No, I left the house on the 12th and was not there since. Anything that happened since I cannot swear to it.

MacCarthy then questions him about the Clyno, Jim Treacy and the guns.

MacCarthy: Would you think it strange for the guards to find traces of your Clyno in Kavaghnas lane in Taghmon?

Jas: I don't know.

MacCarthy: Isn't it strange that Treacy should go into the box and swear you were with him on the bank robbery?

Jas: I don't know.

MacCarthy: He is a decent boy?

Jas: Yes, as far as I know.

MacCarthy: He lives a mile from you and is often at your house?

Jas: Sometimes

MacCarthy: And there is no reason in the world he should swear that you and your brother and he plotted in this robbery?

Jas: He made several statements. (*referring to the two opposing statements Jim made within a few hours of each other*) He believed that by swearing he could get out of it.

MacCarthy: Is he capable of doing that?

Jas: Yes.

MacCarthy: Did he ever see the yokes? (*Irish slang for "thing"*)

Jas: What do you mean by yokes?

MacCarthy: Between ourselves – and don't let the jury hear – did he ever see them? He undoubtedly saw the service rifle. Did he ever see the parabellums?

Jas: There were no parabellums found.

MacCarthy: Did he know anything about your little dump?

Jas: No.

MacCarthy: Or about the car?

Jas: No.

MacCarthy: How would he have invented Mrs Love carrying a lamp around if he wasn't there?

Jas: I don't know.

MacCarthy: Are you able to drive a car?

Jas: No.

MacCarthy: ...but you paid your brother John £5 for a car you couldn't drive - without lamps?

Jack is then called to the dock. He tells the court he was at Coburns until 7ᵗʰ February when he received a letter from Josie telling him that the guards were looking for him. He then travelled to Liverpool to meet his brother off the boat. He crossed back to Dublin, walked to Kilcloney and moved into the dugout the following night. He preferred to stay there because the house was surrounded by detectives. He had been living under an assumed names because an old firearms charge was still active against him. O'Brien had told his wife that the charge would be dropped if he made a statement about the robbery - but he didn't want to risk getting arrested before that. He brought the money found in the dug out there on night of 16ᵗʰ. It was money he'd inherited and earned at Carrick.

MacCarthy: So, you claim the silver is yours How did you carry it around?

Jack: I didn't. I had it in a house I'd bought for £23 (£1656) from John Neil (*the house he'd bought in Ballinagree after being made bankrupt from Carrick on Bannow*). I took the silver to the dugout in Kilcloney in cloth bags. I emptied them out when I got there.

He goes on to add:

I haven't seen the shoes before. I had nothing to do with the raid on the Taghmon bank on 2nd February. Treacy was a very small chap when I left home in 1927 (*he would have been 12*) and I haven't seen him since.

MacCarthy: So, Knowing the police were looking for you, you took the silver to Kilcloney?

Jack: Yes

MacCarthy: That must have been quite a performance?

Jack: No.

MacCarthy: Was it not as safe in an unoccupied house as in the custody of a man wanted for a bank raid?

Jack: No.

MacCarthy: So, Knowing you were wanted for a bank raid you took two stone of silver on your back to the dugout in Kilcloney?

Jack: That's exactly what happened

MacCarthy: What is the explanation of it?

Jack: Prior to my leaving home in 1927 I had considerable trouble with the Guards.

MacCarthy: You're not answering my question There was a quantity of silver taken from the bank in Taghmon...

Jack: I know the bank was raided but I didn't know what was taken.

MacCarthy: Could you not guess?

Jack: No, I was never in a bank (*laughter*)

MacCarthy: What did you expect could be taken from a bank – would it be sealing wax? If there was sealing wax in it, it would be taken You knew if the silver was got with you it would look very bad.

Jack: My conscience did not worry me because the silver was my own

MacCarthy: It didn't occur to you that it could be a dangerous thing for a man wanted for a bank raid to be found in a secret dug out with a bag of silver by his side?

Jack: It did not occur to me.

MacCarthy: There was no reason for you to go into the dugout?

Jack: In 1927 I had a considerable amount of trouble with the police and was continually writing depositions – about 2-3 a week The house was also being raided 2-3 times a week by military and civil guards.

MacCarthy: Was this banking apartment ever found? (*chuckles around courtroom*)

Jack: They never found it in 1927 or 1920 nor 1922. The dump was made for the concealment of arms. It was during the Cosgrave government. Any man that took an active part in trouble in 1922, if Mr Cosgrave got a hitch of it he would give him a run for his money (*Laughter*). I left home because my people were put to great expense to defend me.

MacCarthy: Will you tell us why you went into the dugout?

Jack: That is the reason.

MacCarthy: Why bring it into the dugout?

Jack: Where would I leave it? On the doorstep? (*more laughter*)

MacCarthy: Your wife was the only occupant of the house?

Jack: She was not – she was visited several times by detectives. (*laughter*)

MacCarthy: But you were not a scrap concerned about the silver when you took it into the dugout?

Jack: Where else would it be safe?

MacCarthy: What was the necessity of concealing it in the unoccupied house (*Ballinagree*) before that?

Jack: Where else would I put it?

MacCarthy: How come the bank's half a crown was in the silver?

Jack: The only explanation I can give is that it is a coin I got while in business Anyone in business gets so many freak coins it is impossible to check them.

MacCarthy: Did you hear the Super swear that the first thing you said when you came out of the dugout was "Remember there are no notes in there"?

Jack: I cannot swear I said that.

MacCarthy: Can you explain it?

Jack: I don't remember saying it.

MacCarthy: Do you contradict it?

Jack: I don't contradict or verify it

MacCarthy: Can you give any explanation of your statement "here are no notes in that bag"?

Jack: No.

MacCarthy: I suggest it was because you wanted to indicate it was not the banks silver because the notes were not found?

Jack: I do not make any such suggestion.

Towards the end of the trial MacCarthy brings to the judge's attention that Coburn had been threatened by Nell when entering court the previous day. Davitt orders her to the witness box and asks if it was true.

Nell: No, my lord.

Davitt: You know it would be very wrong if you did?

Nell: I never said it I never mentioned him being bumped off – just that Jack would do him a bad turn – and he will your Lordship - but I never mentioned anything about him being bumped off.

MacCarthy: I suppose you thought that was a friendly observation? Something he could take back to England with pleasant memories of Wexford. That a man charged with bank robbery and an arsenal of guns could do him a bad turn?

Nell: Well, if there was not any reason for it...

Davitt: You made no threat yourself?

Nell: No.

At that, Davitt says that if he'd any absolute evidence he'd have no hesitation in sending her to jail. To threaten a witness he told her, was a very serious offence.

Nell: Coburn addressed me – I didn't even know the man.

Davitt: I hate to think that a Wexford woman like you would threaten murder.

MacCarthy reminds him that Nell is a Carlow woman (laughter). Davitt ends the examination by dismissing her from the witness box with the words "Run away now."

HISTORICAL CHARACTERS

Gerry Adams

(1948-present day). Gerard Adams. IRA politician and nephew of Dominic Adams, who was never arrested for the bombing campaign on the British mainland in WW II. Republican politician and president of Sinn Féin, 1983-2018.

Charles Asgill

(1762-1823). Sir Charles Asgill, 2nd Baronet. Career soldier in the British army. Involved in the suppression of the 1798 rebellion and the subsequent rebellion of 1803. Responsible for rebels being routed at the Battle of Kilcumney.

H. H. Asquith

(1852-1928). Herbert Henry Asquith, 1st earl of Oxford and Asquith. Liberal party politician and PM serving from 1908 - 1916. Forced to resign after failures of the Gallipoli campaign in World War I.

Arthur Balfour

(1848-1930). Arthur James Balfour, 1st earl of Balfour. British statesman and Tory politician who served as PM, 1902-1905. Advocated a home for Jewish people in Palestine. He and his secretary, Wyndham, encouraged British landlords to sell their Irish land by giving them a 12% cash bonus. Tenants were encouraged to buy with a low-interest rate loan with repayments drawn out over sixty-eight years.

Dennis Beresford

(1864-1942). Denis Robert Pack-Beresford. Irish entomologist and arachnologist. Estate owner of Fenagh House from 1881, serving as high sheriff of Carlow, Deputy Lieutenant, and JP. A reviled landlord in the Kilcloney area.

Henry Beresford

(1811-1859). Henry de la Poer Beresford, 3rd Marquess of Waterford. Landlord at Kilcloney during the 1840 evictions. Suspected to have been "Spring-heeled Jack." Frequently in the news for drunken brawling, brutal jokes, and vandalism, and was said to do anything for a bet. His irregular behaviour and his contempt for women earned him the moniker "the Mad Marquess."

John Betjeman

(1906-1984). John Betjeman. An English poet, writer, and broadcaster. Poet Laureate from 1972 until his death.

James Cagney

(1899-1986). James Francis Cagney Jr. American actor, dancer, and film director. Remembered for playing "tough guys" in films like *Public Enemy* (1931) and *Angels with Dirty Faces* (1938).

Edward Carson

(1854-1935). Edward Henry Carson, Baron Carson. Irish unionist, politician, barrister, and judge. Prosecutor in the Oscar Wilde case. First signatory in a petition to resist Home Rule, which threatened to use "all means necessary." Founder of the Ulster Volunteers, the first paramilitary group in Northern Ireland that was to be followed by the UVF.

Howard Carter

(1874-1939). British archaeologist and Egyptologist who discovered Tutankhamun's tomb in 1922.

Roger Casement

(1864-1916). Sir Roger Casement. British diplomat, humanitarian, activist, and poet. Knighted for investigation of human rights violations in Peru. Responsible for gun running from Germany for the 1916 uprisings. Executed by hanging, Pentonville prison.

Neville Chamberlain

(1869-1940). Arthur Neville Chamberlain. British conservative politician serving as PM, 1937-1940. Known for appeasement policy in World War II and Irish negotiations for land annuities and treaty ports.

Charlie Chaplin

(1889-1977). Charles Spencer Chaplin. English comic actor known for his portrayal of *The Tramp*.

Erskin Childers

(1870-1922). Robert Erskin Childers. English-born writer, politician, and militant. Ex-unionist, and then gun smuggler in the Anglo-Irish war. Executed by the Free State during the Civil War.

Winston Churchill

(1874-1965). Sir Winston Spencer Churchill. British statesman, soldier, and writer. Served as British PM, 1940-45 and 1951-1955.

Tom Clarke

(1858-1916). Irish Republican and a leader of the IRB. Possibly the person most responsible for the 1916 uprising. Executed by firing squad.

Tom Cloney

(1773-1850). United Irishman and a leader of the 1798 rebellion in Wexford. He fought in the battles of 3 Rocks and New Ross, led the attack on Borris house, and was generally referred to as General Cloney.

Michael Collins

(1890-1922). Soldier and politician. IRA leader and subsequently head of the pro-treaty Irish Free State. Assassinated by anti-treaty forces. Also known as "Big Fella."

James Connolly

(1868-1916). Irish Republican socialist and trade union leader. Born to Irish parents in Glasgow. Leader of the Irish citizen's army and a leader of the 1916 uprising. Executed by firing squad.

William Cosgrave

(1880-1965). William Thomas Cosgrave. Irish Fine Gael politician and president of the executive council of the Free State from 1922 – 1932. Considered Ireland's first Taoiseach due to having been the Free State's first head of government.

James Craig

(1871-1940). James Craig, 1st Viscount Craigavon. Leading unionist and key architect of Northern Ireland as a devolved region in the UK. During the Home Rule crisis of 1912-14, he defied the British government by preparing armed resistance to an all-Ireland parliament.

Oliver Cromwell

(1599-1658). English statesman, politician, and soldier. Lord Protector of England from 1653-1658. Responsible for the execution of Charles I and bloody campaigns across Ireland.

Austin Curry

(1939-2021). Joseph Austin Curry. Irish politician and active member of the Northern Ireland Civil Rights Association.

Edward Daly

(1933-2016). Bishop Edward Kevin Daly. Irish Roman Catholic priest and author. Took part in numerous civil rights marches during the Troubles. Famous for waving a blood-stained handkerchief while escorting a group carrying a mortally wounded protestor during Bloody Sunday, 1972.

Paddy Daly

(1888-1957). Paddy O'Daly. A veteran of the 1916 uprising. Subsequently held the position of major general in the Free

State army. Implicated in a series of atrocities during the Civil War.

Eamon De Valera

(1882-1975). George de Valero. Commandant in 1916 rising, anti-treaty statesman and political leader. Served several times as head of state. Also known as "Long Fella."

John French

(1852-1925). John Denton Pinkstone French, 1st Earl of Ypres. Commander in Chief of British expeditionary forces in WW I. Hero of the Boer war. Lord Lieutenant of Ireland, 1918. His assassination was attempted at Ashtown Road, Dublin by IRA men, including Sean Treacy, Paddy Daly, and Dan Breen.

Elbridge Gerry

(1744-1814). Elbridge Thomas Gerry. Republican American Founding Father, merchant, politician, and Vice President of the United States from 1813-1814. When governor of Massachusetts. Signed off legislation to redraw senate state districts in Essex Country to maintain Republican control. The shape of the new boundaries resembled a Salamander, coupled with his name, creating the term "Gerrymander."

Arthur Griffiths

(1871-1922). Arthur Joseph Griffiths. Irish writer, newspaper editor, and politician who founded Sinn Féin. He led the delegation at the 1921 treaty negotiations and served as president of Dail Eireann in 1922.

Adolf Hitler

(1889-1945). Austrian-born politician who became dictator of Germany, 1933-1945. Died by suicide.

James I

(1556-1625). James I of England and VI of Scotland, James Charles Stuart. Son of Mary Queen of Scots and successor to Elizabeth I. Responsible for the Protestant plantation of Ulster and American colonisation.

James II

(1633-1701). James II of England and VII of Scotland, James Francis Edward Stuart. Grandson of James I, King of England, Ireland, and Scotland. Believed in religious tolerance but was forced out when William of Orange was invited to seize the throne and maintain the Protestant hierarchy.

Art Kavanagh

(1831-1889). Arthur MacMurrough Kavanagh. Irish politician born in Borris House without arms or legs. Responsible for the building of Borris as it is today. The only dissenter in the House of Commons to the Beesborough Commission, which advocated the three f's for tenants: Fair rent, free sale, and fixity of tenure.

Dermot "Macmurrough" Kavanagh

(1110 -1171). "Dermot of the foreigners." King of Leinster, 1127-1171. Solicited the help of Henry II and subsequently Richard de Clare (Strongbow) to regain his Kingdom. Ultimately responsible for the Anglo-Norman invasion of Ireland.

Thomas Kavanagh

(1767-1837). Father to Art Kavanagh. Irish MP. Considered a "charitable and benevolent" landlord. Voted against the repeal of the Corn Laws. Defended Borris House from attack in the 1798 rebellion.

Mogue Kearns

(Unknown-1798). Fr. Moses Kearns. Irish Roman Catholic priest associated with tenant farmers society "The Defenders" and United Irishmen. Involved in the battle of Enniscorthy and the taking of Bunclody. Hung, drawn, and quartered.

Sean Lemass

(1899-1971). John Francis Lemass. A veteran of the 1916 rising, Anti-treaty Taoiseach, and leader of Fianna Fail, 1959-1966.

David Lloyd George

(1863-1945). 1st Earl Lloyd George of Dwyfor. Liberal PM of Britain, 1916-1922. Known for his roles in social reform, the Paris Peace Conference after WW I, and negotiating the establishment of the Irish Free State.

Martin Luther King

(1929-1968). Martin Luther King Jr. American Baptist minister and activist. One of the most prominent leaders in the black American Civil Rights Movement. Assassinated 1968.

Ramsay MacDonald

(1866-1937). James Ramsay MacDonald. One of the founders of the Labour Party and its first PM. His second government of 1929-1931 was dominated by the Great Depression and he stood down in 1935.

Terence MacSwiney

(1879-1920). Terence James MacSwiney. Irish playwright, author, and politician. Elected Sinn Féin Lord Mayor of Cork during Anglo-Irish war. Arrested for sedition, he was imprisoned in Brixton Prison and died after seventy-four days on hunger strike.

John Maxwell

(1959-1929). Sir John Grenfell Maxwell. British army officer and colonial governor. Responsible for numerous executions after the 1916 Easter rising. Retired in 1922.

Martin McGuinness

(1950-2017). James Martin Pacelli McGuinness. Irish Republican politician and statement for Sinn Féin. Leader of the Provisional IRA during the Troubles. First deputy minister of Northern Ireland from 2007-2008.

Jeremiah Mee

(1889-1953). RIC member and leader of Listowel mutiny. Objected to call for more aggressive action with Black and Tan help during the Anglo-Irish war.

Louis Mountbatten

(1900-1979). Albert Victor Nicholas Louis Francis Mountbatten, 1st Earl Mountbatten of Burma. British statesman, naval officer, colonial administrator, and close relative to the English royal family. Assassinated by the IRA in Sligo.

John Murphy

(1753-1798). Irish Roman Catholic priest in Ferns. Had a significant role as a leader in the 1798 rebellion in Wexford. Tortured, stripped, flogged, decapitated, burnt in tar, and impaled by British forces.

Liam Neeson

(1952-present day). William John Neeson, OBE. Northern Irish actor. Famous for playing Qui-Gon Jinn in *Star Wars: The Phantom Menace* and Michael Collins in the 1996 film of the same name.

Daniel O'Connell

(1775-1847). Acknowledged political leader of Ireland's Roman Catholic majority in the first half of the 19th century. He secured Catholic emancipation in 1929 and fought against the 1801 Act of Union.

Eoin O'Duffey

(1890-1944). Owen Duffey. Irish military commander, police commissioner, and fascist leader of the Blueshirts. Chief of staff in the Free State army, he suggested to Nazi Germany that his men could fight for them on the eastern front.

Kevin O'Higgins

(1892-1927). Kevin Christopher O'Higgins. Minister of Justice in Free State Government, 1922-1927. Responsible for the execution of seventy-seven IRA prisoners during the Civil War. Assassinated by anti-treaty IRA.

Olivia O'Leary

(1949-present day). Journalist and TV news presenter. Granddaughter of Dr. Edward Dundon, brigade leader of Borris 4th Battalion during the Anglo-Irish war.

Ernie O'Malley

(1897-1957). Ernest Bernard O'Malley. Writer and veteran of 1916 rising. Assistant chief of staff of the anti-treaty IRA during the civil war

William of Orange

(1650-1702). William III of England, William II of Scotland, King of England, Ireland, and Scotland after defeating the Catholic James II at the battle of the Boyne in 1690. A staunch Protestant from the Dutch province of Orange.

Charles Stewart Parnell

(1846-1891). Irish nationalist politician who served as MP, 1875-1891. Acting leader of the Home Rule League and leader of the Irish Parliamentary Party, 1882-1891. He held the balance of power in the House of Commons during the 1885-1886 Home Rule debate.

Ian Paisley

(1926-2014). Ian Richard Kyle Paisley, Baron Bannside. Northern Ireland politician and Protestant religious leader.

Served as leader of the DUP, 1971 to 2008. The First Minister of Northern Ireland from 2007-2008.

Patrick Pearce

(1879-1916). Patrick Henry Pearce. Irish teacher, barrister, poet, writer, and revolutionary. One of the leaders of the 1916 rebellion and seen by many as the embodiment of it. Executed by firing squad in Kilmainham Gaol.

Robert Peel

(1788-185). Sir Robert Peel, 2nd Baronet. British conservative statesman serving as PM, 1834-1835 and 1841-1846, during the time of the potato famine. Noted for the repeal of the Corn Laws.

John Redmond

(1856-1918). Irish nationalist politician, barrister, and MP. Leader of moderate Irish Parliamentary Party, 1900-1918. Also leader of the paramilitary Irish National Volunteers.

Richard II

(1367-1400). Richard of Bordeaux. King of England, 1377-1399. Deposed by Henry IV. Starved to death in Pontefract Castle.

Tiernan O'Rourke

(1124-1172). 12th century King of Ireland known for his expulsion of Dermot Kavanagh, King of Leinster in 1166

Seán Russell

(1893-1940). John Angelo Russell. Veteran of 1916 rising. Chief of Staff, IRA, 1938-1939. Responsible for the bombing campaign in England during World War II. Died in German U-boat.

Charles Trevelyan

(1807-1886). Sir Charles Edward Trevelyan, 1st Baronet. British civil servant and administrator. Assistant secretary to the treasury during the potato famine. Known for his laissez-faire economics and reluctance to disburse food and monetary aid.

Moss Twoomey

(1897-1978). Irish son of farm labourers and Volunteer from the age of fourteen. Adjutant of Cork no. 2 brigade. Staff commandant for Liam Lynch. Anti-treaty IRA man who became IRA Chief of Staff in 1927.

George Wallace

(1919-1998). George Corley Wallace Jr. American politician and 45th governor of Alabama. Stood on a platform of "segregation now, segregation forever."

George Wyndham

(1863-1913). British conservative politician who brought the Land Purchase Act of 1903 into law. Before the Act, Ireland's land was largely owned by British landlords. Within years, most of it had reverted to Irish tenants. Perhaps the most radical change in Irish life in history.

JACK'S FAMILY TREE

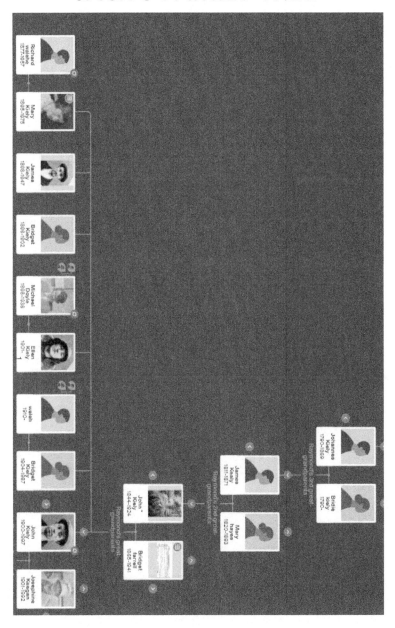

BORRIS

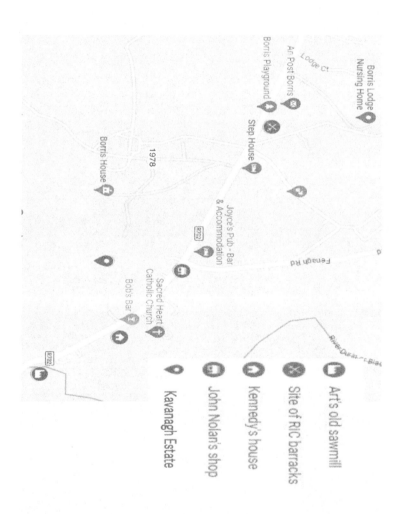

WHERE IT HAPPENED

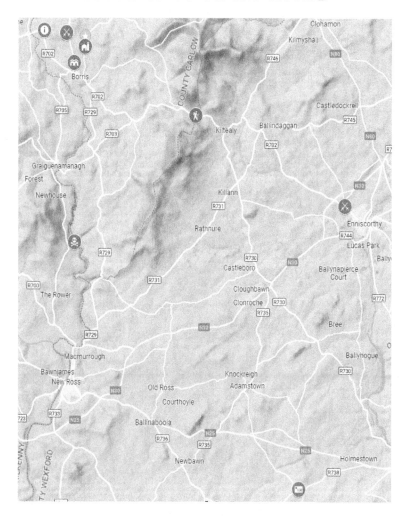

KEY TO "WHERE IT HAPPENED"

- Battle of Kilcumney
- Kilcloney Mill
- Scullough gap
- Dermot's castle
- Taghmon bank
- Jack's grocers at Carrick on Bannow
- battle of vinegar hill (Enniscorthy)
- Jack's bungalow
- Pat's house
- Kiely burial ground

Laurence Keily's letter of 1865

"Excuse mistakes and errors also, bad writing

To oblige, your nephew.

United states of America, Nashville Tennessee

Tuesday evening

August 1st 1865

Dear Uncles and Aunt and cousins,

With pleasure I acknowledge the receipt of your very kind highly interesting and affectionate epistle of the 2nd of July which came to hand yesterday. Let me assure you I have not words to express how much gratified I was to learn the good news and glad tidings of all of my relatives being in good health and prospering in life. And also to know that you have not forgotten me. As I had nearly given up all hopes of ever hearing from my native country again as the one whom was most beloved by me has departed from this life. May her soul rest in peace, amen.

Before I went into the American army I wrote my dear mother a letter each month and I received an answer to them but alas there is no mother to write to now. So uncle I will beg of you hereafter to correspond with me regular. For there is nothing in this life that would afford me more pleasure than to hear from you and home regular.

When I went into the army I could not write to my mother regular for we were marching and battling with the enemy all the time and likewise I did not like to let her know I was in the army for I know if she knowed I was in the army she would fret herself to death about me. And also my intention was to come home as soon as I got discharged from the army to console and be with her in her last days.

Dear Uncle when I look back to days and years gone by I think this cruel world is only a moment to a heavenly world which I hope when we depart from this life that we will be prepared to meet all of our dear kindred where parting is no more. I saw brother John yesterday and allowed him to read your letter. He was very glad to hear from you. I asked him his reason for not replying to your letter that he received while I was in the army which he said he answered it the day after he received it. He is well and doing well. His wages is forty five dollars per month and board. He is taking care of government horses. He says he is going to Louisville Kentucky shortly to live as he can get a better situation there than the one he now holds at the present time. He sends his love and best respects to all relations and friends.

I am still in the same business as I was when I wrote to you last. I am very well satisfied and doing well although I do not know for certain how long I shall remain here in the South as the climate in the north part of America agrees with my health the best. Also dear Uncle when young people come to America they are very disforgetful about home and kindred which they have left behind. But dear uncle that is nor the way with me as home and kindred eternally lives in my memory and will never be forgotten no matter where ere I go. I suppose that is the way with brother Edward and others for not writing home. The last account I had from him he was working in Baltimore, Maryland that was about six months ago. I wrote to him then and I received no answer. Also since then I have advertised in the newspapers to know his whereabouts but could not succeed in finding out where he is. As for uncle Billys family I have not received no account from them for a long time and them they were in Baltimore.

You need not to worry about them as this is a country where nobody suffers from anything and as for my aunts in Richmond I have had no word from them since I came to America. I wrote to them several times before the war broke out and received no answer. Since the war broke out Richmond was the enemy government capital so therefore mail communications was not open between the north and Richmond and consequently I could not write until of later since peace has once again visited out glorious free country as have the privilege of writing anywhere.

I think this is the best country and government ever the sun shone on but still sweet Erin the land of my berth ever lives and is thought of in my bosom. I hope the day is not far distant when I can once again lay my eyes on the emerald land, the land which is so dear beloved by me. As for sister Bridget and family the last I hear from them they were in Wheeling, Virginia. I have not wrote to them since and have received no answer. The last account I had from her she had 3 children, her husband seems to be a very nice person, his name is James Keenan. I was very glad indeed to learn that mother had in a decent wake funeral and that she was buried in St Mullins. May her soul rest in peace amen.

Dear Uncle, the wages here is from 2 and ½ dollars to $5 per day for a labourer. Mechanics get from $5-$10 dollars per day. A person can buy good land here for from $25-$75 per acre. They had very good crops in this country this year. Everything in the line of vegetables is plentiful. Nobody suffers from something to eat and wear in this country.

You requested to know where I shall be back in Ireland. I think if nothing happens between now and Christmas I will pay you a visit. I was very glad indeed to learn of your doing good business at the mill, I hope you will continue to do so. I was likewise glad to hear of my cousins going to school and doing well as there is nothing in this world to a young person like schooling. I know it has served me a great deal since I have left home as I can get a situation in this county no matter where I go.

Give my love and well wishes to Aunty Mary, Uncle Laurence and all my cousins and relatives and friends. You never said anything about Uncle Laurence in your last letter. Please inform me as to his whereabouts. I will conclude for the present hoping *to hear from you soon and I remain dear Uncle your affectionate nephew until death.*

Laurence Keily

Printed in Great Britain
by Amazon